SQL Server 2017 Administrator's Guide

One stop solution for DBAs to monitor, manage, and maintain enterprise databases

Marek Chmel

Vladimír Mužný

BIRMINGHAM - MUMBAI

D1261720

SQL Server 2017 Administrator's Guide

First published: December 2017

Production reference: 1081217

Published by Packt Publishing Ltd.
Livery Place
35 Livery Street
Birmingham
B3 2PB, UK.

ISBN 978-1-78646-254-1

www.packtpub.com

Credits

Authors
Marek Chmel
Vladimír Mužný

Copy Editor
Safis Editing

Reviewer
Tomaž Kaštrun

Project Coordinator
Manthan Patel

Commissioning Editor
Amey Varangaonkar

Proofreader
Safis Editing

Acquisition Editor
Vinay Argekar

Indexer
Tejal Daruwale Soni

Content Development Editor
Tejas Limkar

Graphics
Tania Dutta

Technical Editor
Dharmendra Yadav

Production Coordinator
Shraddha Falebhai

About the Authors

Marek Chmel is an IT consultant and trainer with more than 10 years of experience. He's a frequent speaker who specializes on Microsoft SQL Server, Azure, and security topics. Marek writes for Microsoft's TechnetCZSK blog, and since 2012 he's been an MVP: Data Platform. Marek is also recognized as a Microsoft Certified Trainer: Regional Lead for Czech Republic for few years in a row, he holds many MCSE certifications, and on the top of that he's a ECCouncil Certified Ethical Hacker and holder of several eLearnSecurity certifications.

He earned his MSc (business and informatics) degree from Nottingham Trent University. He started his career as a trainer for Microsoft server courses. Later, he joined AT&T as a senior database administrator with a specialization in MSSQL Server, data platforms, and machine learning.

Vladimír Mužný has been a freelance developer and consultant since 1997. His first steps with SQL Server were done on version 6.5 and from that times the working with all next versions of SQL Server has been never stopped.

Now Vladimir teaches Microsoft database courses and also participates on SQL Server adoption in companies and also on projects for production tracking and migrations.

SQL Server 2017 Administrator's Guide is his first attempt to share his knowledge and experience with people around the world, but writing is a strong drug and if possible, Vladimir is interested to share other namely his development experiences with others.

I wish to thank my colleague, Marek, my friend, and coauthor; without him, this book would have never been written. Also, I would like to thank all the team members behind this book; I especially thank them for their never-ending passion.

Last but not least, I would say thank you to my family for their support not just during writing the book but also throughout my career.

About the Reviewer

Tomaž Kaštrun is an SQL Server developer and data analyst with more than 15 years of experience in the field of business warehousing, development, ETL, database administration, and query tuning. He also has more than 15 years of experience in data analysis, data mining, statistical research, and machine learning. He is a Microsoft SQL Server MVP for data platform and has been working with Microsoft SQL Server since version 2000. Tomaž is a blogger, the author of many articles, the co-author of a statistical analysis book, a speaker at communities and Microsoft events, and an avid coffee drinker.

I would like to thank you, the authors, and Packt Publishing, especially Manthan Patel, for making this a great book. A Big thanks to the readers and the SQL Server community as well.

www.PacktPub.com

For support files and downloads related to your book, please visit `www.PacktPub.com`. Did you know that Packt offers eBook versions of every book published, with PDF and ePub files available? You can upgrade to the eBook version at `www.PacktPub.com` and as a print book customer, you are entitled to a discount on the eBook copy. Get in touch with us at `service@packtpub.com` for more details. At `www.PacktPub.com`, you can also read a collection of free technical articles, sign up for a range of free newsletters and receive exclusive discounts and offers on Packt books and eBooks.

`https://www.packtpub.com/mapt`

Get the most in-demand software skills with Mapt. Mapt gives you full access to all Packt books and video courses, as well as industry-leading tools to help you plan your personal development and advance your career.

Why subscribe?

- Fully searchable across every book published by Packt
- Copy and paste, print, and bookmark content
- On demand and accessible via a web browser

Customer Feedback

Thanks for purchasing this Packt book. At Packt, quality is at the heart of our editorial process. To help us improve, please leave us an honest review on this book's Amazon page at https://www.amazon.com/dp/1786462540.

If you'd like to join our team of regular reviewers, you can email us at customerreviews@packtpub.com. We award our regular reviewers with free eBooks and videos in exchange for their valuable feedback. Help us be relentless in improving our products!

Table of Contents

Preface

SQL Server is a very complicated set of end-to-end data processing technologies, and its correct functioning is crucial for every business. This book leads the reader through all the substantial topics a good administrator has to know in a professional job of provisioning, securing, maintaining, and monitoring SQL Server.

What this book covers

Chapter 1, *Setting Up SQL Server 2017*, is a reader's guide through the SQL Server installation process. This chapter also covers all the prerequisites needed for a successful installation of SQL Server. Overview of the SQL Server technology set is also provided in order to show the reader which services and features are used for particular tasks.

Chapter 2, *Keep Your SQL Server Environment Healthy*, is about maintaining a healthy database environment on SQL Server 2017. This can be used as a complete guide on what to check when you need to manage a new database server, find the root cause of an issue, or start at a new DBA job. You'll immediately get a good feeling and view of what's going on.

Chapter 3, *Backup and Recovery*, provides comprehensive information about all the backup and disaster recovery options offered by SQL Server 2017. Many complex examples are shown and explained throughout this chapter.

Chapter 4, *Securing Your SQL Server*, is about securing SQL server 2017. This is a very important chapter on the basics, on how to secure your data with different factors.

Chapter 5, *Disaster Recovery Options*, is where the available disaster recovery options are discussed in detail. Replication will be discussed in detail, with different options. Log shipping and mirroring are the options available options for disaster recovery. Also, database snapshot is discussed. Later in the chapter, which option should be selected is also discussed.

Chapter 6, *Indexing and Performance*, introduces a wide set of tools and techniques for performance monitoring in its first section alongside with some usage scenarios. The second section describes types of indexes and their internal structures.

Chapter 7, *Troubleshooting SQL Server Environment and Internals*, covers troubleshooting, a wide and diverse subject. In this book, this chapter will mainly focus on troubleshooting Windows Server and the SQL Server database engine. Troubleshooting queries/indexes is taken care of by Chapter 6, *Indexing and Performance*.

Chapter 8, *Migration and Upgrade*, explains migration, upgrading, and consolidation, a very important part of working with SQL Server.

Chapter 9, *Automation – Using Tools to Manage and Monitor SQL Server 2017*, shows how SQL Server 2017 helps to automate a routine and regularly repeated administrator tasks.

Chapter 10, *Always On High Availability Features,* covers the free tools available to monitor and manage a SQL Server installation. This will include health reviews, performance monitoring, backup, and so on.

Chapter 11, *In-Memory OLTP – Why and How to Use it,* In-Memory OLTP is quite new approach of data handling when the data contention is huge. This chapter goes through several use cases for In-Memory OLTP, with detailed descriptions of each feature used.

Chapter 12, *Combining SQL Server 2017 with Azure*, explains that using a cloud environment fully or partially is very advantageous and SQL Server does not stay aside. The last chapter goes through many scenarios of cooperation between SQL Server and Azure. Every scenario is shown as a working example.

What you need for this book

To be able to learn hands-on while reading this book, the reader needs at least SQL Server 2017 Evaluation Edition and also a client toolset called SQL Server Management Studio. Both programs are provided by Microsoft for free.

If you want to do experiments with Azure, an Azure subscription will be needed as well. It can be done for free at https://azure.microsoft.com/en-us/.

Who this book is for

This book targets database administrators with an interest in SQL Server 2017 administration. Readers are expected to have some experience with previous versions of SQL Server.

Conventions

In this book, you will find a number of text styles that distinguish between different kinds of information. Here are some examples of these styles and an explanation of their meaning.

Code words in text, database table names, folder names, filenames, file extensions, pathnames, dummy URLs, user input, and Twitter handles are shown as follows: "Internally, this task is executed as the DBCC SHRINKDATABASE() function."

Any command-line input or output is written as follows:

```
DBCC CHECKDB(<database_name>, REPAIR_ALLOW_DATA_LOSS)
```

New terms and **important words** are shown in bold.

Words that you see on the screen, for example, in menus or dialog boxes, appear in the text like this: "It's actually a button in the **Regressed Queries** window under the **Query Store** node."

Warnings or important notes appear like this.

Tips and tricks appear like this.

Reader feedback

Feedback from our readers is always welcome. Let us know what you think about this book-what you liked or disliked. Reader feedback is important for us as it helps us develop titles that you will really get the most out of.

To send us general feedback, simply email feedback@packtpub.com, and mention the book's title in the subject of your message.

If there is a topic that you have expertise in and you are interested in either writing or contributing to a book, see our author guide at www.packtpub.com/authors.

Customer support

Now that you are the proud owner of a Packt book, we have a number of things to help you to get the most from your purchase.

Downloading the example code

You can download the example code files for this book from your account at `http://www.packtpub.com`. If you purchased this book elsewhere, you can visit `http://www.packtpub.com/support` and register to have the files emailed directly to you. You can download the code files by following these steps:

1. Log in or register to our website using your email address and password.
2. Hover the mouse pointer on the **SUPPORT** tab at the top.
3. Click on **Code Downloads & Errata**.
4. Enter the name of the book in the **Search** box.
5. Select the book for which you're looking to download the code files.
6. Choose from the drop-down menu where you purchased this book from.
7. Click on **Code Download**.

Once the file is downloaded, please make sure that you unzip or extract the folder using the latest version of:

- WinRAR / 7-Zip for Windows
- Zipeg / iZip / UnRarX for Mac
- 7-Zip / PeaZip for Linux

The code bundle for the book is also hosted on GitHub at `https://github.com/PacktPublishing/SQL-Server-2017-Administrators-Guide`. We also have other code bundles from our rich catalog of books and videos available at `https://github.com/PacktPublishing/`. Check them out!

Errata

Although we have taken every care to ensure the accuracy of our content, mistakes do happen. If you find a mistake in one of our books-maybe a mistake in the text or the code-we would be grateful if you could report this to us. By doing so, you can save other readers from frustration and help us improve subsequent versions of this book. If you find any errata, please report them by visiting http://www.packtpub.com/submit-errata, selecting your book, clicking on the **Errata Submission Form** link, and entering the details of your errata. Once your errata are verified, your submission will be accepted and the errata will be uploaded to our website or added to any list of existing errata under the Errata section of that title. To view the previously submitted errata, go to https://www.packtpub.com/books/content/support and enter the name of the book in the search field. The required information will appear under the **Errata** section.

Piracy

Piracy of copyrighted material on the internet is an ongoing problem across all media. At Packt, we take the protection of our copyright and licenses very seriously. If you come across any illegal copies of our works in any form on the internet, please provide us with the location address or website name immediately so that we can pursue a remedy. Please contact us at copyright@packtpub.com with a link to the suspected pirated material. We appreciate your help in protecting our authors and our ability to bring you valuable content.

Questions

If you have a problem with any aspect of this book, you can contact us at questions@packtpub.com, and we will do our best to address the problem.

1
Setting up SQL Server 2017

Microsoft SQL Server is not just a database engine, it has become a very complex and robust technology set for data management, analysis, and visualizations over the years. As the progress of technologies incorporated with SQL Server grows, it is more complicated to decide which specific technology is actually needed, how to prepare the environment for its installation, and which configuration properties administrators should be aware of.

In this chapter, we will cover the following topics:

- **Microsoft SQL Server 2017 technology overview**: What SQL Server technology set contains and what is the purpose of each technology
- **Preparing for installation**: Which prerequisites and preinstallation steps are needed
- **Installation process**: What happens during installation, which settings are the most important ones, and which post-installation steps are necessary and recommended

Microsoft SQL Server 2017 technology overview

Microsoft SQL Server provides an extremely strong end-to-end data processing platform. In other words, data can be gained from a wide set of sources, securely and reliably managed, transformed, processed, analyzed, and visualized under an all-in-one license.

It's good to know what the bigger picture of the SQL Server looks as follows:

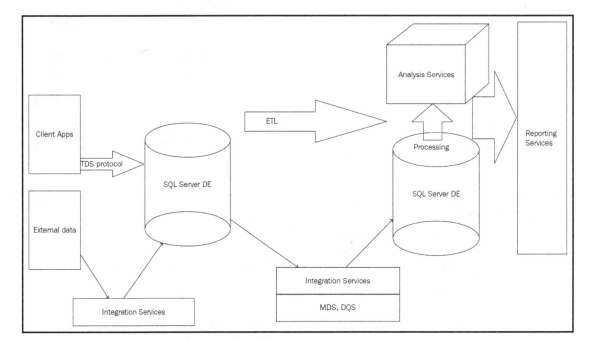

Overview of SQL Server technology set on-premise

Understanding SQL Server DE

The core and most important service in the SQL Server technology set is the **SQL Server Data Engine** (**DE**). This service has the three most important responsibilities aside of storing data:

- **Handling recovery**: This responsibility means that after any sudden as well as planned breakdown of the service or database, the service will recover every database to its last consistent state without any undone transactions
- **Handling transactions**: Transaction is mentioned as a single unit of work and SQL Server DE has to guarantee that transactions will be durable and isolated one from another and correctly finished on COMMIT or ROLLBACK

- **Handling security**: SQL Server DE resolves every request for authentication or authorization and decides if the user or application is known (authenticated) and if the user or application has permission for certain actions (authorization)

SQL Server does not provide its capabilities to end users only, but it's necessary to keep in mind that SQL Server DE serves as a base service not just for users, but also for almost every other service in the SQL Server technology set and it sets the next important points:

- Every BI service such as analysis services or reporting services are actually clients of SQL Server DE.
- Some services like machine learning services can be installed within or independently of SQL Server DE.
- SQL Server agent (not seen in the previous figure) plays an exceptional role in the SQL Server ecosystem. This service exists as an indivisible part of every SQL Server DE.

Why do we need this information? It's one of the crucial moments when planning SQL Server installation. For example, analysis services are heavily resource consuming and their deployment along with SQL Server DE could lead to big performance problems and user disappointment with responses on their requests.

SQL Server integration services

SQL Server integration services (**SSIS**) are used as a data pump of SQL Server. SSIS is used to maintain data movements and transformations between a wide scale of heterogeneous data sources and destinations as well as migrating or transforming data between several instances of SQL Server. A very common use case is using SSIS in data warehousing to extract, transform, and save data from **online transactional processing** (**OLTP**) databases to a data warehouse.

The working unit of this technology is the **SSIS** package. It's a runnable unit of integration services and we can think about it as one simple program. Its definition consists of the so called **Control Flow** task set such as creating a temporary folder, if it succeeds in downloading CSV files from some FTP site, and so on. One of the most crucial tasks in control flow is called the **Data Flow** task. This Data Flow task causes the execution of the SSIS package to switch to a Data Flow transform set.

The integration service itself is not mandatory for SSIS package execution but the service is used for integration services packages management. It's installed for backward compatibility with older versions of SSIS packages deployment model. SSIS packages are now commonly placed into a database called SSISDB. The database is not often accessed directly by users or administrators; it is maintained using integration services catalogs part of management studio.

From an administrator's point of view, the SSIS service installation could be omitted if all existing SSIS packages can be deployed to the integration services catalog, which can be created anytime just by a few clicks in the Management Studio.

Integration services often cooperate with two features for data cleansing, validating, and deduplicating. These services are called Master Data Services and Data Quality Services.

Master Data Services

Master Data Services (MDS) is a technology providing a very efficient way to manage data that has to be maintained centrally for more applications (for example, organizational structure) or data that should be cleansed and validated before it is sent to other data destinations like a data warehouse. From an administrator's perspective, it's a database usually called MDS, MDM, or master_data_services (administrator can choose the database name) and a website created on IIS. Master Data Services are not installed within SQL Server installer; a graphical tool called Master Data Services configuration manager is used for their installation and configuration.

Loading data into Master Data Services database is often done using SSIS. Then the data is optionally cleansed by data stewards. Clean and consolidated data could be subscribed via **subscription views**. Definitions of these views are stored in the Master Data Services database.

Data Quality Services

Data Quality Services (DQS) is a technology providing you with a way to **deduplicate** and correct data that originates from several sources. Actually, DQS is not a service installed within SQL Server installer, but it's created by an independent application.

The SSIS package has a special control flow task called DQS cleansing task, which is used when some a DQS knowledge base (set of rules created by the data steward) has to be used for data cleansing before the data is written to a target.

Using SSIS, MDS and DQS is complex discipline behind topics covered by this book. The only information needed is that described ETL technologies are more like standalone applications using SQL Server databases.

SQL Server Analysis Services

The Microsoft **SQL Server Analysis Services (SSAS)** is a very robust and scalable service that steps behind relational database limits by precalculating data that has been read from a relational data source and saving the data to a multidimensional storage called a **storage model**.

This approach is even more efficient for further analysis and visualizations than just the usage of relational data because the multidimensional format allows users to drill down and pivot actions as well as advanced aggregations or period-to-date queries. From this perspective, it is obvious that SSAS forms the core component of corporate as well as self-service BI solutions.

Analysis Services can be installed within SQL Server installer but it is not a good idea to have both SQL Server DE and SSAS service installed on the same computer. We must remember that SSAS is an extremely complicated engine with a lot of physical I/O operations when accessing a storage model, a lot of memory cache is used for data processing and data querying, and entails big CPU consumption for computations. One more important thing is that results from SSAS are often consumed in applications such as decision support, management reports, and so on, and it's crucial to get responses fast without waiting.

As mentioned previously, it's obvious that SSAS has to be installed on its own computer. The only disadvantage is that separate installations of SQL Server services lead to separate licensing. In other words, the more computers that are used to spread SQL Server technologies across an infrastructure, the more licensing expenses will grow.

SSAS can be installed in two distinct modes:

- Multidimensional mode: this mode is used for centrally created data cubes and mining models.
- Tabular mode: this mode is called also in-memory mode. It's used to host PowerPivot models.

If both modes are needed, the SQL Server installer has to be executed twice and two instances of SSAS have to be installed.

Multidimensional mode of SSAS installation

Multidimensional mode is used for corporate BI scenarios. Dimensions, data cubes, and mining models are developed by IT departments.

Multidimensional mode requires regular data processing so its approach is for bigger centralized analysis, trend predictions, longitudinal studies, and so on. Multidimensional mode is seen as a bigger, more robust, and scalable mode but often with data delay (existing storage model called **real-time ROLAP** can be used for real-time analysis, but has a lot of constraints. An overview of a real-time operational analysis scenario will be described later in this book).

PowerPivot mode of SSAS installation

SQL Server as well as other Microsoft technologies support BI solutions created by business users. This approach is intended for users who are subject matter experts more than IT experts, who have simple but strong enough tools to create their own analysis and visualizations. The toolset is known as power BI. A part of power BI is the **PowerPivot** technology--compressed and somehow precalculated data used to build data models similar to data cubes.

For the possibility of sharing our own data models with other users in a well-managed and secured environment, the PowerPivot mode of SSAS was originated. Data models can be deployed with almost no adjustments to the server environment and then can be accessed by authorized users.

One big advantage of PowerPivot mode is that data models are held in memory and when some additional data is needed to fulfill user requests, it can be read from the data source directly.

A detailed description of how Analysis Services work is beyond this book, but combining Analysis Services--no matter which installation mode--with other SQL Server services will lead to big performance problems.

SQL Server Reporting Services

Data, either relational or multidimensional, does not have its own visible face--data is not visual. To have a complete end-to-end data management platform, Microsoft offers a service called **Reporting Services (SSRS)** as a part of the SQL Server technology set. This service is designated to access data from variety of sources and visualize the data to users. Reporting Services is a favorite service for centralized and managed reporting.

From an architectural point of view, the SSRS is a Windows (or newly Linux) service that offers HTTP/HTTPS endpoints for human-readable as well as web service content consuming. The human-readable endpoint is called **Report Portal**. It is just a web application for report consumption and management. (Formerly, the report portal was called report manager.)

Reporting Services can be installed in two modes:

- Native mode
- SharePoint mode

Reporting Services have almost the same features in both modes, including report deployment, report previews, subscriptions, or report exports to formats such as MS Excel or PDF. The only feature not present in the native mode of installation is **data alerts**. A data alert is a user's option to be informed when something is changed in the report's data.

 SQL Server 2017 Reporting Services installation is no longer a part of SQL Server installer. From now, SSRS is installed and versioned separately. Linking to the installer is accessible from the SQL Server installation center or from the setup wizard step with **Feature Selection**.

When SQL Server 2016 was up to date, it had two installation modes for Reporting Services. This approach has completely changed since SQL Server 2017. Reporting Services can still be installed in both modes, but by separate installers.

When installing SSRS in native mode, web installer allows only installation of the service itself without creating the `ReportServer` and `ReportServerTempdb` databases for services metadata:

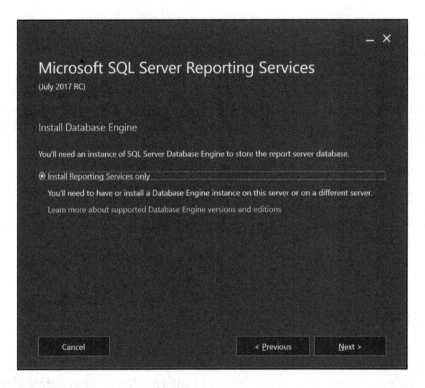

In production environments, it is a better option to install an instance of SQL Server DE on its own computer and then install SSRS on its own computer as well. Metadata databases are created later by a visual configuration tool called **reporting services configuration manager**.

Compared to the native mode installation, the SharePoint mode requires that SharePoint farm already exists and the downloaded installer runs on it. The installer just installs the SharePoint service application and SharePoint features containing certain SSRS web parts and features. After installation, SSRS in SharePoint mode is not working because SharePoint does not know that new components were added. The SharePoint administrator has to run two simple PowerShell commandlets to assign SSRS to SharePoint.

PowerShell commands to install SSRS in SharePoint mode are as follows:

```
Install-SPRSService
Install-SPRSServiceProxy
```

As a last step of making SSRS work on SharePoint, the content manager of certain SharePoint sites should create new custom libraries called report library. Data sources, shared datasets, report parts, and reports are then delivered to the report libraries.

Machine learning services

Predictive analysis profits from efficient and enlarged languages such as Python or R. SQL Server 2016 was the first version of SQL Server that incorporated new features called **R Services**. This feature is not seen in SQL Server 2017 installation anymore because it was renamed to **Machine Learning Services**. The renaming reflects the new Python support.

Machine learning services can be installed **in-server**. In this installation mode, Python and R support is incorporated directly into SQL Server DE. When the **in-server** mode is chosen, developers can call the SQL Server stored procedure, `sp_execute_external_script`, with R command or Python command as a parameter.

The second possible mode of installation is the machine learning server, which is an independent server consuming and executing R as well as Python scripts and visualizations.

SQL Server Agent

SQL Server Agent is a service installation is done along with SQL Server DE installation. Only exception is SQL Server Express Edition which does not enable SQL Server Agent service.

SQL Server Agent is a service to plan, execute and monitor regular tasks (jobs). The first approach that we can imagine is the planning and execution of regular administration tasks like those contained in maintenance plans (backups, reindexing, and so on). However, SQL Server and its services also need to execute other automated actions, for example:

- Master Data Services jobs for the internal maintenance of the MDS database
- Reporting Services (in native mode) jobs for regular subscriptions
- SQL Server replications are internally represented as sets of jobs
- When data collection diagnostics are configured, collection jobs are created and executed

We will discuss features of SQL Server Agent throughout the book.

Conclusion

The technology overview tried to answer the principal questions: What are certain SQL Server services and features for? Do I need every service or feature? Is it a good idea to install everything on one operating system? Now let's go on to prepare our computers to start the SQL Server 2017 installation on Windows.

Preparing for installation

The previous section described the whole set of services and features contained in SQL Server. From now, we will pay attention to on-premise SQL Server DE installed on Windows only.

In this section, we will discuss the following topics:

- Which edition of SQL Server to buy with respect to the features and performance capabilities
- How to prepare our Windows operating system and other prerequisites
- Installation options such as installation wizard, command prompt, and sysprep

Edition comparison

Microsoft provides SQL Server in several editions. Each edition has its supported features and with these features allocation of resources will differentiate. This can be seen in terms of performance, price, runtime and service availability. A complete edition comparison matrix is published on `Microsoft's site`. The core editions are as follows:

- **Enterprise edition**: Intended for big enterprise environment
- **Standard edition**: Contains almost all services (except Master Data Services and Data Quality Services) but has some limited hardware resource consumption as well as some internal limits in SQL Server DE
- **Developer edition**: edition containing all enterprise features, but for development purposes only! Must not be provisioned to production environment
- **Express edition**: Express Edition of SQL Server published for free but with a lot of limitations; for example, analysis services, integration services, and SQL Server Agent are not contained in this edition

Preinstallation tasks

When planning to install SQL Server 2017, there are three important points to be considered:

- Amount of memory
- Disk set
- Security consequences

Planning memory

Every edition of SQL Server has its limit of maximum consumable memory. It's needed to give SQL Server correctly because SQL Server consumes as much memory as possible. Every request to SQL Server needs memory. When preparing the server for SQL Server installation, we must consider two main memory usages:

- **Interpreted queries**: This is the traditional approach where SQL Server processes user requests. Data is stored on disk and, when some portion of data is needed by any query, it's cached to a memory area called buffer cache. Buffer cache with many other memory areas like procedure cache, user connections ,and others is a matter of memory limit given by the edition of SQL Server.

- **In memory OLTP**: In memory OLTP is relatively new SQL Server DE technology that was introduced with SQL Server 2014 Enterprise edition. Later in SQL Server 2016 SP 1, in memory OLTP has ceased to be an enterprise feature and now its memory capacity depends on memory limit determined by certain editions. For example, SQL Server standard edition has maximum memory set to 128 GB and in memory capacity is set to 1/4 of maximum SQL Server memory, which means 32 GB of memory up to the regular limit. In memory area is used for in memory tables--tabular structures for extremely fast access, especially in conjunction with native compiled stored procedures. If any application supposes to use in memory technology, be aware of this extra memory need.

When planning the amount of memory, we must keep in mind any concurrent service or application that will be present on the same server.

Planning disk capacity

No simple formula exists to calculate disk capacity. We can just estimate the amount of disk space needed from similar applications or from older databases. Disk space needs described on MSDN are sufficient for empty SQL Server installation, not for production environment.

When preparing disks, we have to consider the following points:

- Using directly attached disks is very common approach. Only possible issue is that the server itself does not have a sufficient number of controllers and disks don't have enough space for large scale real-world production databases.
- The best way is to use SAN storage, which has a sufficient number of controllers and allows you to spread every database across more disks.
- Let its own disk be present for the `tempdb` database; this database is used internally by SQL Server as well as explicitly by developers as an optimization helper for complicated queries (however this is not best practice).
- If the server has a low amount of memory (less than 64 GB) and more memory is needed especially for read-intensive OLTP databases, the administrator can set up a **buffer pool extension** (**BPE**). It is a file supplying more memory area for so called clean pages. SQL Server enhances the buffer cache and stores data pages intended to be read only from database to this file. The best practice is to place the BPE on its own SSD disk.
- Data files and log files of databases should always be separate. SQL Server uses write-ahead logging. This means that SQL Server caches data from data files and, at the moment, describes to the transaction log file what will be done with the data. When data and log files are not separate, overhead could occur on the disk controller.

Software and other requirements

When installing SQL Server 2017 on Windows, a 64-bit system is mostly preferred. Supported versions of the operating system are from Windows Server 2012 higher for non-enterprise editions; desktop operating systems such as Windows 8.1 or Windows 10 (including Home edition) are supported as well.

SQL Server uses the .NET framework for some features. The .NET framework of versions 2.0 and 3.5 SP 1 must be present before installation.

The easiest way to check whether everything is in place is to start the SQL Server installation center. It starts automatically when installation media is added to the server or it can be reached from Windows Explorer by clicking on the setup.exe file. This tool provides a central point to find resources about SQL Server as well as tools needed for standalone installation, cluster installation, adding or removing SQL Server components, and so on. The installation center is divided into sections and every section contains a list of links. The first section shown when the installation center starts is called planning. There is a link to a tool called **System Configuration Checker** (**SCC**):

SQL Server Installation Center

The SCC is a tool that checks all prerequisites needed for successful installation of SQL Server. The following image shows how it looks when every requirement is fulfilled:

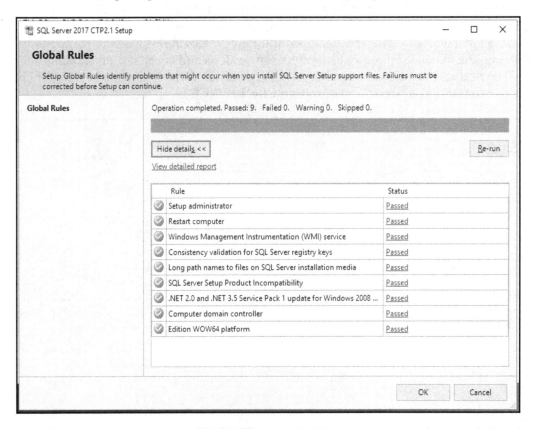

System Configuration Checker successful result

Besides the requirements, SCC checks the overall state of the server and other prerequisites such as whether the installation is running with administrator's privileges or whether a restart is needed.

Security accounts for SQL Server

SQL Server as well as other technologies within the SQL Server technology set need to log in to the operating system. From a security point of view, it is important to set an account for every service correctly. The general recommendation is to create a login account for every service of SQL Server separately with the weakest permissions. As the installation process itself is run in administrator security context, the installer will set permissions for every account correctly within the installation. The following are the most used scenarios:

- **Built-in service accounts**: This type of account provides less control from the administrator's side and it's good enough for small, standalone installations of SQL Server. In a bigger domain environment, it's not recommended at all.
- **Dedicated domain account**: This option means that the domain administrator prepares dedicated domain accounts with regular user rights (no elevated permissions needed) and during installation (or after the installation), prepared domain accounts are set. A big concern is that such domain accounts must fulfill security policies, namely password expiration, and SQL Server as a machine cannot create its own password for, say, every three months.
- **Managed service accounts**: Managed service accounts are domain accounts similar to regular domain accounts. Unlike domain accounts, managed service accounts create and change their passwords without any action needed from live administrators. That's why a managed service account is usually the best approach to setting security accounts for SQL Server and its services.

Installation process

Microsoft provides several options to install SQL Server and its technologies as simply as possible. Almost everything is done through the SQL Server installation center, which is opened via the autorun property of the installation media. The next chapter describes typical scenarios of installation and first post-installation checks and configurations.

Installation options

The SQL Server installation center provides several ways on how to install SQL Server. The most common method of installation is to use the wizard for standalone installation as well as for cluster installation of SQL Server.

For situations when more SQL Servers are propagated into the environment (for example, new departments or sales points are created often and every department or sales point has its own SQL Server), SQL Server provides a possibility to be installed through the command line, which is the only approach possible for installations on core editions of Windows or sysprep installation.

Installation wizard

The installation wizard is started from the SQL Server installation center from the second tab called **Installation**. There are several wizards (shortened):

- New SQL Server standalone installation
- Install SQL Server Reporting Services (new on SQL Server 2017; the version 2016 installation of SSRS was added to SQL Server's installation wizard directly)
- Install SQL Server Management Tools (means **SQL Server Management Studio** (**SSMS**); beginning in version 2016, management and data tools are not installed within SQL Server installation process, they are installed and versioned separately)

The first option called **New SQL Server stand-alone installation** is the right way to install SQL Server on a clean machine just with the operating system. When a user clicks on this option, the wizard starts.

The first two steps of installation ask for the license key and EULA acceptation. In the third step, the **Global Rules** installer checks the state of the computer again. Two product update steps try to connect Microsoft update for **news**. Until now, everything is very clear and almost automated, the administrator just uses the **Next** button.

The fifth step called **Install setup files** sets up the installation runtime. After this, the setup wizard checks that the computer is not a domain controller and then the actual installation begins:

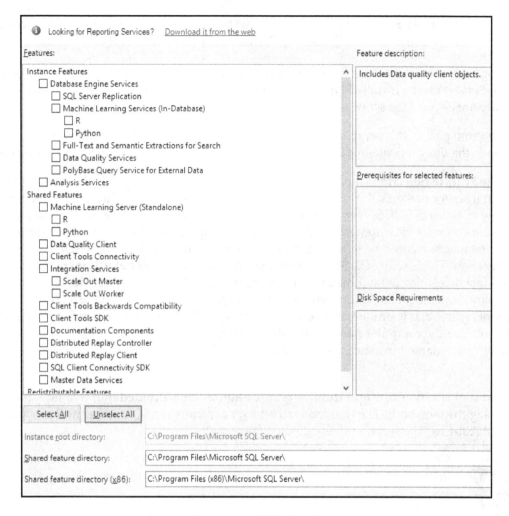

Setup wizard step with Feature Selection

As shown in the preceding screenshot, the setup wizard offers a wide set of features to be installed at once. For administrators who already installed previous versions of SQL Server, the setup step writes an information message about SQL Server Reporting Services. This service is newly installed separately from SQL Server installation.

When Installing SQL Server DE, administrator selects these options:

- **Database Engine Services**: This is the core component, DE itself
- **Optionally SQL Server Replication**: For the possibility of setting up replication scenarios

- **Optionally Full-Text and Semantic Extractions for Search**: Full text is a strong feature provided by SQL Server DE and it could be very useful for users.

Other options such as machine learning services (provides support to run external scripts on SQL Server) can be installed later or in a standalone separated setup. Features such as PolyBase are beyond the scope of this book.

In the bottom part of this setup step, the user decides where to place program files, not data files. So in the *System Configuration Checker successful result default* screenshot, location is set.

After the **Feature Selection** step, the **instance configuration** step appears that enables you to set an instance name. SQL Server can run in multi-instance mode. This means that more than one instance of SQL Server could be installed on the same machine. It's a good for example for side-by-side upgrades when on the same operating system. Another scenario for several instance could be when some information system needs its own SQL Server configuration. That's why SQL Server provides an ability to install **default instances** and **named instances**. The default instance has no special additional name provided by the administrator during installation; whereas every named instance must have its own additional name that is unique on a certain computer. When connecting a default instance, clients just use the computer name or IP address (such as MYSQLSERVER01); when connecting to a named instance, users must provide the instance name (for example, MYSQLSERVER01\MYADDITIONALNAME).

The next step is **server configuration**. Server configuration is divided into two tabs. Never miss going through both! The first tab is to set user accounts for SQL Server and all other installed features. The second tab is called collations.

 Collations contains only a configuration value, which cannot be changed after installation easily! When mismatched, it leads to a reinstalling of system databases.

The setting called collation describes which code page, sort rules, and case sensitivity will be used as the server's default way of handling string characters. This server default is inherited by databases as a database default collation, and every character column in the database has its own collation inherited from database default collation. On database as well as on column level, the collation setting could be overridden, but it's not good practice. It is crucial for the proper working of SQL Server to set the server default collation correctly. It's not simple to say which collation is the correct one. The only idea is that, if not sure, it's a better approach to use ANSI compatible collation with case insensitivity in a combination of unicode SQL Server data types such as nchar or nvarchar.

The next steps could vary--their set and order depends on features selected in the **Feature Selection** step. For our database administration purposes, the step called **database engine configuration** is the most important one. In this step, all crucial configurations are done by an administrator. As shown in the following screenshot, the step is divided into tabs. Never miss going through all these tabs!

Crucial part of Database engine configuration step

In the first tab called **Server Configuration** are basic settings for SQL Server security from a client's perspective. The first setting is **Authentication Mode**. It has two options:

- **Windows authentication mode**: In this mode, logins to SQL Server can be established in a trusted way only. It means that only logins created from Windows (domain or local accounts of groups) can connect to the SQL Server.
- **Mixed mode**: For cases when every user comes with its domain identity, SQL Server can manage **Standard logins** or **SQL logins**--logins with passwords managed directly by SQL Server. This was considered as a minor security risk, but since SQL Server 2005 (this was the first version of SQL Server able to consume **Group Policy Object** (**GPO**)), this is not a problem any more.

When the administrator selects mixed mode, he must provide a strong password for standard system SQL Server login called **sa**. This is the standard administrator login on SQL Server.

Authentication mode is the configuration value that can be changed later during SQL Server instance's lifetime, but then it needs restarting so it's a better approach to set it directly during installation.

In the last part of this tab is a list of sysadmin server role members of the SQL Server instance being installed. Add yourselves to the list and add another users to the list of principals who will have administrator access to the SQL Server.

The **Data directories** tab is very important as well. It's a set of paths to the filesystem where system databases, user databases, and backups will be placed when the user will not provide their actual paths:

- **Data root directory**: This is the base path to all data files (with .mdf or .ndf extensions). All system databases will be placed to this path (with the exception of the tempdb database). It's not recommended to use the default path to the program files, as was explained in the *Planning disk capacity* section; the best practice is to have a disk prepared just for data files.
- **User database directory**: This is the default base directory for user database data files. For certain data files this path can be overridden.
- **User database log directory**: In this, all log files (with the .ldf extension) of every database will be placed. Never mix data and log files in the same place.

User as well as system databases could be moved to a different location.

The third tab called **TempDB** precalculates the best configuration settings for the tempdb database. The tempdb database has a very special position in SQL server as well as for developers using it in some optimization tasks. The optimized execution of the tempdb database roughly depends on the following:

- Number of data files
- Their location
- Their symmetric growth

The number of data files is calculated from the number of CPUs. The best practice is to have 1/4 to 1/2 data files to the number of CPUs (even logical CPUs). The best location of data files is on a fast separate disk. In the case of tempdb failure due to a disk failure, tempdb is regenerated every time SQL Server starts.

The symmetric growth of all data files is carried out by the SQL Server engine automatically. Unlike the prior versions that had trace flags set in startup parameters, this is not needed from SQL Server 2016.

The last tab in the database engine configuration is called **FILESTREAM**. The **FILESTREAM** itself is a type of storage for binary data like documents or pictures saved in the database. If you have no idea about saving **FILESTREAM** data at the moment of installation, the **FILESTREAM** should remain disabled. It can be enabled and configured properly later without the need for restarting SQL Server.

After database engine configuration, additional wizard steps could occur depending on other features selected in **Feature Selection**.

 Maybe some readers are concerned about where SQL Server Agent configuration is. SQL Server Agent doesn't have any special settings in the installation process and its installation is automatically done along with every instance of database engine installation.

The installation wizard is almost complete now. After a short recap of what was selected by the administrator, the setup operation starts and shows its progress.

Command line

Installing SQL Server directly from the command line is possible but when searching the **Install SQL Server from the Command Prompt** topic on MSDN, the user will obtain a huge set of options that need to be added to the command prompt (or to the bat file) directly. It leads to a big risk of misspellings and other mistakes.

A better approach is to use configuration files for command prompt installations. It contains the same options as the command prompt itself, but we can find very good working examples from any setup already run from the wizard. When the wizard setup finishes, it leaves the setup log and configuration on disk. If SQL Server is installed in the default location, the path is `C:\Program Files\Microsoft SQL Server\140\Setup Bootstrap\Log`. In this location is a file called `Summary.txt`, which contains the actual path to the `ConfigurationFile.ini` file. The configuration file can be copied and adjusted as needed and then run using the following command from the command prompt:

```
setup.exe /ConfigurationFile=<path to my config file>.ini
```

The SQL Server installation wizard allows you to prepare a configuration file without installing. When the administrator goes through the wizard, everything is saved in the newly created configuration file. In the summary step of the wizard, the path to the configuration file is shown. So the administrator can cancel the wizard without the actual installation of SQL Server.

New installation possibilities

With the release of SQL Server 2017, administrators are very excited about the following new installation scenarios:

- SQL Server on Linux
- SQL Server in a container

The SQL Server on Linux installation scenario was a big highlight when SQL Server 2017 was announced for the first time. The installation process is managed via the command prompt, from downloading the SQL Server installer to starting the newly installed instance. Access to the instance is done by the `sqlcmd` command line almost in the same way as on Windows. Right now, SQL Server DE, as well as SSRS and SSIS services, support running on Linux.

Container is quite a new term supported by Microsoft. We can think about containers as lightweight virtual machines with less isolation of processes (for example, service running in a container can be stopped from the host operating system). Another approach of container is to create a sandbox for an isolated amount of system resources. Container installation of SQL Server is done via command prompt.

When SQL Server is installed on Linux or in some container, it's accessed by clients in exactly the same way as any other instance of SQL Server. More detailed information about these new installation scenarios is beyond the scope of this book.

Checking the completed installation

We have taken all the necessary steps to install standalone instance of SQL Server DE. Next step is to check if the installation was successful, if the instance is up and running. After the installation completes, administrators have to check whether everything is working as expected.

If any error occurs during installation, additional diagnostics is needed. Every single task of the setup process is described in the setup log (in the case of default installation path, the log is placed on the `C:\Program Files\Microsoft SQL Server\140\Setup Bootstrap\Log` path).

However, it is still good practice to check whether everything works as expected. Those simple post-installation checks could be done using **Sql Server Configuration Manager**:

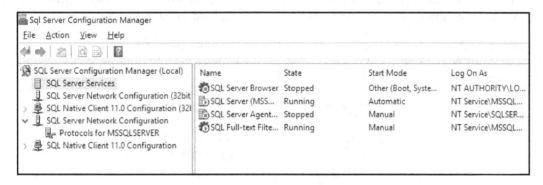

Sql Server Configuration Manager

The **Sql Server Configuration Manager** is the only visual client tool actually installed in the SQL Server setup. Configuration manager is a snap-in to Microsoft Management Console and consists of two main sections:

- **SQL Server Services**: When selected in the left pane, the right detail pane shows every SQL Server service or feature installed with its state, start-up mode, and logon account. These settings can be changed by right-clicking on a certain row and selecting **Properties** from the pop-up menu. The properties modal dialog appears and we can go through it to correct any setting as needed.
- **SQL Server Network Configuration (32-bit)**: In this section, administrators view a list of instances (the MSSQLSERVER instance name seen in **Sql Server Configuration Manager** picture above is the internal name for the default instance of SQL Server) and, when clicked on any instance in the left, a list of network protocols appears in the right pane.

There are also other nodes in the tree shown in the left pane of **Sql Server Configuration Manager** such as **SQL Native Client configuration**, which provides the ability to set client aliases for SQL Server instances (for example, when SQL Server is accessible only via its IP address, which is almost non-readable to users), but the preceding two sections are the most important ones.

SQL Server services configuration node

The administrator can call for a pop-up menu from every record shown in the right pane. Special attention should be focused on SQL Server itself and on SQL Server Agent.

SQL Server may be shown in several records because every instance has its own configurations so the first good thing is to select the right record. Following image shows the properties dialog box.

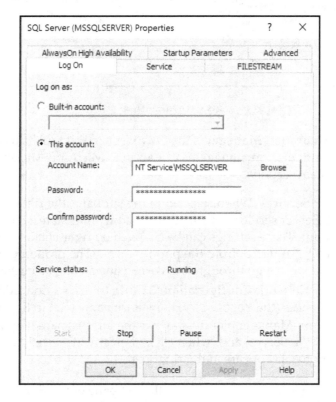

As shown on preceding image, Properties dialog box for every instance allows you to set the following:

- **Log On** tab: The context of the Windows account that will be used by the instance to log in to the operating system. This configuration needs restarting if changed.
- **Service** tab: The only setting enabled on this tab is Startup mode, which should be set to automatic.

- **FILESTREAM** tab: This tab contains **FILESTREAM** settings. As described earlier, **FILESTREAM** is a special kind of storage for binary data such as pictures or documents stored in relational data directly to a database. From administrator's point of view, **FILESTREAM** must be enabled for at least T-SQL Access. When enabled, databases can contain **FILESTREAM** file groups, which are actual representations of the binary storage. There's enhancement called file tables for which the second two textboxes (**allow for I/O...** and **enable remote clients...**) must be switched on.
- **Startup Parameters** tab: This tab contains three startup parameters as default:
    - d: The location of the primary data file of the database master (must be reconfigured when the master database is moved)
    - l: The location of the log file of the database master (must be reconfigured when the master database is moved)
    - e: The default path for error logs written by SQL Server
    - Additional parameters like trace flags and others can be added if needed.
- **AlwaysOn High Availability** tab: AlwaysOn is an advanced concept of data availability and reliability built on top of **Microsoft Cluster Service (MSCS)**. When certain instances would attend to the AlwaysOn group, it must be enabled on this tab. MSCS must already be present before this configuration is done.
- **Advanced** tab: This tab actually has no advanced settings, just error reporting and usage feedback to Microsoft.

Special attention should be given to SQL Server Agent. SQL Server Agent is installed with every single instance of SQL Server. In other words, every instance of SQL Server has its own SQL Server Agent. Immediately after installation, SQL Server Agent is set to manual startup mode, which is not good enough for production environments.

That's why one of the first post-installation configurations should be to change SQL Server Agent's startup mode to automatic because SQL Server Agent is an invaluable service for a lot of regular administrator tasks as well as automated tasks done by SQL Server itself (for example, data collection, strong diagnostics tool, and collecting performance statistics using SQL Server Agent jobs).

SQL Server network configuration node

SQL Server communicates with clients on its own network application protocol called **Tabular Data Stream** (**TDS**). Under this network application layer, TCP/IP and Named Pipes (now deprecated) network protocols are supported. The third option called **Shared Memory** is always enabled and allows communication between server and client when the client is running locally on the same machine as SQL Server.

SQL Server supports both 32-bit and 64-bit protocols so configuration for both modes is the same. Under the **SQL Server Network Configuration** node (even if it's the 32-bit node), network protocols for every instance of SQL Server already installed on the machine are placed. The administrator selects certain instances (for example, Protocols for MSSQLSERVER, which is the default instance) and, in the right pane of the **Sql Server Configuration Manager**, selects the property window for certain network protocols by right-clicking on properties.

The most complex configuration has to be made on the TCP/IP protocol. When SQL Server 2017 is installed, the protocol is enabled, so the administrator just checks whether the proper TCP ports are used. The default TCP port used for SQL Server communication is port number 1433. For additional named instances, ports starting with numbers 1450, 1451, or similar are often used. The ability and port number has to be set for every variant of IP address of every network interface.

After this configuration is done, instance of SQL Server needs to be restarted.

Testing connection to a fresh SQL Server

As mentioned earlier, SQL Server does not contain a client management toolset in its installation. It's a good idea to install SQL Server Management Studio directly on the server where SQL Server service is already running because a lot of administrator's tasks will be done directly on the server, but for a quick check whether SQL Server is accessible to clients, the command prompt can be used. Its name is sqlcmd and it's the only client tool installed with SQL Server directly. This tool is very useful in some scenarios:

- When SQL Server Management Studio is not present or cannot be used (for example, when restoring the master database)
- When the express edition of SQL Server was installed and SQL Server Agent cannot be used (when planning regular tasks, it can be done by PowerShell or by sqlcmd in conjunction with **Windows Task Scheduler**)

The most simple way to use `sqlcmd` is as follows:

```
sqlcmd
```

When running `sqlcmd` as shown in the preceding code example, it tries to connect the local default instance of SQL Server using the current user's Windows account. When successfully connected, rows in the command prompt window start to be numbered.

A better approach is to call `sqlcmd` with parameters precisely set:

```
sqlcmd -E -S localhost
```

In domain user context or with SQL login context:

```
sqlcmd -U <user name> -P <password> -S localhost
```

The E parameter (beware that all parameters of all command line tools provided by SQL Server are case-sensitive) says to the connection that Windows login context of the user currently logged in the desktop will be used; U and P parameters are used when user wants to connect via mixed authentication mode of SQL Server. Then user and password created on the SQL Server are used, not the Windows identity.

The S parameters is used for the name of the server. If connected locally on a default instance of SQL Server, shortcuts such as . or (localhost) could be used.

All the preceding examples start the `sqlcmd` tool in interactive mode. When successfully connected, rows start numbering and the user can start to write queries. Every query must be followed by the GO keyword. This keyword (sometimes called **batch terminator**) causes the text written to the console to be sent to SQL Server and then processed with some result.

Results returned back to the console are not so readable in many cases, so the `sqlcmd` could be started with the command parameter, o, followed by the path to the output file. The output file is just a text file catching all results from all queries sent by the user in the session.

When the user wants to run `sqlcmd` in unattended mode, the i parameter followed by the path to the input file may also be very useful. A complete example may look the following. The first piece of code shows the correctly created input file (for example, `demo.sql`):

```
--      content of demo.sql file
use master
go
select @@version as VersionOfMySQL
go
```

The first line (`use master`) establishes the correct database context in the connection and it is highly recommended to never commit this row because very often, the database context is not the default database context set for login.

The third line is just an example of doing something meaningful.

When the administrator wants to run a script file like this, he can add the following command to the command prompt:

```
sqlcmd -E -S (localhost) -i "c:\demo.sql" -o "c:\demo_output.txt"
```

The command will run and it will save all results (even if error will occur) to the file called `demo_output.txt`.

There are more useful command parameters for `sqlcmd` but this set, especially the first three examples, are sufficient to test an instance's accessibility locally.

For remote testing of accessibility, very common way is to use SQL Server Management Studio. Common issues (followed by error No. 40 - Network Related Error) are as follows:

- **SQL Server instance is not running**: In **Sql Server Configuration Manager**, this error is seen if service is running or not. When it's not running, we can try to start it up manually and diagnose additional errors.
- **TCP/IP protocol is disabled**: This issue may be corrected by **Sql Server Configuration Manager** (requires restart after reconfiguring).
- **Other than default TCP port number is used**: It can be corrected on user's side by adding the port number after server name (for example, `MYSQLSERVER:12345`).
- **Firewall rules are not set**: It must be resolved on firewall's side by enabling certain ports for communication.

Summary

The SQL Server ecosystem provides you with a wide set of technologies and the first problem is to know what is the responsibility of every single technology of SQL Server. When this is clear and we recognize our needs, we can start preparing our operating system and the complete infrastructure to install SQL Server.

The most important decision before starting the installation is which technologies to install and how many computers will be needed to distribute SQL Server services appropriately across an infrastructure.

Before installing SQL Server DE itself, we need to ensure that sufficient set of disk storage is in place, that appropriate security accounts are prepared, and that all software prerequisites are fulfilled.

After installation, it's highly recommended to check whether SQL Server is running, and if not, check logs in the `Setup Bootstrap` folder. When SQL Server is successfully running, we need to check SQL Server accessibility locally and remotely.

Last but not least, is a check of the SQL Server Agent state because, for administrators, this service is an invaluable helper when performing day-to-day administrative tasks. SQL Server Agent should have the startup mode set to automatic and should be running all the time when SQL Server DE does.

It is very useful to do more configuration after installation. The next chapter talks about these configuration settings and more about how to keep SQL Server healthy.

2
Keeping Your SQL Server Environment Healthy

In the first chapter, we have seen that SQL Server is a complex tool consisting of many services that work together. Based on the deployment scenario, we can even have more instances of the SQL server running on the same host. SQL Server is usually a key service in the enterprise environment because many other applications and tools depend on SQL Server as their primary data storage. It's a crucial task to keep our SQL Server healthy with proper maintenance and monitoring but also with proper post-installation configuration. Installation, as we have seen in the first chapter, is not configuring many of the settings and keeping the default values. Default configuration might not be ideal for your production environment and it's important to understand the benefits of the modification to the default values.

This chapter will cover the following points:

- Understanding SQL Server patching
- Post-installation configuration of the SQL Server
- Creating a performance baseline
- Understanding the monitoring tool set

Understanding SQL Server patching

Once you install SQL Server, you need to watch for future updates released by Microsoft. You can recognize what updates were installed to your server by checking the build number of the SQL Server. You can find the build number in the SQL Server Management Studio as you can see in the following screenshot or via the `SELECT @@VERSION` command. There are several types of updates released for SQL Server:

- Service packs
- Cumulative updates
- Security updates

Service packs are usually the largest update option for your SQL Server. They frequently include updates released by more cumulative updates and should be tested more thoroughly regarding performance and stability of the system. It's also important to keep your environment with recent service packs due to system support by Microsoft. Service packs not only fix issues, but often also bring new features to SQL Server. A good example was the service pack 1 for SQL Server 2016, which enabled many features previously available only in enterprise and standard editions. This had a tremendous impact on many smaller environments that were not utilizing enterprise edition, as DBAs and developers were able to start using many new features that were previously unavailable to them.

Cumulative updates are smaller compared to service packs and released more frequently. Cumulative updates usually fix many errors and include more updates, and undergo the same comprehensive tests as service packs. As an example, we can see that SQL Server 2014, by the time of writing this book, had only two service packs available, but for the first service pack, Microsoft had already released twelve cumulative updates with additional fixes for errors, performance, and stability. You can now install cumulative updates proactively with the same level of confidence as you would with service packs. Cumulative updates are incremental in nature so cumulative update 4 includes all the updates that were released in cumulative updates 1 to 3.

Security updates are smaller than cumulative updates and are usually fixing some sort of error or security vulnerability. These are released usually in a monthly cycle along the regular Windows updates and should be evaluated for your environment. Usually, a **Chief Security Office** (**CSO**) team or security team in general may request you to install such a security update in a reasonable time frame to your SQL Servers, which may be a complex task if you're managing larger environments.

You can find a nice list of updates for all SQL Server versions at `http://sqlserverbuilds.blogspot.com/` where you can identify the correct build of your SQL Server.

Installing updates

If you need to install an update to your SQL Server, you first need to download the correct bits from the Microsoft site and store them locally in your SQL Server. Some updates are downloaded as `.exe` files and some are available as `.zip` files, so you need to extract the installation first.

When you first start the installation, it will automatically extract to a random folder on one of your drives on the SQL server, as shown in the following screenshot:

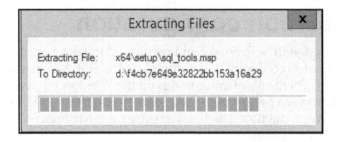

This folder will automatically get deleted once the installation is over.

When you accept the license terms for the installation, you need to select the instance from the list to which you would like to install the update. You can see the list of features installed for each instance and the last installation option is **shared services**. These include integration services and, on older systems, SQL Server Management Studio as well. Via the update installer, you can also see the current build and whether the update was installed or only partially installed due to some error.

Once you select the instance to which you'd like to install the update, you can proceed to the installation. It's common practice to restart the server after the installation. If you're installing more updates in a sequence, they perform system checks and one of them is restart pending anyway. After the restart, you need to verify that applications can correctly connect to the SQL Server and there are no impacts after the update installation.

For any high availability solution like fail-over clusters and mirroring or availability groups, you need to take special consideration to install updates and follow proper sequence between primary and secondary nodes (with respective naming for all the HA/DR options). For any more information, consider checking books online to find detailed procedures.

If you are deploying many SQL Servers at once or very frequently, you might consider customizing your installation media to include the latest updates.

In complex environments, you can integrate the installation bits of service packs and cumulative updates in your installation source and use this modified installation to install new SQL Servers directly with proper service packs or cumulative updates. This will speed up your deployment as the installation will already include the required service packs, updates, or security updates that may be required by your security or architecture team.

Post-installation configuration

Once you have installed your SQL Server and performed the patching to the current patch level required, you need to configure basic settings on the SQL Server and also on the Windows Server itself. There are several settings on the Windows Server that have an impact on your SQL Server's performance and security and these need to be updated before you put the server into production. The following are the basic options that you need to configure on the operating system:

- Security rights for your SQL Server account
- Power settings
- Firewall rules

Configuring security rights for a SQL Server account

During the installation of the SQL Server, you're choosing an account that will be used to run all SQL Server services. There are quite a few considerations for a proper choice but, in this chapter, we'll focus more on the follow-up configuration. Such an account needs to have proper rights on the system. System rights can be configured via **Group Policy Editor** in the **Computer Configuration** segment of the policy. To open up the console for the rights configuration, perform the following steps:

1. Run `gpedit.msc`.
2. Expand `Computer Configuration` | `Windows Settings` | `Security Settings` | `Local Policies`.

2. Double-click on the system right that you want to edit.
3. Add the account or group to which you want to grant the rights.

There are several rights that we'll consider for the SQL Server. The first one will be `Perform volume maintenance Tasks`. This right can be granted directly during the installation of the SQL Server, but if you skip this, here's where and how you can add this right to your SQL Server account. The reason for granting this right is to enable `Instant File Initialization`, which can speed up disk operations to allocate new space for data files on the disk. `Instant File Initialization` does not work for log files, which in any case have to be zeroed out.

`Instant File Initialization` is used when the data file for the database is growing and allocating new space on the disk drive and also during the restoring of the database to create all files on the disk, before data can be copied from backup to the data files:

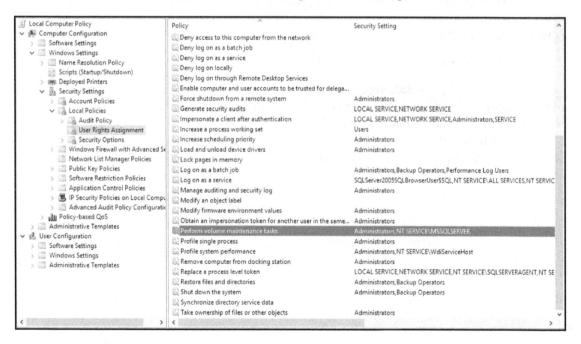

Another system right that we will assign as part of post-installation configuration will be `Generate Security Audits`. As you can see in the previous screenshot, this right is granted to two accounts, `Local Service` and `Network Service`. Our SQL Server is running with a different account and this account needs to be added to the list. This right will, later on, allow our SQL Server to store audit events in `Windows Event Log` to the security log portion. This may come handy once we see how SQL Server audit is working and what are the options to audit.

The last system right that we will assign is `Lock Pages In Memory`. This right will allow SQL Server to lock the memory pages and prevent Windows OS to page out memory in a case of memory pressure on the operating system. This one has to be taken with careful consideration and more configuration on the SQL Server engine and proper system monitoring. We'll talk about the SQL Server settings later.

Configuring power settings

When you install Windows Server operating system, you need to check for power settings, which are configured on such systems. There are several options for how you can verify which power setting plan is currently in use. If you open a command prompt or PowerShell, you can use the `powercfg` utility to see what plan is used on your server:

```
powercfg.exe -list
```

By default, you will see a **Balanced** plan selected, which is great for most servers and offers a lot of power-saving features, but usually this plan is not optimal for SQL Servers. SQL Server can put quite some load on the CPU and switching between CPU speeds may cost you precious time and performance. If you open the **Task Manager** tool, you can see that your CPU is not running on the maximum speed and may be running with a much lower value.

As an example, you can see the following screenshot from one of the physical servers with 2.4 GHz CPU, which is running on 1.25 GHz due to a power-saving plan:

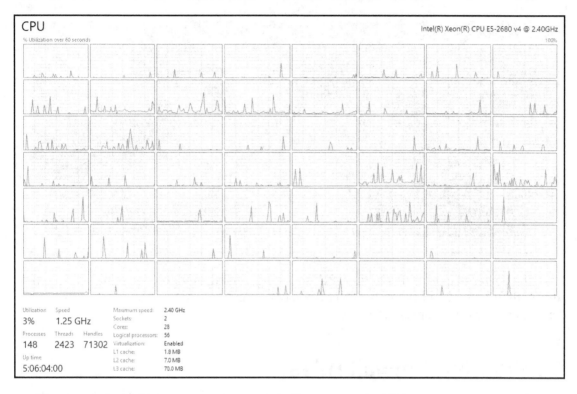

You can verify this with tools like CPU-Z or similar, and the best option we have here is to update the power plan to high performance, which is common for SQL Server workloads. To update the power plan setting, you can either use a control panel where you can find settings for power options or use a command line again. When we listed the plans on the server with the previous command, you have seen in the output that they come with name and GUID. To update the plan via the command line, we need to use the GUID with the `powercfg` tool:

```
powercfg.exe -SETACTIVE <GUIDofThePlan>
```

The following screenshot gives an illustration of updating the plan via the command line:

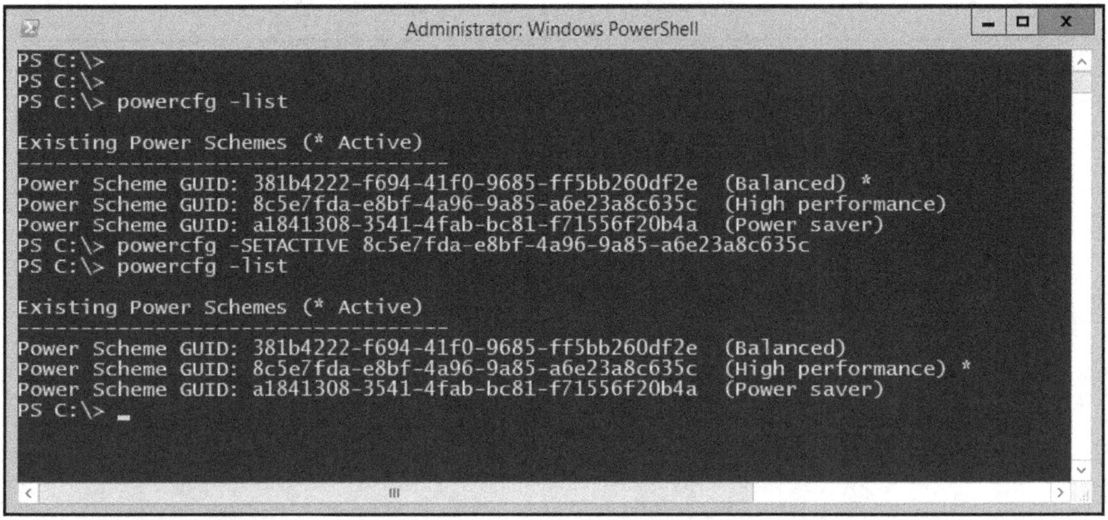

```
Administrator: Windows PowerShell                                    _  □  x

PS C:\>
PS C:\>
PS C:\> powercfg -list

Existing Power Schemes (* Active)
---------------------------------
Power Scheme GUID: 381b4222-f694-41f0-9685-ff5bb260df2e  (Balanced) *
Power Scheme GUID: 8c5e7fda-e8bf-4a96-9a85-a6e23a8c635c  (High performance)
Power Scheme GUID: a1841308-3541-4fab-bc81-f71556f20b4a  (Power saver)
PS C:\> powercfg -SETACTIVE 8c5e7fda-e8bf-4a96-9a85-a6e23a8c635c
PS C:\> powercfg -list

Existing Power Schemes (* Active)
---------------------------------
Power Scheme GUID: 381b4222-f694-41f0-9685-ff5bb260df2e  (Balanced)
Power Scheme GUID: 8c5e7fda-e8bf-4a96-9a85-a6e23a8c635c  (High performance) *
Power Scheme GUID: a1841308-3541-4fab-bc81-f71556f20b4a  (Power saver)
PS C:\> _
```

Once the power plan is updated, the CPU is no longer using any power-saving mode and runs with full speed and possibly even turbo boot for extreme loads while performing complex queries on your server.

Configuring firewall rules

Each SQL Server instance running on your server is using a different port number to listen for incoming connections, but during the installation of the SQL Server, there are no firewall rules created on your local firewall. So SQL Server is perfectly accessible locally, but not from remote hosts if the local firewall is active. You can run with a built-in firewall on the Windows Servers or have some third-party software in your environment, which requires additional configuration.

During the installation of the SQL Server, you had to make a choice between deploying SQL Server as a default instance or a named instance. SQL Server default instance is listening on port 1433, which you can verify in the SQL Server configuration manager tool. This port is set as static and will not change over time. Named instances, on the other hand, use a randomly selected port, which may not be fixed and can change after a system reboot, because named instances use dynamic ports as a default option.

It's advised to change the dynamic port to static so that the port number does not change and this does not have any impact for any security configuration like service principal name, which we'll discuss in another chapter.

The following screenshot gives a good idea of the default instances:

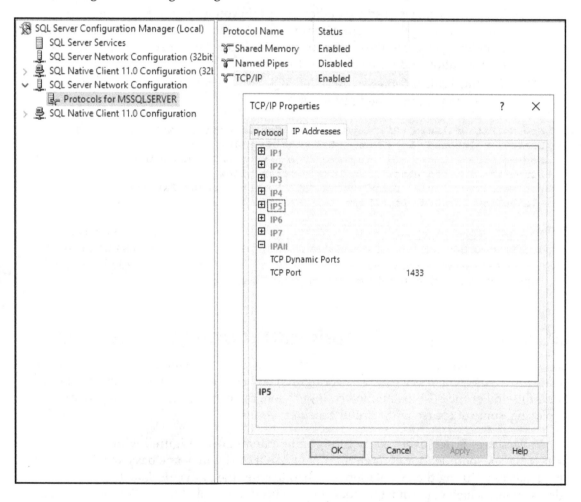

Once we know what port our SQL Server instance is listening to, we need to configure the firewall to allow the traffic to our SQL Server service. Windows Server comes with a built-in firewall that can be controlled via GUI, command line, and PowerShell.

We will add three different rules to the firewall with the PowerShell tool:

- The first rule is for the SQL Server service with the proper port number. We have seen the port number in the configuration manager. For a default instance, this is 1433; for a named instance, the port number would be mostly random on each system.
- The second rule is used for dedicated admin connection, which is used for troubleshooting the system. Enabling just the firewall rule does not allow you to remotely connect to DAC session; this also has to be turned on in the SQL Server configuration and we'll cover this topic later.
- The third rule is for a service called SQL Server browser, which is used for connection to the named instances:

```
New-NetFirewallRule -DisplayName "SQL Server Connection" -Protocol TCP -
Direction Inbound -LocalPort 1433 -Action allow
New-NetFirewallRule -DisplayName "SQL Server DAC Connection" -Protocol TCP -
Direction Inbound -LocalPort 1434 -Action allow
New-NetFirewallRule -DisplayName "SQL Server Browser Service" -Protocol UDP
-Direction Inbound -LocalPort 1434 -Action allow
```

If you're running more instances on the server, or any other services such as analysis services or reporting services, or you use any solutions for HA/DR such as mirroring or always on, then you need to carefully examine what firewall rules are needed and the list may get much longer than the three basic rules we have seen.

SQL Server post-installation configuration

So far, we have configured our Windows Server and we have made a few configurations related to SQL Server, but we haven't configured any SQL-specific items inside the SQL Server itself. For the post-installation configuration, there are plenty of settings worth exploring, some of course with careful consideration.

When the server is deployed, many configuration items are configured with default values, which may be modified for your environment. We'll start with some basic configuration for the databases. During the installation, you had to enter the paths for data, log, and backup file locations, which you can later modify if you need to update the location of the default files.

In the **Database Settings** section of the server configuration, you can again configure all three paths, as shown in the following screenshot:

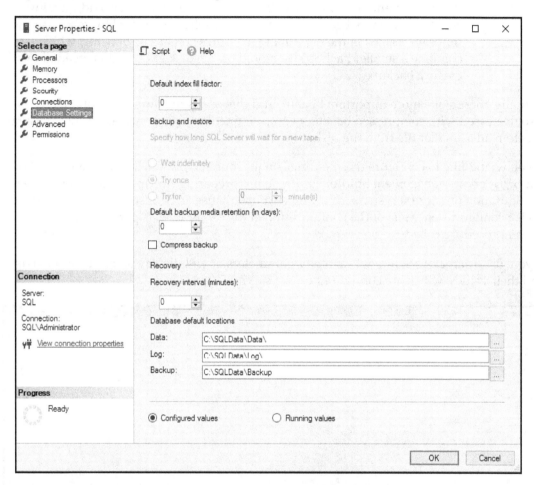

On this same settings page, you can configure two additional important parameters. The first one is the backup compression. We'll talk more about the backup settings and methods to perform backup in a different chapter, but as part of post-installation configuration, you can configure this setting on most servers.

Bear in mind that turning on backup compression puts additional load on the CPU while performing the backup, so this may cause higher peaks in the performance monitor. Also if the server is under heavy load, causing additional load by backup compression might not be ideal for response times for users. On the other hand, compression has its benefits, which combine a smaller backup size stored on the disk and the time needed to create a backup.

Actually, there's one more important benefit, and this one is the time to restore, which is also decreased with compressed backup versus an uncompressed one, because the system gets to read a smaller file from the disk.

If you would like to configure these settings on just one server, you'll be fine with GUI of our SQL Server Management Studio, but if you are preparing a script for post-deployment configuration on more servers, you will most probably use an SQL script that can perform such a configuration. Most of the configuration at the server level is performed with a stored procedure called `sp_configure`.

If you just run the procedure without any parameters, it will display all basic parameters and their values, which are configured on the server:

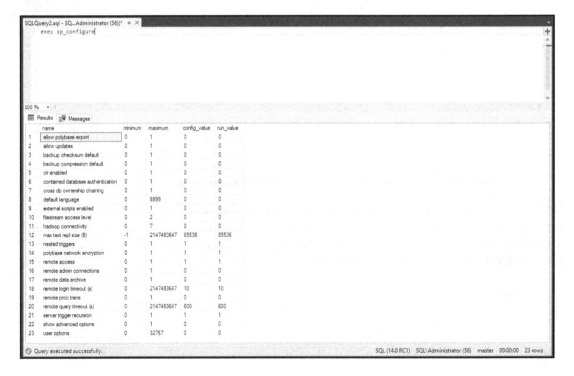

You don't need to memorize all the options as we won't configure all of these. It's just a basic set of the items; as you can see, the second from the bottom is an option called **show advanced options**, which will display more of the items for configuration. Backup compression is listed in the basic set and can be configured with the following code:

```
USE master
GO
EXEC sp_configure 'backup compression default',1
GO
RECONFIGURE
GO
```

Some other options that we will explore are visible only when you display the advanced features. To display all the advanced features, you can simply run `sp_configure` again and you'll set the option for show advanced options as in the previous example. With advanced options displayed, SQL Server will let you configure 77 (on SQL Server 2017; with other versions, this may be different) options in contrast to 23 when you display only the basic set.

With regards to post-installation configuration, we'll configure the memory and CPU settings for our server too. By default, SQL Server is allowed to use as much memory as possible and Windows OS won't make any larger reserve of other applications or even for itself, so you can limit the amount of memory available to SQL Server. You should reserve memory to the operating system so that it does not get unresponsive under heavy load on SQL Server.

There have been many situations when DBA could not connect to the SQL Server operating system because all the memory was allocated to SQL Server itself. You can limit the memory available to the SQL Server with a setting called **max server memory**. This setting has to be considered carefully as you need to keep some memory to the OS. As a general guideline, you need to keep 1 to 2 GB for the OS and then one 1 GB for each 8 to 16 GB on the system. So for a SQL Server with 256 GB RAM, you would configure the max server memory setting to a value between 224 to 240 GB. The code to perform the configuration is as follows. Don't forget that the procedure is using megabytes as a unit of measure:

```
sp_configure 'max server memory',245760
```

SQL Server editions provide different limits to use system memory to SQL server. Standard edition can use only up to 128GB RAM for the SQL Server buffer pool, whereas enterprise edition can use all the system memory available on the server. You can find different limits for the editions available in the online documentation. The differences in the editions are not only about RAM, but also about CPU and core support for different SQL Server SKUs.

There is another setting that can be very useful when you're troubleshooting your SQL Server and it gets unresponsive--it is called dedicated admin connection. By default, such a connection is not allowed remotely and you can connect to DAC only locally while being logged onto the server. If the system faces performance issues and even the Windows Server won't allow you to connect via **Remote Desktop**, you can connect to DAC remotely if you have enabled this setting. To enable remote DAC, you need to run the following procedure:

```
sp_configure 'remote admin connections',1
GO
RECONFIGURE
```

Additional items that we will configure have an effect on the SQL Server performance and require deeper understanding of your workload, hardware, and requirement of your applications. These will include configuring parallelism on your server.

There are two main configuration items that we're using to control parallelism on the server level and these are as follows:

- Max degree of parallelism (default is 0)
- Cost threshold for parallelism (default is 5)

The first one sets the maximum amount of threads to be used in a query when it's processed in parallel. It does not mean that each query will be processed with multiple threads, and if it will be, it can be a lower amount. It's a default server setting, which you can later override on different levels, but as a general option, it's a good idea to configure this value. What is the proper value depends greatly on several factors and they are as follows:

- Your hardware: CPUs and cores
- Your workload: OLTP versus OLAP
- Your environment: Physical versus virtual

In most cases, you can examine the amount of CPUs and cores on your system and assign a value that determines the amount of cores on one CPU. So for example, if you have two 8-Core CPUs used for your SQL Server, you will configure the max degree of parallelism to value 8. Again, you can use the SQL Server Management Studio or the `sp_configure` procedure. At the same time, in the GUI, you can also update the cost threshold for parallelism value, which is something like a virtual cost of a query when the query optimizer component is generating a serial or parallel plan.

If the cost is too low, there might be too many parallel plans, which can increase the load on the CPU and memory of your SQL Server. This configuration is subject to test, but you can start with values ranging from 20 to 50 and evaluate the load on your SQL Server and your application performance:

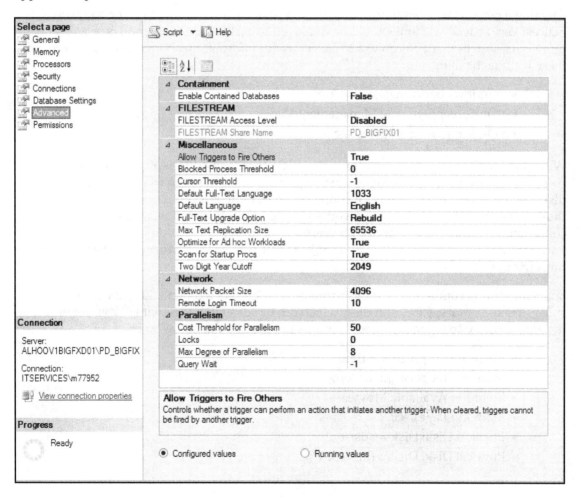

Creating a performance baseline

Once you have deployed and configured your SQL Server, you can create a performance baseline. This baseline is very important for you for numerous reasons and they are as follows:

- When you start troubleshooting the server, you need to know how your server will behave to something odd
- You can proactively tune the system if you find a weak spot in the baseline
- When you plan to upgrade your server, you know how the load was increasing over time, so you can plan properly

Creating a performance baseline and capturing performance information for your server is hence a very crucial task and should be deployed to each of your servers. There are numerous sources that you can use to collect useful information about your SQL Server and these include the following:

- Windows performance monitor
- SQL Server Dynamic Management Views
- SQL Server extended events

With Windows performance monitor, you can capture many different performance counters that are related not only to the SQL Server, but also to the whole system--CPU, disk, network, and so on. The list of counters can be quite large, but you should select only those counters that are important to you and keep yourself from overwhelmed data collection. Performance monitor can be very useful for log correlation as you can load the performance data to other tools such as SQL Server profiler or **Performance Analysis of Logs** (**PAL**) tool.

Some interesting counters worth capturing on the OS level would include the basic subsystems--memory, CPU, and disk, which can be correlated together to have better insights to the system performance. These would include the following:

- Processor: % processor time
- System: Processor queue length
- Memory: Available Mbytes
- Memory: Pages/sec
- Physical Disk: Disk reads/sec
- Physical Disk: Disk writes/sec

These counters will give you a very basic overview of the system performance and have to be combined with more information to get any conclusion from the values. As a starting OS performance baseline, these will be very useful and can be tracked and stored for historical overview and troubleshooting. Of course, you need to consider many factors such as change in the system load during business hours, after business hours, and weekends. There may be some peaks in the values in the mornings, during some maintenance, backup, and so on. So understanding what your system is doing over time is an essential part in reading the performance baseline.

There are numerous SQL Server counters available in performance monitor and it's not needed to include them all, so we'll again see some basic counters worth monitoring over time to have a baseline that we can use for troubleshooting. These would include the following:

- SQL Server: Buffer manager--buffer cache hit ratio
- SQL Server: Buffer manager--page life expectancy
- SQL Server: Memory manager--total server memory (KB)
- SQL Server: Memory manager--target server memory (KB)
- SQL Server: Memory manager--memory grants pending
- SQL Server: Access methods--full scans/sec
- SQL Server: Access methods--index searches/sec
- SQL Server: Access methods--forwarded records/sec
- SQL Server: SQL statistics--SQL compilations/sec
- SQL Server: SQL statistics--batch requests/sec
- SQL Server: General statistics--user connections

Another tool that you can use is SQL Server **Dynamic Management Views** (**DMV**), which can return the state of SQL Server and it's objects and components. You can query the DMVs with SQL language like any other table and most of the time, you'll combine several of the views to have better information:

```
SELECT * FROM sys.dm_exec_requests er
JOIN sys.dm_exec_sessions es
ON er.session_id = es.session_id
-- remove all system sessions and yourself
WHERE es.session_id > 50 and es.session_id != @@SPID
```

This simple query as an example will combine two DMV views together and filter out all system sessions connected to SQL Server and your query window and display all user requests/sessions with all information stored in these two views. For a baseline, you shouldn't use all the columns as you will store quite a lot of data and you should limit your queries only for important parts.

Some important DMVs worth investigating and capturing for a baseline would include the following:

- `sys.dm_io_virtual_file_stats`
- `sys.dm_db_index_physical_stats`
- `sys.dm_db_missing_index_detais`
- `sys.dm_os_wait_stats`

> You can find many ready-to-use DMV queries online; an awesome source is a list of queries compiled by Glenn Berry, which are available on his blog, `https://www.sqlskills.com/blogs/glenn/category/dmv-queries/`.

If you schedule a data collection of these values to some monitoring database with a reasonable schedule, you can see how the performance of the system is changing over time; by combining all of these, you can have a comprehensive view over your system.

Summary

In this chapter, we have seen how to build a healthy SQL Server environment and how to configure not only the SQL Server, but also a Windows Server for stable and secure SQL Server workload. Keeping your server up to date, secure, and monitored is extremely crucial for the stability of the applications and your ability to perform any troubleshooting at the SQL Server level.

In the next chapter, we will build on our healthy SQL Server and introduce backup and recovery procedures so that you will understand how to keep your server safe and how to recover from failures.

3
Backup and Recovery

To maintain data reliability is one of the most important of an administrator's responsibilities. SQL Server helps in fulfilling this responsibility via very sophisticated backup and restore features. This chapter is going to describe in detail what's needed to choose an appropriate database backup strategy in conjunction with its usage and configuration, and how to use stored backups to restore a database in case of failure.

At the end of this chapter, we will understand the following points:

- **Data structures and transaction logging**: How SQL Server handles data. This knowledge is highly welcome for good understanding of what, when, and why should be backed up.
- **Backup**:
  - How to configure the server and database properly for certain backup types
  - What kind of backups are on the playground and how to use them
- **Restore**:
  - How to prepare the database for restore and the restore process itself
  - Sample restore scenarios

Data structures and transaction logging

We can think about a database as of **physical database structure** consisting of tables and indexes. However, this is just a human point of view. From the SQL Server's perspective, a database is a set of precisely structured files described in a form of **metadata** also saved in database structures.

A conceptual imagination of how every database works is very helpful when the database has to be backed up correctly.

How data is stored

Every database on SQL Server must have at least two files:

- The **primary data file** with the usual suffix, `mdf`
- The **transaction log file** with the usual suffix, `ldf`

For lots of databases, this minimal set of files is not enough. When the database contains big amounts of data such as historical tables, or the database has big data contention such as production tracking systems, it's good practise to design more data files. Another situation when a basic set of files is not sufficient can arise when documents or pictures would be saved along with relational data. However, SQL Server still is able to store all of our data in the basic file set, but it can lead to a performance bottlenecks and management issues. That's why we need to know all possible storage types useful for different scenarios of deployment. A complete structure of files is depicted in the following image:

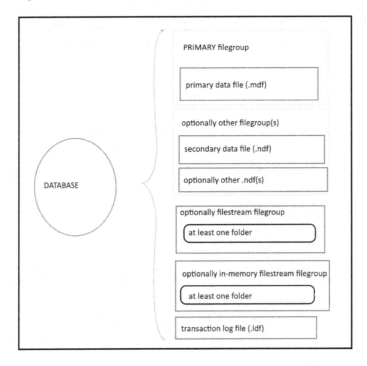

For many administrators who never care about databases on SQL Server before, this tree of objects could be unclear and confusing. It's time to explain every single node in the preceding tree.

Database

A **relational database** is defined as a complex data type consisting of tables with a given amount of columns, and each column has its domain that is actually a data type (such as an integer or a date) optionally complemented by some constraints.

From SQL Server's perspective, the database is a record written in metadata and containing the name of the database, properties of the database, and names and locations of all files or folders representing storage for the database. This is the same for **user databases** as well as for **system databases**.

System databases are created automatically during SQL Server installation and are crucial for correct running of SQL Server. We know five system databases.

Database master

Database master is crucial for the correct running of SQL Server service. In this database is stored data about logins, all databases and their files, instance configurations, linked servers, and so on. SQL Server finds this database at startup via two startup parameters, -d and -l, followed by paths to `mdf` and `ldf` files.

 These parameters are very important in situations when the administrator wants to move the master's files to a different location. Changing their values is possible in the SQL Server Configuration Manager in the SQL Server service Properties dialog on the tab called **startup parameters**.

Database msdb

The database `msdb` serves as the SQL Server Agent service, Database Mail, and Service Broker. In this database are stored job definitions, operators, and other objects needed for administration automation. This database also stores some logs such as backup and restore events of each database. If this database is corrupted or missing, SQL Server Agent cannot start.

Database model

Database model can be understood as a template for every new database while it is created. During a database creation (see the CREATE DATABASE statement on MSDN), files are created on defined paths and all objects, data and properties of database model are created, copied, and set into the new database during its creation. This database must always exist on the instance, because when it's corrupted, database tempdb can be created at instance start up!

Database tempdb

Even if database tempdb seems to be a regular database like many others, it plays a very special role in every SQL Server instance. This database is used by SQL Server itself as well as by developers to save temporary data such as table variables or static cursors. As this database is intended for a short lifespan (temporary data only, which can be stored during execution of stored procedure or until session is disconnected), SQL Server clears this database by truncating all data from it or by dropping and recreating this database every time when it's started.

As the tempdb database will never contain durable data, it has some special internal behavior and it's the reason why accessing data in this database is several times faster than accessing durable data in other databases. If this database is corrupted, restart SQL Server.

Database resourcedb

The resourcedb is fifth in our enumeration and consists of definitions for all system objects of SQL Server, for example, sys.objects. This database is hidden and we don't need to care about it that much.

It is not configurable and we don't use regular backup strategies for it. It is always placed in the installation path of SQL Server (to the binn directory) and it's backed up within the filesystem backup. In case of an accident, it is recovered as a part of the filesystem as well.

Filegroup

Filegroup is an organizational metadata object containing one or more data files. Filegroup does not have its own representation in the filesystem--it's just a group of files. When any database is created, a filegroup called primary is always created. This primary filegroup always contains the primary data file.

Filegroups can be divided into the following:

- **Row storage filegroups**: These filegroup can contain data files (`mdf` or `ndf`).
- **Filestream filegroups**: This kind of filegroups can contain not files but folders to store binary data.
- **In-memory filegroup**: Only one instance of this kind of filegroup can be created in a database. Internally, it is a special case of filestream filegroup and it's used by SQL Server to persist data from in-memory tables.

Every filegroup has three simple properties:

- **Name:** This is a descriptive name of the filegroup. The name must fulfill the naming convention criteria.
- **Default**: In a set of filegroups of the same type, one of these filegroups has this option set to on. This means that when a new table or index is created without explicitly specified to which filegroup it has to store data in, the default filegroup is used. By default, the primary filegroup is the default one.
- **Read-only**: Every filegroup, except the primary filegroup, could be set to read-only. Let's say that a filegroup is created for last year's history. When data is moved from the current period to tables created in this historical filegroup, the filegroup could be set as read-only, and later the filegroup cannot be backed up again and again.

 It is a very good approach to divide the database into smaller parts-- filegroups with more files. It helps in distributing data across more physical storage and also makes the database more manageable; backups can be done part by part in shorter times, which better fit into a service window.

Data files

Every database must have at least one data file called **primary data file**. This file is always bound to the primary filegroup. In this file is all the metadata of the database, such as structure descriptions (could be seen through views such as `sys.objects`, `sys.columns`, and others), users, and so on. If the database does not have other data files (in the same or other filegroups), all user data is also stored in this file, but this approach is good enough just for smaller databases.

Considering how the volume of data in the database grows over time, it is a good practice to add more data files. These files are called **secondary data files**. Secondary data files are optional and contain user data only.

Both types of data files have the same internal structure. Every file is divided into 8 KB small parts called **data pages**. SQL Server maintains several types of data pages such as data, data pages, index pages, **index allocation maps** (**IAM**) pages to locate data pages of tables or indexes, **global allocation map** (**GAM**) and **shared global allocation maps** (**SGAM**) pages to address objects in the database, and so on. Regardless of the type of a certain data page, SQL Server uses a data page as the smallest unit of I/O operations between hard disk and memory. Let's describe some common properties:

- A data page never contains data of several objects
- Data pages don't know each other (and that's why SQL Server uses IAMs to allocate all pages of an object)
- Data pages don't have any special physical ordering
- A data row must always fit in size to a data page

These properties could seem to be useless but we have to keep in mind that when we know these properties, we can better optimize and manage our databases.

Did you know that a data page is the smallest storage unit that can be restored from backup?

As a data page is quite a small storage unit, SQL Server groups data pages into bigger logical units called **extents**. An extent is a logical allocation unit containing eight coherent data pages. When SQL Server requests data from disk, extents are read into memory. This is the reason why 64 KB NTFS clusters are recommended to format disk volumes for data files. Extents could be **uniform** or **mixed**. Uniform extent is a kind of extent containing data pages belonging to one object only; on the other hand, a mixed extent contains data pages of several objects.

Transaction log

When SQL Server processes any transaction, it works in a way called **two-phase commit**. When a client starts a transaction by sending a single DML request or by calling the BEGIN TRAN command, SQL Server requests data pages from disk to memory called **buffer cache** and makes the requested changes in these data pages in memory. When the DML request is fulfilled or the COMMIT command comes from the client, the first phase of the commit is finished, but data pages in memory differ from their original versions in a data file on disk. The data page in memory is in a state called dirty.

When a transaction runs, a transaction log file is used by SQL Server for a very detailed chronological description of every single action done during the transaction. This description is called **write-ahead-logging**, shortly WAL, and is one of the oldest processes known on SQL Server.

The second phase of the commit usually does not depend on the client's request and is an internal process called **checkpoint**. Checkpoint is a periodical action that:

- searches for dirty pages in buffer cache,
- saves dirty pages to their original data file location,
- marks these data pages as **clean** (or drops them out of memory to free memory space),
- marks the transaction as **checkpoint** or **inactive** in the transaction log.

Write-ahead-logging is needed for SQL Server during **recovery process**. Recovery process is started on every database every time SQL Server service starts. When SQL Server service stops, some pages could remain in a dirty state and they are lost from memory. This can lead to two possible situations:

- The transaction is completely described in the transaction log, the new content of the data page is lost from memory, and data pages are not changed in the data file
- The transaction was not completed at the moment SQL Server stopped, so the transaction cannot be completely described in the transaction log as well, data pages in memory were not in a stable state (because the transaction was not finished and SQL Server cannot know if COMMIT or ROLLBACK will occur), and the original version of data pages in data files is intact

SQL Server decides these two situations when it's starting. If a transaction is complete in the transaction log but was not marked as checkpoint, SQL Server executes this transaction again with both phases of COMMIT. If the transaction was not complete in the transaction log when SQL Server stopped, SQL Server will never know what was the user's intention with the transaction and the incomplete transaction is erased from the transaction log as if it had never started.

The aforementioned described recovery process ensures that every database is in the last known consistent state after SQL Server's startup.

It's crucial for DBAs to understand write-ahead-logging when planning a backup strategy because when restoring the database, the administrator has to recognize if it's time to run the recovery process or not.

Backup

Backup can be understood as a copy of used data pages or a copy of transaction log records. Backup has to be done regularly. Backup is needed not only to restore databases in case of physical or logical failure, but it is also useful when, for example, we want to make a copy of the database or migrate the database to another SQL Server instance. To have our backups proper and complete, we need to consider the following points:

- How to configure the database
- Which types of backups combine together
- How to use backup strategies in conjunction with database usage

Recovery model

Every database has a property called **recovery model**. The recovery model determines how transactions are logged, and for how long time committed transactions will be stored in the transaction log. The recovery model is set by T-SQL command, ALTER DATABASE:

```
-- setting full recovery model
ALTER DATABASE <database_name> SET RECOVERY FULL
```

The recovery model has three possible options:

- SIMPLE
- BULK_LOGGED

- FULL

When the recovery model is set to SIMPLE, SQL Server clears transactions from the transaction log when they are checkpoint. This approach leads to a relatively small transaction log file, which seems to be a good behavior, but, on the other hand, the transaction log does not hold transaction descriptions so we are not able to use more sophisticated strategies to minimize data loss.

The SIMPLE recovery model is a good option when data stored in the database is not mission-critical, or when potential data loss is not critical for users, or for databases that could be reloaded from other sources. As an example of a database where data is not crucial for business, we can imagine development databases where data is sometimes damaged intentionally.

As an example for a database where content could be reloaded repeatedly, we can imagine data warehouse for statistical purposes loaded periodically from an operational database such as accounting, order processing, or production tracking.

When recovery model is set to SIMPLE, SQL Server keeps transaction log records in the transaction log file to the checkpoint only. When the recovery model set to FULL, SQL server keeps transaction log records in the transaction log file until BACKUP LOG statement is executed. It provides the ability for complex and sophisticated backup strategies. With recovery model set to full, SQL Server keeps all transaction records indefinitely until the transaction log file is full, then the database stops its work and becomes inaccessible. That's why we need to back up the transaction log regularly because the backup clears the transaction log, keeps it a manageable size, and defends the database against stopping work. As an advanced point, we have to say that when the recovery model is set to full, we can restore the database at any point in time.

What is the BULK_LOGGED recovery model for? This option has almost the same behavior as a full recovery model, but bulk-logged operations (for example, BULK INSERT of flat files into database tables) are described briefly in the transaction log file. The BULK_LOGGED recovery model doesn't provide the ability to restore the database at any point in time. It is used only on databases where some small data loss is allowed and one example of usage can be as follows:

- Before periodical data load, set recovery model to BULK_LOGGED
- Load flat files, images, or other LOBs
- Set the recovery model back to full
- Back up the database

Backup types

SQL server supports three main types of backup:

- Full backup
- Differential backup
- Transaction log backup

Each of these types has several variants and we will go through each of them.

Full backup

A **full backup** is simply the backup of a complete database. When performing a full backup, SQL Server stores metadata of the database (its name, creation date, all options set to the database, paths to all files belonging to the database, and so on), used data pages of every data file, and also the active part of the transaction log (which means all transactions that are not checkpoint yet and all running transactions even if they are not finished).

At the end of the backup process, SQL Server stores the last **Log Sequence Number** (**LSN**) for possible additional backups.

A full backup never clears the transaction log file!

A full backup can be performed with no respect to the recovery model set but the correct option is to have a `SIMPLE` recovery model if we don't intend to add additional backups to our backup strategy.

The command for a full database backup is generally as follows:

```
BACKUP DATABASE <database name> TO DISK = '<full path to backup>'
```

We can write the following as an example to back up an `AdventureWorks` database:

```
BACKUP DATABASE AdventureWorks TO DISK = 'D:\myBackups\AdventureWorks.bak'
```

Let's describe the preceding example in more detail. A database called `AdventureWorks` must exist on the server and it must be in consistent state; in other words, we never cannot back up a database (with any kind of backup) that is not online and working normally. The second mandatory condition is that the path `D:\myBackups` must exist on the filesystem. Backups are not installers, they never create folders.

The filename for the backup is arbitrary, the `.bak` extension is recommended. The file itself need not exist, it's created with the first backup. It's possible to store more backups in one file. When we want to have more backups in one file, we have to add a new option to the `backup` command:

```
BACKUP DATABASE AdventureWorks TO DISK = 'D:\myBackups\AdventureWorks.bak'
WITH NOINIT
```

When the preceding example is run for the first time and the `.bak` file doesn't exist, it will be created. When the same command is executed a second time with the same path and filename, the backup file will grow in volume because additional backup will be added to it. Recursively, when we want to erase all backups from the backup file and start a new backup cycle, we can change the `NOINIT` option with the `INIT` option. The `INIT` option causes all backups to be erased from the backup file and only the new backup will be stored in it.

Full backups tend to have a big volume. It could lead to disk insufficiency as well as too much time spent by the backup operation. That's why it's good and highly welcome to compress backups. There are two ways for doing this. The first way is to set the server level to default for backup compression. The command for this server setting is as follows:

```
EXEC sp_configure 'backup compression default', 1
GO
RECONFIGURE
GO
```

The `sp_configure` system stored procedure is used in many cases, as seen in the preceding example. The first parameter `'backup compression default'` is the name of the configuration property. It's actually hard to remember all configuration parameters, the simplest way is to call `sp_configure` just as is, without parameters, and the procedure will return the result set with a list of parameter names and currently configured values.

The second parameter (number 1) is a bit value; in this case, indicating that we want to switch the backup compression on. For some configuration values, only bit is used; for example, when setting the maximum degree of parallelism, the integer value indicating how many CPUs can be used for parallel processing of one T-SQL request.

The `RECONFIGURE` command causes the load of the configured property immediately without the need of service restart.

If we don't need to explore the default server setting of compression, we can simply add another option directly to the BACKUP command:

```
BACKUP DATABASE AdventureWorks TO DISK = 'D:\myBackups\AdventureWorks.bak'
WITH NOINIT, COMPRESSION
```

Can you believe how simple it is? Just keep in mind that compressed backups cannot be stored in the same file as uncompressed backups because SQL Server compresses the backup file when it is written. In other words, we cannot have a part of file uncompressed and the rest of the same file compressed. If we don't want to compress some backup, the opposite option is NO_COMPRESSION.

Let's have some uncompressed backup and we want to use backup compression. In this case, the INIT option of the BACKUP command is too weak. We need to replace the INIT option with the stronger FORMAT option. The Format option deletes the backup file and creates a new one. Use the FORMAT option carefully because it will cause all your backups in certain backup files to be lost forever.

A full backup serves as a baseline for more advanced backup strategies. It is often combined with transaction log backups and the dependency is driven by the last LSN written to every backup. When additional transaction log backup is executed, SQL Server remembers the last backup LSN from the previous backup and starts the current backup operation from the next LSN in order. Hence, when a full backup is executed, the last remembered LSN is replaced with a new one and the backup strategy obtains a new baseline.

In some cases, this is undesired behavior. For example, in situations when we need to create a copy of a certain database with a full backup, but without breaking out of the backup sequence. For this case, one more full backup variant exists:

```
BACKUP DATABASE AdventureWorks TO DISK =
'D:\myBackups\tempBackupOfAdventureWorks.bak'
WITH COPY_ONLY
```

The COPY_ONLY option in the preceding command causes that the LSN sequence tracked for backup consequences is not restarted and the exceptional full backup doesn't establish a new baseline for the backup strategy.

Full backup is relatively straightforward but less efficient when we need to minimalize potential data loss. That's why we need to have some stronger mechanism on how to keep our data safe and sheltered against physical as well as logical damage.

Transaction log backup

As written in the previous section, full backup establishes a baseline for more efficient backup strategies. In other words, at least one full backup must be created before we can start a backup transaction log. A **transaction log** backup is a consequencing backup that backs up all transaction log records from the last LSN, which is contained in any previous backup.

In other words, a full backup is a backup of state of the database while transaction log backup is a backup of additional changes. Using transaction log backup ensures that the **recovery point objective** (**RPO**) point to which the database could be restored, will be very close to the moment when the database was damaged.

Another important property of transaction log backups is, that this backup type erases inactive virtual log files of the transaction log file. It keeps the transaction log file at a reasonable size.

To be able to use a transaction log backup, the database's recovery model property has to be set to the BULK_LOGGED or FULL value. Remember that the BULK_LOGGED value does not allow you to restore the database at a certain point in time.

When the recovery model is set correctly and a full backup is executed, we can start a backup of the transaction log on a regular basis. The basic syntax for a transaction log backup is as follows:

```
BACKUP LOG AdventureWorks TO DISK = 'D:\myBackups\AdventureWorksLog.bak'
WITH <additional options>
```

As seen in the preceding code example, the BACKUP LOG syntax is very similar to the BACKUP DATABASE syntax. The database must already exist and it must be in online state and the path to the .bak file must exist in the filesystem, but if the .bak file does not exist, it will be created when the BACKUP LOG statement is executed for the first time.

Additional options are basically almost the same as the full backup statement:

- INIT/NOINIT pair controls whether the content of the backup file will be replaced
- FORMAT/NOFORMAT pair is a stronger variant for INIT/NOINIT options
- COMPRESSION/NO_COMPRESSION pair controls the backup compression

The meaning of these options is completely the same for all backup types.

This is the moment when we have sufficient information about basic backup types and we can go through more complex examples. The following code sample shows you a set of backup statements and their sorting. The only difference in the real world is that every statement is executed separately and typically the execution is planned by SQL Server Agent (note: SQL Server Agent will be described later in Chapter 9, *Automation - Use Tools to Manage and Monitor SQL Server 2017*).

Let's see this assignment: The AdventureWorks database is used as a typical operational database with lots of incoming transactions. These transactions must not be lost because clients of the database write their data through a sales web application. The backup cycle will be restarted every day. The AdventureWorks database is relatively small so all backups could be stored in the same file. An important business need is that the database must be recoverable to a certain point in time. How do we prepare the AdventureWorks database for proper backups and which backup statements do we use?

```
-- 1. we have to ensure if the database is in FULL recovery model
--     this statement will be run once only
--     if database is in FULL recovery model already, nothing happens
ALTER DATABASE AdventureWorks SET RECOVERY FULL
GO

-- 2. every day, for example at 3 a.m. we will run full backup
--     following statement will reset content of the backup file
BACKUP DATABASE AdventureWorks TO DISK = 'D:\backups\AdventureWorks.bak'
WITH INIT
GO

-- 3. every hour or more often we will repeat the transaction log backup
--     following statement will apend the backup to the backup file and
clears
--     transaction log
BACKUP LOG AdventureWorks TO DISK = 'D:\backups\AdventureWorks.bak'
WITH NOINIT
GO
```

As seen in the previous code sample, it is not so complicated to create a simple and strong enough backup strategy. The transaction log backup itself has to be executed often; in some cases, more than every hour, because the transaction log file is maintained well and the backup operation itself is fast, relatively small, and not in conflict with regular user requests.

Until this moment, everything is just routine, but what if some damage appears? A very common mistake is that the only kind of damage is physical damage, for example, file corruption. However, we have to keep in mind that another damage is also logical damage, for example, accidental deletion of data or some structures. When such logical damage occurs, the database itself is still online and, from SQL Server's perspective, no problem occurred; but from user's perspective, the database is useless and damaged.

For either type of corruption, SQL Server provides a special transaction log backup called **tail-log** backup. The tail-log backup is a variant of the transaction log backup. It backs up transaction log records written to the transaction log file up to the moment of the corruption, that's why it's called backup of tail of the transaction log. Tail-log backup switches the state of the database to **restoring**. The restoring state of the database causes inaccessibility of the database to users. It's very important to use the tail-log backup in the case of logical corruption. It is not so probable that all data in the database will be logically damaged at the same moment and that's why we need to stop any user working on the rest of the data because we know that the database is going to be restored and all user changes will be lost. An example syntax to execute tail-log backup is as follows:

```
BACKUP LOG AdventureWorks TO DISK = 'D:\backups\tailLog.bak' WITH
NORECOVERY
```

The NORECOVERY keyword is the option that forms the tail-log backup. The preceding syntax is sufficient just for logical accidents such as unwanted deletes of data. But for every backup operation, the database must be in consistent and online state. What if the database is in **suspect** state?

Suspect state of a database is set by SQL Server in situations when the database is somehow corrupted physically and not accessible to users. In this case, we have two additional options that can be added to the BACKUP LOG statement:

```
BACKUP LOG AdventureWorks TO DISK = 'D:\backups\taillog.bak'
WITH
NORECOVERY, NO_TRUNCATE, CONTINUE_AFTER_ERROR
```

Let's describe these new options in more detail. When the database is corrupted, no backup could be executed with the exception of the preceding code. The CONTINUE_AFTER_ERROR option says to SQL Server that we know about the corruption, but we want to keep all possible transaction log records captured by the transaction log until the moment of damage even if the transactions are incomplete or some of the transaction log records are not readable. If we don't use the CONTINUE_AFTER_ERROR option, SQL Server expects that the database is in consistent online state and the BACKUP LOG statement will fail.

The second `NO_TRUNCATE` option causes no maintenance to be done by SQL Server on completion of the backup. It's intended behavior because we know that the database is in an unstable state and it's probable that any write operation will fail. We also know that after the tail-log backup completion, we will start the restore process of the database so any additional maintenance is wasteful.

Differential backup

SQL Server maintains an internal structure called a **differential map**. This structure maps all changes are done in database extends from the last full backup. This is very useful in cases when a transaction log backup is executed often. Let's see an example where the administrator needs to back up a database on a daily basis, similar to our example in the transaction log backup section, but the transaction log backup is executed every ten minutes. It leads to six transaction log backups every hour and to more than a hundred transaction log backups every day. Such an amount of backup raises a risk of unreadability or loss of certain backups and also increases time spent by the restore process. To reduce the risks and the time of restore, the administrator can add the **differential backup** to his backup strategy. Differential backup has these characteristics:

- It is a kind of full backup (backups extents changed from the last full backup and do not maintain the transaction log)
- It is cumulative (backup extents changed from last full backup, hence allows you to skip more transaction log backups during restore)
- It is faster and smaller than full backup (does not slow down the database for too long and can be executed against user work without decisive influence on performance)
- It does not need any additional settings on the database or server level

The syntax for differential backup is as follows:

```
BACKUP DATABASE AdventureWorks TO DISK =
'D:\myBackups\AdventureWorksDiff.bak'
WITH DIFFERENTIAL
```

From the syntax point of view, differential backup is just a database backup with one more option. Other options such as INIT/NOINIT are also possible. If the use of differential backups is recognized, the timeline of backups will be according to the following table. This table describes a daily-based strategy for smaller databases with all backups stored in the same backup file:

Time of day	Backup type	INIT/NOINIT
3:00 a.m.	FULL	INIT
3:15 a.m.	LOG	NOINIT
3:30 a.m.	LOG	NOINIT
...		
8:45 a.m.	LOG	NOINIT
9:00 a.m.	DIFFERENTIAL	NOINIT
9:15 a.m.	LOG	NOINIT
...		
12:00 a.m.	DIFFERENTIAL	NOINIT
...and so on...		

Advanced backup scenarios

Now that we have all three basic backup types described, we have sufficient information to decide how to summarize our needs and choose the right backup strategy. It's also very important to ensure that backup is reliable and fast. We also have to maintain backups for larger databases composed of more files or filegroups. SQL Server provides you with a set of features covering all three needs.

Backup media

In previous chapters, we worked with backups stored to disk files. It's a very common destination of backup because tape drive as a backup destination must be attached directly to the server. Due to the usual usage of backup tape devices to back up overall company infrastructures, SQL Server does not improve tape backup possibilities and relies on third-party backups. That's why all the following examples will use disk files as the backup device.

If SQL Server databases are going to be backed up by third-party backup devices, never mix the execution of these backups with SQL Server native backup!

When we need to improve the speed of the backup, we can join more backup places into one set called **media set**. The media set is formed of one or more devices of the same type. SQL Server spreads data across all devices in the media set evenly. We can imagine the media set as a striped disk. The media set is created the first time the backup is executed. The following example creates a media set:

```
BACKUP DATABASE <database name> TO
DISK = '<path to first file>',
DISK = '<path to second file>'
WITH
MEDIANAME = '<name of the media set>'
```

Every backup saved to the same media set is then called backup set. Once the media set is created, it must be used as a whole. An attempt to use one of the files for additional backup without using the whole media set will fail. Using media sets makes backup operations faster, but it also increases the risk of backup loss.

Let's see the following example:

```
BACKUP DATABASE <database name> TO
DISK = '<path to first file>'
-- second file from previous example is not used
WITH
FORMAT
```

The FORMAT option causes the media set to break and all backups saved there are lost! So use media sets carefully.

Backup reliability

Everything saved on disk could be somehow broken or unreadable. That's why SQL Server provides you with two features to improve backup reliability. The first option is to use backup with the CHECKSUM option. This option of backup is very simple to use and causes computation of checksum value on backup completion. This value is saved in the backup and, when we prepare for the restore process, we can test backup readability using the CHECKSUM option:

```
BACKUP DATABASE <database name> TO DISK = '<path to file>'
WITH
```

CHECKSUM

Another option is to distribute backups across more devices. It's called **mirrored backup**. Mirrored backup is an enterprise feature of SQL Server and, when it's used, two identical backups are written synchronously to two backup devices. When backup mirroring is used, the syntax looks as follows:

```
BACKUP DATABASE <database name> TO
DISK = '<path to file>'
MIRROR TO DISK = '<path to file>'
WITH <additional options like CHECKSUM>
```

File or filegroup backup

One of the reasons why a database should be distributed into more files or filegroups is better manageability. As the database's size grows from time to time, the backup size also increases even if backup compression is used. For this case, SQL Server provides a very useful feature called file backup or filegroup backup. All the following examples will be shown for filegroup backups because file backups are almost the same but use the FILE keyword instead of the FILEGROUP keyword. The syntax of file/filegroup backup uses the logical file names or filegroup names respectively in the header of the backup. Let's see an example database called BiggerSystem with these filegroups:

- PRIMARY (mandatory in every database)
- OPERDATA (filegroup containing hot data instantly used for transactions)
- ARCHIVE2016 (filegroup containing cold data without any DML operations on it)

The proper setting of the recovery model option for this database is FULL.

Filegroup backup syntax is as follows:

```
BACKUP DATABASE <database name>
FILEGROUP = <filegroup name>, FILEGROUP = <another filegroup name>
TO DISK = '<file path>'
WITH
<additional options>
```

The following near real-life example will use the `BiggerSystem` database and its filegroups:

```
-- monday 3 a. m.
BACKUP DATABASE BiggerSystem
FILEGROUP = 'PRIMARY'
TO DISK = 'L:\backups\bigsysprimary.bak'
WITH INIT, CHECKSUM, COMPRESSION
-- monday every hour
BACKUP LOG BiggerSystem TO DISK = 'L:\backups\bigsyslogs.bak'
WITH NOINIT, CHECKSUM, COMPRESSION

-- tuesday 3 a. m.
BACKUP DATABASE BiggerSystem
FILEGROUP = 'OPERDATA'
TO DISK = 'L:\backups\bigsysoper.bak'
WITH INIT, CHECKSUM, COMPRESSION
-- tuesday every hour
BACKUP LOG BiggerSystem TO DISK = 'L:\backups\bigsyslogs.bak'
WITH NOINIT, CHECKSUM, COMPRESSION

-- wednesday 3 a. m.
BACKUP DATABASE BiggerSystem
FILEGROUP = 'ARCHIVE2016'
TO DISK = 'L:\backups\bigsysarch2016.bak'
WITH INIT, CHECKSUM, COMPRESSION
-- wednesday every hour
BACKUP LOG BiggerSystem TO DISK = 'L:\backups\bigsyslogs.bak'
WITH NOINIT, CHECKSUM, COMPRESSION

-- and so on, thursday we start to backup the PRIMARY filegroup again
```

As seen in the preceding example, we must not miss any filegroup from a certain database.

Let's assume that the filegroup called `ARCHIVE2016` is not used for DML operations and in such cases, its repeating backup becomes unnecessary. SQL Server provides an enterprise feature called **partial backup**. The partial backup saves the primary filegroup, all read-write filegroups, and explicitly written read-only filegroups. That's why it is very useful to set filegroups containing historical or other read-only data as read-only.

Let's go through one more example (for the sake of simplicity, transaction log backups in following code sample will be omitted):

```
-- run once: set the ARCHIVE2016 filegroup as read-only
ALTER DATABASE BiggerSystem MODIFY FILEGROUP ARCHIVE2016 READONLY

-- first time backup after setting the filegroup read-only
BACKUP DATABASE BiggerSystem
READ_WRITE_FILEGROUPS, FILEGROUP = 'ARCHIVE2016'
TO DISK = 'L:\backups\bigsys.bak'
WITH INIT, CHECKSUM, COMPRESSION

-- transaction backups follow for the rest of day

-- next daily backups
BACKUP DATABASE BiggerSystem
READ_WRITE_FILEGROUPS
TO DISK = 'L:\backups\bigsysadd.bak'
WITH INIT, CHECKSUM, COMPRESSION

-- transaction backups follow
```

Backup system databases

In simple words, system databases need backup as user databases do. Backup strategies for system databases are often much more straightforward than for user databases. Let's describe common backup strategies for every system database:

Database name	Recovery model	Backup description
master	SIMPLE	Full backup once a week
msdb	User settable (SIMPLE recommended)	Full backup every day
model	User settable (affects newly created user databases)	Full backup once a week
tempdb	SIMPLE	N/A

Backup summary

Managing our backups properly is very important task that we must perform. As was described in this chapter, we need to decide which type of backups, how often, how reliable, and where to store them. This decision has a strong impact on the ability of restoring the data in minimal time with minimal loss. The following table describes several types of databases and example backup strategies:

Data contention	Recovery model	Backups used
Smaller (for example, up to 20 GB) OLTP database	FULL	FULL TRANSACTION LOG (optionally DIFFERENTIAL)
Big OLTP database with read-only archive filegroups	FULL	FULL or FILEGROUP (partial backup if possible) TRANSACTION LOG
OLAP database with periodical data load (data load can be repeated)	SIMPLE	FULL or FILEGROUP (partial backup highly welcome)

In the next chapter, we will work with database backups and restore corrupted databases in many scenarios.

Restore

The restore feature in SQL Server is used for data recovery in the case of its corruption and heavily relies on how data is backed up. In this section, we will cover the following topics:

- Preparation steps before restore starts
- Restore scenarios depending on backup strategies

Preparing for restore

Before a database is being restored, we have to decide the type of corruption and backup sets already available for restore. If we have more backups to be restored (full backup combined with other backup types), we need to handle the recovery process as well.

The recovery process was described in the *Transaction log* section, but let's recall the recovery process one more time. SQL Server uses **write-ahead-logging** (**WAL**) for very detailed transaction actions. These transaction log records are written before the action is actually done against data pages in the buffer cache (transaction log records are buffered for a short time and written in batch actually, but for a conceptual view, it does not matter). In every moment, a certain transaction can be in these states:

- Transaction is not committed by user yet; **transaction is running**
- Transaction is committed by user, but its data pages are in dirty state (different version of the data page in memory and on disk); **transaction is active**
- Transaction is committed by user, SQL Server executed the checkpoint, and data pages in memory are in clean state (the memory version of data page was persisted on disk); **transaction is inactive**

When SQL Server runs a backup, running and active transactions are saved within the backup even if they are not finished yet. Backups go one after the other; we must remember that incomplete transactions saved in the first backup will continue in the consequential backup. This is true mainly when transaction log backups are used in the backup strategy. If we don't specify explicitly, after each restore of the database (or transaction log), recovery process is executed by SQL Server, even though it's not wanted in many situations.

> The first and the most important decision is when to enable the recovery process. Written shortly--after the last restore is executed in the line of restores used.

Great, but which backups do we have? Are they readable? Where were the files of my database originally placed? These questions could be answered by simple preparation RESTORE statements.

The first action is to check whether the backup files are readable. The following statement is often placed directly after the BACKUP statement to ensure that nothing accidental happened when backup files were copied:

```
RESTORE VERIFYONLY FROM DISK = 'D:\myBackups\AdventureWorks.bak' WITH
CHECKSUM
```

The preceding statement tests the readability of the backup file. The CHECKSUM option can be used only when it was also used during the backup operation. The result of this command is just saying that the backup set on file 1 is valid.

The second piece of information needed is the content of a certain backup file. The following command explores a valid backup file and returns the result set with a list of backups saved:

```
RESTORE HEADERONLY FROM DISK = 'D:\myBackups\AdventureWorks.bak'
```

The result set contains many columns such as LSNs needed for internal restore purposes and database properties such as the version of database, collation, and others, but from an administrator's perspective, the main columns are as follows:

- `BackupType`: This column contains enumeration (1--full backup, 2--transaction log backup, 4--filegroup backup, and so on)
- `Position`: This column contains the numeric ordering of backups; this value is used in the `RESTORE` statement to address correct backup to be restored
- `BackupStartDate`: This is the date and time when backup was started
- `BackupFinishDate`: This is the date and time when backup was finished

As we will go through restore scenarios, we will use this statement heavily to recognize what to restore.

Last but not least, metadata `RESTORE` statement is used in situations when restoring the database recovers files to different locations. In such situations, we need to know logical filenames to be able to reference to them in order to set different places on disks:

```
RESTORE FILELISTONLY FROM DISK = 'D:\myBackups\AdventureWorks.bak'
```

The result of this statement returns more columns for internal purposes. For the administrator, just the first three columns are interesting:

- `LogicalName`: The name of the file used as a reference
- `PhysicalName`: The full path of the file
- `Type`: D for data files, L for logs

Voila! Now we know how to be prepared for the restore process. In the next sections, we will go through several sample scenarios and we will perform complete restores.

Executing restores

A backup strategy is the main criteria that determines how a database should be restored to the most up-to-date point. In the next sections, we will go through several restore scenarios.

Using the full backup strategy

The restore process consists of several phases. The first phase is called **safety check**. If we are attempting to restore a database with the same name but different files, the restore process is terminated. When the database does not exist on the instance of SQL Server but some file on disk is in name conflict with some filename that is going to be restored, the restore process is terminated as well.

 If restore is used for database creation, don't create an empty database before. SQL Server will do it for you using information from the backup device.

The second phase tries to remove the rest of the corrupted database. After this phase, the database is recreated and recovered from backup.

 Never try to delete physically corrupted databases before RESTORE. Even if DROP DATABASE is the last action in the database's lifetime, SQL Server expects its consistent state so it's a high probability that the DROP DATABASE statement will fail. The RESTORE statement is prepared for this case and will remove the debris of the corrupted database correctly.

Repeating full backups regularly is the best approach of a backup strategy when the database is small, has a small amount of transactions ,and is not so mission-critical. A crucial requirement is to have this database in the SIMPLE recovery model. We can think of databases used for development or testing purposes.

In this case, we can imagine an every day full backup. When the database is corrupted, the only point to which the database can be restored and also recovered is the time when the backup (often the last full backup) was created. This is also the simplest restore that can be done:

```
RESTORE DATABASE <database name> FROM DISK = '<path to backup file>'
WITH RECOVERY
```

The preceding statement attempts to restore the database with the given name even if it does not exist. All files are placed in the original locations, but if some file with the same name exists for a different database, the restore fails (the initial part of the restore process is called **safety check**). If a database with the same name exists already with an identical set of files, it's overwritten by this statement. The RECOVERY option ensures that the recovery process will be executed by SQL Server on restore completion and that the database will be online and consistent after restore.

If the database was backed up with, for example, **read-only** state, it will be in this state after restore.

If we want to skip the safety check, say, in situations where the database is completely lost from SQL Server but some file remained on the disk, we can add the REPLACE option to the restore statement.

Let's see a database called DevDemo. This database is small and is used just for development purposes, so data in it is not so important as it is full of test values created during development and testing. Backup is executed every night. Corruption of the database occurs some morning and we need to recover it. The statement will be as follows:

```
RESTORE DATABASE DevDemo FROM DISK = 'L:\backups\devdemo.bak'
WITH RECOVERY
```

Let's imagine that we have one devdemo.bak file recycled every week. In other words, we start our backup strategy every Monday morning (for example, at 3 a.m.) so seven backups are potentially contained in the file. The corruption occurs Wednesday at 10 a.m. We need to find the last and freshest backup from the backup file and then use it. The complete example is as follows:

```
-- this statement will return result set with backups in the file
-- our backup will have value 3 in column Position (Monday's backup will be
1,
-- Tuesday's backup will be 2, our corruption occurred at Wednesday)
RESTORE HEADERONLY FROM DISK = 'L:\backups\devdemo.bak'

-- we need to provide the value of desired backup to actual RESTORE
statement
RESTORE DATABASE DevDemo FROM DISK = 'L:\backups\devdemo.bak'
WITH
FILE = 3,
RECOVERY
```

The preceding example shows the restore process of a simple database. Let's see another example. Our DevDemo database has to be moved to another instance of SQL Server. On the original instance, the data file of the database was placed on disk D, but on the new server, data file disk is E. We need to use the following sequence of statements:

```
-- this statement will return result set with backups in the file
-- as in previous example (remember that Wednesday = 3)
RESTORE HEADERONLY FROM DISK = 'L:\backups\devdemo.bak'
```

```
-- this statement will show LogicalName and physical location of each file
-- in the database
-- for example LogicalName of .mdf file is "devdemo_Data"
-- and LogicalName of .ldf file is "devdemo_Log"
RESTORE FILELISTONLY FROM DISK = 'L:\backups\devdemo.bak'

-- we need to provide the value of desired backup to actual RESTORE
statement
-- and also we need to say where to place files
RESTORE DATABASE DevDemo FROM DISK = 'L:\backups\devdemo.bak'
WITH
FILE = 3,
MOVE 'devdemo_Data' TO 'E:\data\devdemo.mdf',
MOVE 'devdemo_Log' TO 'L:\logs\devdemo.ldf',
RECOVERY
```

This example moves database files to their new locations. The MOVE .. TO pair is used just for files that have to be moved, it's not necessary to write this option for every file.

In this chapter, usage of the simplest backup/restore strategy was shown and common options of the RESTORE statement were described. Now let's dive deep into more sophisticated scenarios.

Using full and transaction log backup strategy

For this and the next backup strategies, we must consider two conditions:

- At least the BULK_LOGGED recovery model must be set on the database
- Correct handling with the RECOVERY/NORECOVERY pair has to be done

Combining full and transaction log backups in the backup strategy is the best approach for OLTP databases with continual data contention. This strategy also provides an ability to restore the database to a certain point in time. It covers situations of logical corruptions such as accidental delete statement, failed structure update, and so on. For the ability to recover the database to some point in time, we need to have the database's recovery model option set to FULL.

The restore process usually starts with the BACKUP statement. Maybe this action looks strange but it's used for the latest possible transaction rescue. Yes, this is the tail-log backup. If the database is damaged logically, the tail-log backup sets its state to **restoring;** if the database is damaged physically (and is in **suspect** state so far), the tail-log backup saves all readable transaction log records from the active portion of the transaction log.

The following statement does the tail-log backup when logical damage of the database occurs:

```
BACKUP LOG <database name> TO DISK = '<path to tail log .bak file>'
WITH NORECOVERY
```

The next statement is better for physical damage of the database:

```
BACKUP LOG <database name> TO DISK = '<path to tail log .bak file>'
WITH NORECOVERY, NO_TRUNCATE, CONTINUE_AFTER_ERROR
```

The `CONTINUE_AFTER_ERROR` option is crucial because when omitted, SQL Server fails our tail-log backup due to inconsistency of the database.

All right, everything what was possible is saved now and we can start to write `RESTORE` statements in correct order. Every restore starts with `RESTORE DATABASE` as it was described in the Using the full backup strategy chapter. The only but very important difference is that we don't want to execute the recovery process. That's why we must use the `NORECOVERY` option. Let's see a database called `accounting`. This database has its full backup every morning at 3 a.m. and then transaction log backup every hour. All backups are saved to the same file on a daily basis. The physical corruption appeared at 9:30 a.m. The following code example describes the full process of the data rescue:

```
-- try to save the latest user work
BACKUP LOG Accounting to DISK = 'L:\backups\taillog.bak'
WITH NORECOVERY, NO_TRUNCATE, CONTINUE_AFTER_ERROR

-- let's check out backup ability
RESTORE VERIFYONLY FROM DISK = 'L:\backups\accounting.bak' WITH CHECKSUM

-- It's readable, what about content?
RESTORE HEADERONLY FROM DISK = 'L:\backups\accounting.bak'

-- now we have full backup on position 1
-- and six following trans. log backups on positions 2 - 7

-- restoring initial state of database
-- note: the FILE position need not to be written because 1 is the default
RESTORE DATABASE Accounting FROM DISK = 'L:\backups\accounting.bak'
WITH NORECOVERY

-- restoring incremental states from backups 2 - 7
RESTORE LOG Accounting FROM DISK = 'L:\backups\accounting.bak'
WITH
FILE = 2,    -- this value changes for every additional log backup
NORECOVERY
```

```
-- restoring the tail-log backup
RESTORE LOG Accounting FROM DISK = 'L:\backups\taillog.bak'
WITH RECOVERY  -- this option recovers the database and sets its state
ONLINE
```

As seen in the example, only the last backup restored has the RECOVERY option. We can think about the NORECOVERY/RECOVERY pair as a TV series. The NORECOVERY says that the restore process will continue by restoring next log backup and the RECOVERY is the happy end.

As NORECOVERY is used in every RESTORE statement except the last one, it's simple to make a mistake and use the NORECOVERY in the last RESTORE. Fortunately, it's simple to correct this mistake; just repeat the last backup with the correct option.

The full backup and transaction log backup strategy has one big advantage because it can be used for point-in-time recovery. However, every coin has two sides and the disadvantage of this strategy is relatively big amount of backups that need to be maintained readable and complete. The next two sections will describe how to profit from the advantage and how to handle the issue.

Point-in-time recovery

In most situations, the right point in time for a database restore is the most recent state of the database before failure. Sometimes the database becomes incorrect in a little different way, for example, when some tables or other objects are lost. When such a situation occurs, it is recommended that you know how to recover the database. SQL Server provides very useful mechanisms to restore a database to the desired but not the last moment. The first option is to set a date and time for data recovery, and the second is to use a transaction log mark. We will go through both options in the form of examples.

Let's see a database called accounting. It is the same database as in the previous section. Full backup executed is every morning at 3 a.m.; transaction log backups are executed every hour. The problem appears at 9:30 a.m. The following list of steps have to be performed:

- Obtain the current time from SQL Server
- Create a tail-log backup
- Restore the database as in a regular full and transaction log backup strategy
- Stop the recovery process, not at the end of the last transaction log backup but earlier

As seen in the checklist, we have two exceptional moments, the first one and the last one. Obtaining the current time is very simple:

```
SELECT SYSDATETIME()
--or
SELECT GETDATE()
```

We need to consider that the time returned is the time when we noticed the problem, so depending on the actual situation we will subtract some time from the current time (for example, 30 seconds).

The second and third steps are a regular way of working on the restore process. It means to obtain the available backup files, explore their quality and content, and then start the restore process step by step.

When the restore process comes closer to the moment of failure, we need to pay attention to the correct transaction log backup covering the time interval with the failure. When we touch this backup (for example, the backup executed on 9:45 a.m. so the interval is from 9 a. m. to quarter to ten), we will use following syntax:

```
RESTORE LOG Accounting FROM DISK = 'L:\backups\somelog.bak'
WITH
STOPAT = '2017-08-01 9:30am', RECOVERY
```

The STOPAT option says to the SQL Server that we want to recover the database exactly to this point. The RECOVERY option is then needed because the rest of the transaction log backups (if they exist) is useless because the time interval from 9:30 a.m. will be ignored and we cannot omit part of transactions.

If we are not sure which transaction log backup contains the desired point in time, we can write STOPAT = 'time', RECOVERY to each restore log statement. When a certain transaction log backup ends before the time, SQL Server reports a warning and the database will stay in restoring state. When the time is within the transaction log backup, point-in-time restore is successful and the database is recovered to online state. If the time set in the RESTORE statement is before the current transaction log backup executed, restore fails with an error.

This feature has one more option. Sometimes we know that some transaction is risky (for example, some unusual data update). We can mark such a transaction in the transaction log. The mark of the transaction is writen as a part of BEGIN TRAN statement. The complete syntax is BEGIN TRAN myRiskyTran WITH MARK. The myRiskyTran is our text called transaction name. The transaction naming could be helpful for developers when they have more transactions; it's just a kind of an orientation place in source code, but it has no impact on SQL Server and it's not saved to the transaction log. However, WITH MARK changes the situation completely. The name is written to the transaction log and can be read back from within the transaction log backup. In this case, we can use the transaction name to determine where to execute the recovery process. The syntax for this is similar to the STOPAT option:

```
RESTORE LOG Accounting FROM DISK = 'L:\backups\somelog.bak'
WITH
STOPATMARK = 'myRiskyTran', RECOVERY
```

When we need to exclude the transaction from restore, we should write next statement:

```
RESTORE LOG Accounting FROM DISK = 'L:\backups\somelog.bak'
WITH
STOPBEFOREMARK = 'myTiskyTran', RECOVERY
```

The STOPATMARK option includes the marked transaction into recovery and STOPBEFOREMARK executes the recovery process exactly before the marked transaction started.

The rest of the restore process is almost the same. If we are not sure in which transaction log backup the marked transaction is, we can use the same approach as when using STOPAT. It means we could write STOPATMARK = 'my risky tran', RECOVERY (STOPBEFOREMARK = 'my risky tran', RECOVERY respectively) to every RESTORE LOG statement. The only difference is that SQL Server cannot recognize if the desired mark is in future log backups or if the mark is left behind. When the mark is not present in the current transaction log backup already restored, SQL Server never fails this backup but issues a warning and the database will not be recovered.

The described procedures report a very good value of RPO--recovery point objective. It is a measure showing how much data was lost (a lesser value is better). In the next section, we will show you how to reduce **recovery time objective (RTO)**.

Using full, transaction log, and differential backup strategies

The only possible issue when using transaction log backups is that the amount of backups becomes quite big. It has an impact on RTO. This is a measure determining how long the downtime will be noticed before the database is recovered.

In previous sections, we went through a set of backups beginning with full backup and continuing with transaction log backups one by one. The differential backup is added to the backup strategy for better jumps in time. As it was described in the backup part of this chapter, differential backup contains all extents changed from the last full backup. When using this strategy, we can have a set of backups, as shown in the following list:

- 3 a.m.: Daily full backup (backup position 1)
- 4 a.m. to 8:30 a.m.: Transaction log backup twice an hour (backup positions from 2 to 11)
- 9 a.m.: Differential backup (backup position 12)
- 10 a.m. to 1:30 p.m.: Transaction log backup twice an hour (backup positions from 13 to 20)
- 2 p.m.: Differential backup (backup position 21)
- 3 p.m. to 6:30 p.m.: Transaction log backup twice an hour (backup positions from 22 to 29)
- 7 p.m.: Differential backup (backup position 30)
- 8 p.m. to 2:30 a.m. next day: Transaction log backup twice an hour (backup positions 31 and so on)

Let's imagine that our `Accounting` database will fail at 5 p.m. The only difference from the previous examples is that we don't need to restore every backup from our set. The restore process consists of the first, fifth, and partially sixth point from the preceding list. Let's describe the syntax (the following example will omit the preparation steps):

```
-- rescue last user transactions
BACKUP LOG Accounting TO DISK = 'L:\backups\taillog.bak'
WITH NORECOVERY

-- restore initial state of the database
RESTORE DATABASE Accounting FROM DISK = 'L:\backups\accounting.bak'
WITH NORECOVERY

-- restore the most recent differential backup created before 5 p.m.
RESTORE DATABASE Accounting FROM DISK = 'L:\backups\accounting.bak'
WITH FILE = 21, NORECOVERY
```

```
-- restore trans. log backups between the last diff. backup and failure
point
-- this statement is repeated with changing FILE option
RESTORE LOG Accounting FROM DISK = 'L:\backups\accounting.bak'
WITH FILE = 22, -- and 23, 24 and so on until 26
NORECOVERY

-- restore tail-log backup and recover the database
RESTORE LOG Accounting FROM DISK = 'L:\backups\taillog.bak'
WITH RECOVERY
```

As seen in the preceding example, the restore from differential backup is just a kind of database restore with no extras. The only reason for using differential backups in a backup strategy is the shorter time of the restore process.

In the next section, we'll take a look at a partial database recovery from a file or filegroup backups.

Using file or filegroup backups

As the database becomes large over time, it's very complicated to hold a short maintenance window for its backups. This is one of the reasons why we use file or filegroup backups. In this section, we will show you how to recover a certain filegroup in the case of failure:

The task list is as follows:

1. Execute the `tail-log` backup of the database.
2. Restore every corrupted data file/filegroup from its last backup.
3. Restore transaction log backups from the oldest file/filegroup backup.
4. Restore the `tail-log` backup and recover the database.

Let's see a database called `BiggerSystem`. The database consists of filegroups: `PRIMARY`, `OPERDATA`, and `ARCHIVE2016`. One filegroup is backed up every day at 3 a.m.. During each day, transaction log backups are created every hour. The backup process is planned as follows:

- Monday 3 a.m.: `PRIMARY` filegroup backup
- Monday from 4 a.m. to Tuesday 2 a.m.: Transaction log backups
- Tuesday 3 a.m.: `OPERDATA` filegroup backup
- Tuesday from 4 a.m. to Wednesday 2 a.m.: Transaction log backups
- Wednesday 3 a.m.: `ARCHIVE2016` filegroup backup

The failure occurs in the OPERDATA filegroup on Wednesday, 10:30 a.m. The process of restore will be as follows:

```
-- create tail-log backup
BACKUP LOG BiggerSystem TO DISK = 'L:\backups\taillog.bak'

-- restore the damaged filegroup
RESTORE DATABASE BiggerSystem
FILEGROUP = 'OPERDATA'
FROM DISK = 'L:\backups\bigsysoper.bak'
WITH NORECOVERY

-- restore all trans. log backups from Tuesday 4 a.m. until most recent
RESTORE LOG BiggerSystem FROM DISK = 'L:\backups\bigsyslogs.bak'
WITH
FILE = x,    -- where "x" is the position of backup in backup file
NORECOVERY

-- recover the database
RESTORE LOG BiggerSystem FROM DISK = 'L:\backups\taillog.bak'
WITH RECOVERY
```

As seen in the example, the only difference from a regular full restore is the FILEGROUP keyword used to address the filegroup that is to be restored. This restore procedure ensures the most recent consistent state of all the database.

Until this moment, we restored whole database or its important part. In the next section, we will switch our attention to the smallest recoverable part of the database.

Restoring data pages

SQL Server provides an enterprise feature called page restore. It's the ability to shorten the restore time to minimum and restore just the corrupted data pages. The process of page restore is very similar to file or filegroup restore. It needs a full or file/filegroup backup and transaction log backups.

The most challenging part is how to find out which data pages are corrupted. The answer is quite simple. SQL Server maintains a table called suspect_pages in the msdb database. This table is used by SQL Server to hold information about data page corruptions. Consider that the table has up to 1,000 rows, so if it's not monitored for a long time and then exactly 1,000 rows are returned on a query, we never know how many corrupted data pages we have in our database.

The most important columns in this table are as follows:

- `database_id`: The ID of the database containing suspect pages
- `file_id`: The ordinal position of file containing suspect pages
- `page_id`: The page identifier

The `file_id` and `page_id` identifiers are used together to address the page that has to be recovered. If, for example, page number 12345 is corrupted in the primary data file (it has always number 1) in database ID 13, we can use this statement:

```
-- list of potentially corrupted data pages
-- result will be for example AdventureWorks, 1, 12345
SELECT DB_NAME(database_id) AS databaseName
, file_id
, page_id
FROM msdb..suspect_pages
```

From this moment, the restore process starts using almost the same task list as in the filegroup restore. The only exception is in the identification of the database part that is restored. This is seen in the following syntax:

```
RESTORE DATABASE AdventureWorks
PAGE = '1:12345'
FROM DISK = 'L:\backups\aw.bak'
WITH NORECOVERY
```

The page identifier is provided in a form of `file_id:page_id`; in our example, it is page number 12345 of the primary data file. The rest of the restore process stays unchanged.

After restoring all data pages, we should remove all records from the `suspect_pages` table.

Until this moment, attention was paid to user databases, but system databases also need some care and this last section will show extras when restoring them.

System database restore

System databases are databases created during SQL Server installation and have special meanings. That's why a special section is dedicated to restoring them.

The most simple situation is when restoring the `tempdb` database. The `tempdb` database is never backed up, so no restore operation is possible. When some damage appears, we just need to restart the SQL Server service. SQL Server recreates the `tempdb` database at startup.

Restoring the `msdb` database is quite simple as well. It often has a (recommended) simple recovery model, so in case of failure, we restore `msdb` in a similar way to every user database, using the `RESTORE DATABASE .. WITH RECOVERY` statement.

Restoring a database model is a little more complicated. When the database model is corrupted, the first task is to restart SQL Server with the trace flag `-T3608` in the startup parameters. Then the restore process is the same as a simple restore process of every user database, but with the trace flag switched on, the database model is sheltered by SQL Server against restoring.

The last and most complicated way of restore is the restoring of the database master. If SQL Server cannot start, we must start the restore process by rebuilding the master database from SQL Server Setup. When SQL Server is able to start, we will use two command prompt windows. In the first command prompt, we start SQL Server in single user mode with minimal configuration:

```
sqservr.exe -m -f
```

When SQL Server is started, we must not close the window. Then we'll use the second command prompt with the `sqlcmd` utility:

```
sqlcmd.exe -E -S myServerName\instanceName
```

When the `sqlcmd` utility is started (where `-E` means Windows login and `-S` means server name), we'll just execute a regular restore statement for the database master with recovery. When the restore is successfully executed, SQL Server is stopped in the first command prompt. We can then restart it normally.

Summary

When working with databases, we always need to have an ability to recover them when some damage occurs. This chapter was intended mostly as a syntactical guide for correct backup planning and performing for several types of databases such as OLTP user databases, big databases, and system databases. A GUI alternative is also possible but using syntax is a better approach when automating backup tasks and also in stressful situations when some corruption occurs. Who knows syntax is never lost in dialogs of the SQL Server Management Studio.

In the introduction, internal data handling was described. This knowledge is an advantage not only when performance backups and restores, but also for better understanding when we are going to optimize a database.

The second part describes backup capabilities of on-premise SQL Server instance. The third part shows how to used backups to restore database in many scenarios. It also reflects impact of backup procedures already used on restore abilities measured by RPO and RTO criteria.

Another big task is to secure SQL Server properly. It will be described in detail in next `Chapter 4`, *Securing Your SQL Server.*

4
Securing Your SQL Server

Securing SQL Server is a crucial task, as SQL Server usually holds very important and sensitive information in your environment. You need to apply many principles in order to properly secure your databases. Fortunately, SQL Server offers you many options in order to help you with securing your data stored on the SQL Server. Securing a SQL Server is quite a complex task; you need to consider that SQL Server is a client application running on the Windows server, which is accessible via a network. In order to fully secure the environment, you need to secure the Windows OS too and put proper security measures on the network as well.

In this chapter, we will be covering the following topics:

- SQL Server service accounts
- Authentication and authorization
- Encrypting SQL Server data

SQL Server service accounts

An important part of the configuration of your SQL Server environment is the service accounts used to run your SQL Server services. Many of these can be configured immediately during the installation of your SQL Server. There are several options for you to select from while configuring an account for SQL Server services:

- Virtual accounts
- Managed service accounts
- Built-in system accounts
- Group managed service accounts

  • Domain user accounts
  • Local Windows accounts

Virtual accounts

The default choice of any OS higher than Windows Server 2008 R2 is a virtual account. A virtual account is a managed local account for the simple administration of your services. One of the important benefits of virtual accounts is their auto management, so you don't need to worry about regular password updates on your accounts like you have to with domain and local accounts, where you're bound with your enterprise account and password policy.

A virtual account has two forms depending on whether the account is used for named or default SQL Server instances. If you're using a default instance, then the account is as follows:

  • `NT SERVICE\MSSQLSERVER` for the MS SQL database service
  • `NT SERVICE\SQLSERVERAGENT` for the MS SQL Agent service

If you are using named instances, then the instance name is a part of the account name. If your instance name is SQL1, then the accounts will be as follows:

  • `NT SERVICE\MSSQL$SQL1` for the MS SQL database service
  • `NT SERVICE\SQLAGENT$SQL1` for the MS SQL Agent Service

If you're also running SQL Server integration services under virtual account credentials, then account `NT Service\MsDtsServer140` is used for this service.

When you're configuring the account for SQL Server and you would such as to use the virtual account, supply a blank password during configuration in the SQL Server configuration manager, as shown in the following screenshot:

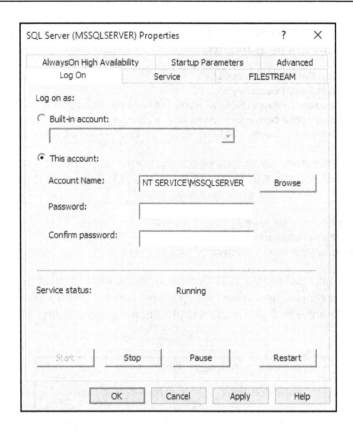

Managed service accounts

Another option to run SQL Server services are **managed service accounts** (**MSA** for short) and **group managed service accounts** (**gMSA**). MSAs are an older implementation compared to group managed service accounts, which were introduced later with Windows Server 2012, whereas MSAs are supported from Windows Server 2008 R2.

MSAs allow you to create an account in the `ActiveDirectory` and tie that account to a specific computer. Such an account has its own complex password, which is, such as a virtual account, managed automatically. As an MSA is used only for services running on the computer, you can't use such an account for interactive login. As this account is tied to just one computer account in the `ActiveDirectory`, one of the big limitations of MSA is that it can't be used together with failover cluster configuration.

To create an MSA, we need to use PowerShell with the `ActiveDirectory` module loaded. The code to create MSA will be as follows:

```
#run this on the Domain Controller
Import-Module ActiveDirectory
New-ADServiceAccount -Name SQLService -Enabled $true
Add-ADComputerServiceAccount -Identity SQL -ServiceAccount SQLService
#SQL will be the host here, SQLService is the name of the MSA account
```

Once you run this command, we will have one account ready and tied to a computer account SQL. Now we need to add this account to the SQL Server so that we can use the account for services:

```
#run this on the SQL Server
Import-Module ActiveDirectory
Install-ADServiceAccount -Identity SQLService
```

Now we can use the account for the SQL Server services. We will update the configuration again via the SQL Server configuration manager and we will use the name in the form of domain name\MSA$ name, and you don't supply the password again like with virtual account:

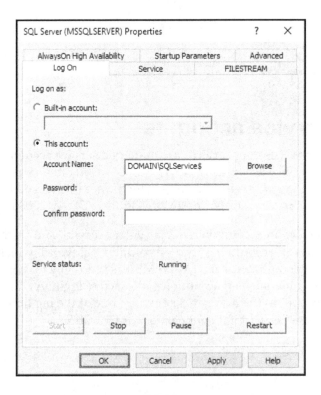

Group managed service accounts

The group managed service accounts provide the same functionality as the MSAs, but they can be used on multiple servers. gMSAs provide a single identity for services running on a farm, cluster, or behind a load balancer, so they are a perfect fit for the failover cluster scenario, where the previous type of managed service accounts couldn't be used. gMSAs have the same benefit as the older MSAs where ActiveDirectory is automatically managing the account password without any service disruption.

You can create gMSAs with a similar PowerShell script, like with the MSAs:

```
#run this on the Domain Controller
Import-Module ActiveDirectory
New-ADServiceAccount -name SQLService -DNSHostName sql.contoso.com -
PrincipalsAllowedToRetrieveManagedPassword sql.contoso.com
```

Once you have created the gMSA, you need to install the account again on the server where you would like to use the account. This time, you can install the account on multiple servers. If you would like to use the account on more servers, you have to specify this in the PrincipalsAllowedToRetrieveManagedPassword parameter of the PowerShell command, where you have to specify multiple hosts or a group of hosts. These have to be created as computer objects and, if you would like to use the group, you need to add them to the ActiveDirectory security group:

```
#run this on the SQL Server
Import-Module ActiveDirectory
Install-ADServiceAccount -Identity SQLService

#test the account with
Test-ADServiceAccount SQLService
```

This module is available as a part of Remote Server Administration Tools, and you can verify the availability of the module via PowerShell

```
Get-Module -ListAvailable ActiveDirectory
```

Once you have installed the account, you can add the account via the SQL Server service configuration manager or even specify the account directly during installation of the SQL Server. As this account has to be created by your ActiveDirectory administrator, you can ask for such an account in advance and use the account for the installation.

Domain accounts and local accounts

If you would like to use a Windows account to run SQL Services, make sure that you're using a minimally-privileged local or domain account to run your SQL Server. Once you have designated your account to be used with the SQL Server services, SQL Server Setup will automatically configure all the required permissions and user rights to your service account so that SQL Server will run correctly.

To change the account you can again use the configuration manager tool. One disadvantage of the domain or local account over the virtual or managed accounts is the required password maintenance. You need to supply the password to the SQL Server services in the configuration manager and your account will adhere to the Windows password policy.

 Windows password policy is configured on the `ActiveDirectory` domain level with group policy objects, which apply to the whole `ActiveDirectory` domain, or with more detailed password setting objects, which can be linked to specific accounts. By default, passwords for domain accounts have to be updated and, if the password expires, your SQL Server environment may stop working. You need to take special consideration, especially in larger environments if you're using domain accounts with non-expiring passwords.

Authentication and authorization

SQL Server security works in layers. As a first step, SQL Server will perform authentication, where SQL Server is determining who you are and if you can log in. If you're successfully logged on, then SQL Server will perform authorization, determining if you can do what you're trying to do. In the next part of the chapter, we will see how to configure the server authentication, how to work with server objects, and how to assign server-level permissions.

Authentication

SQL Server comes with two authentication modes--**SQL Server and Windows Authentication** mode and **Windows Authentication** mode. You can choose the authentication mode during installation and you can always change the mode afterward in the SQL Server configuration, which requires a service restart after the change. The following image gives a good idea of authentication options:

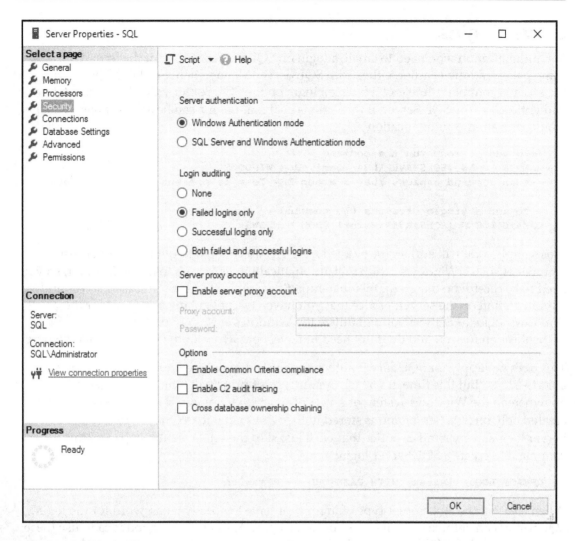

If the **Windows Authentication mode** is turned on, then SQL Server can use several different principals to evaluate your access:

- Local Windows account
- Local Windows group
- Domain account
- Domain group

Server logins

For authentication, you need to create a login on SQL Server for one of the four Windows principals mentioned earlier, either with SQL Server Management Studio, TSQL or with the `sqlcmd` command-line tool. Having a login on the SQL Server will allow a user to authenticate on the SQL Server, if the login is enabled. Logins can be also disabled, which would prevent the authentication.

```
--to add a group run the command
CREATE LOGIN [SQLSERVER\DBA Team] FROM WINDOWS
--this command expects that a group DBA Team is present on the SQL Server

--to add a single user run the command
CREATE LOGIN [SQLSERVER\Marek] FROM WINDOWS
```

This sample code will add a group called `DBA Team` as a login to our SQL Server. Any member of such a Windows group will automatically have access to the SQL Server, so you need to be careful on the group membership. It's a simple start for role-based access and administration on the server. Notice that you haven't supplied any password for the Windows login, as SQL Server will utilize the Windows system to perform the authentication for you and does not need to have a password of the login stored anywhere.

This does not apply for SQL Server authentication mode, where you create the same type of object--`LOGIN`, but this time, it's a SQL Server type of principal, which is not created anywhere in the Windows system or `ActiveDirectory` domain. The SQL Server login is created only on SQL Server and is stored in the `master` database. Syntax to create the SQL Server login is very similar; notice that we'll just skip the `FROM WINDOWS` part of the command to create a SQL Server login:

```
CREATE LOGIN [Marek] WITH PASSWORD = 'P@ssw0rd'
```

When creating the SQL Server type of login, you have to specify a password for the login. SQL Server can enforce several checks on such a password and it's a good idea to use these, so the passwords for SQL Server logins will comply with Windows password policy or your `ActiveDirectory` domain password policy. To create a login with these checks, you can use the following command:

```
CREATE LOGIN [Marek] WITH PASSWORD='P@ssw0rd', CHECK_EXPIRATION=ON,
CHECK_POLICY=ON
```

Domain password policies are configured on the `ActiveDirectory` level and are outside the scope of this book. Such a policy usually controls the length of the password, maximum password age, which enforces the changes on the password, and complexity setting to force using more character types such as uppercase, lowercase, and numbers.

Managing login properties

Many logins could have been created without the policy and expiration checks, so if you would like to find them all, you can use the following query to list all SQL Server types of login, where the checks are not in place:

```
SELECT serverproperty('machinename') as 'Server Name', [name],
[is_policy_checked], [is_expiration_checked] FROM master.sys.sql_logins
WHERE ( [is_policy_checked] = 0 OR [is_expiration_checked] = 0 ) and name
not like '##MS_%'
```

One more option that you can select while creating a SQL Server type of login is to force the login to change the password during the next login, which is useful when the SQL login is utilized by a developer or administrator, but not particularly useful if the login is used by some application, which just needs to log in to the SQL Server. By selecting the SQL Server authentication, you are actually extending the options of the authentication as you can't turn off the Windows authentication at all.

You can check many of the parameters of the login with the `LOGINPROPERTY` function, which can list more than a dozen attributes of your login. The following sample script will check for all SQL logins where the password has not been updated for more than six months. Taking this script into a scheduled task, which can check for such logins on a weekly or monthly basis and report those, for example, via email to system DBA, is just a matter of creating a SQL Agent job with a proper T-SQL job step.

```
SELECT name,loginproperty([name], 'PasswordLastSetTime')
FROM sys.sql_logins
WHERE loginproperty([name], 'PasswordLastSetTime') <
DATEADD(month,-6,GETDATE())
```

For more information about the built-in function, refer to the Microsoft Books Online documentation at `https://docs.microsoft.com/en-us/sql/t-sql/functions/loginproperty-transact-sql`, which lists all the parameters for the function.

Such a regular check on your logins is not the only one you can do on your server. If you create a SQL Server login and you don't enforce any policies, you can actually create the login with any password you want, despite the complexity or the length. You'll be surprised how many logins are created with a password the same as the login name on many systems. The following script will help you find all those logins on your machine:

```
SELECT SERVERPROPERTY('machinename') AS 'Server Name', name AS 'Login With
Password Same As Name'
FROM master.sys.sql_logins
WHERE PWDCOMPARE(name,password_hash) = 1
ORDER by name
```

A worst case scenario is that the logins with blank passwords can be found as well with the same PWDCOMPARE function. The following code will reveal all SQL Server logins with a blank password:

```
SELECT name FROM sys.sql_logins
WHERE PWDCOMPARE('', password_hash) = 1 ;
```

Authorization

Once you have successfully logged in to SQL Server, SQL checks your access level with each operation--in other words, if you're authorized to perform any operation. This is controlled via the permissions that are assigned to the logins, or the server roles.

Roles are there to simplify the administration for us as they include many permissions on the server and can speed up the securing of the server. Server role is a principal, which groups other principals like logins together on the server level. There is a default set of nine server roles, which are configured automatically on each SQL Server installation.

Fixed server roles

There are nine predefined fixed server roles on each server, which you can use as a starting point for securing the SQL Server environment. These roles can't be dropped, you can only update the role membership.

sysadmin	**Members of this role can perform any activity on the server**
bulkadmin	Members can run BULK INSERT and use the bcp.exe tool
diskadmin	Members can manage disk files
processadmin	Members can KILL processes running on SQL Server
public	Each login is a member of the public role; if a principal is not granted any permission on an object, it inherits the permissions from the public role
securityadmin	Members can manage logins and their properties
serveradmin	Members can change server-level configuration and shut down SQL Server

| setupadmin | Members can create linked servers with TSQL commands |
| dbcreator | Members can create, alter, drop, and restore databases |

If you would like to assign a login to a role, you can update the role membership via TSQL or SQL Server Management Studio. With Management Studio, you can select multiple roles at the same time via the checkboxes and clicking on **OK,** as shown in the following screenshot:

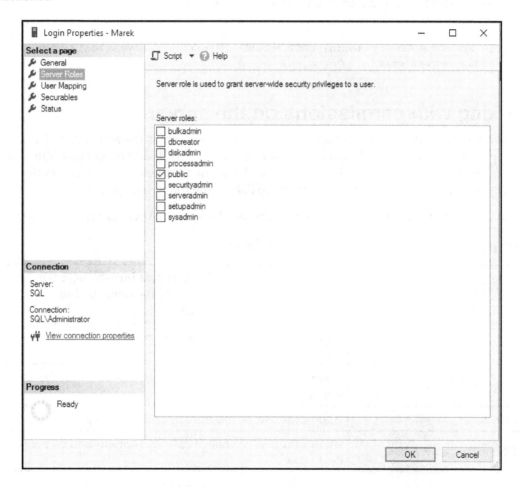

With TSQL, it's quite simple; to add a login to any role, you just enter the following command:

```
ALTER SERVER ROLE [sysadmin] ADD MEMBER [Marek] --for SQL Login type
ALTER SERVER ROLE [sysadmin] ADD MEMBER [DOMAIN\Marek] --for Windows Login
type, including the domain name
```

To remove a member from a role, you can use a similar command with just the DROP MEMBER syntax:

```
ALTER SERVER ROLE [sysadmin] DROP MEMBER [Marek] --removes login Marek from
sysadmin server role
```

Working with permissions on the server

Another option for controlling authorization on the server level is the server permissions. Server permissions can be assigned to your logins via TSQL or the Management Studio to allow the login to perform a specific operation. The list of permissions available on the server is quite long and you can find the whole list via the following query:

```
SELECT * FROM sys.fn_builtin_permissions('') where class_desc = 'SERVER'
```

Server permissions that you can grant are as follows:

ADMINISTER BULK OPERATIONS	**Allows the user to bulk insert data into the SQL Server via the** bcp.exe **tool,** BULK INSERT **statement, and** OPENROWSET(BULK) **statement**
ALTER ANY AVAILABILITY GROUP	Right to failover any availability group, including to create one
ALTER ANY CONNECTION	Allows the user to terminate any connection with the KILL statement
ALTER ANY CREDENTIAL	Allows the user to modify any credential objects
ALTER ANY DATABASE	Allows the user to change database options and create new databases
ALTER ANY ENDPOINT	Allows the user to modify endpoints, including creating new ones
ALTER ANY EVENT NOTIFICATION	Allows the user to modify event notifications and create new ones
ALTER ANY EVENT SESSION	Allows the user to modify event traces and create new traces

`ALTER ANY LINKED SERVER`	Allows the user to create new linked servers, but only with T-SQL commands; via GUI, it's available only to sysadmin role members
`ALTER ANY LOGIN`	Allows the user to modify logins on the instance, reset passwords, and create new logins
`ALTER ANY SERVER AUDIT`	Allows the user to modify and create audits and server audit specifications
`ALTER ANY SERVER ROLE`	Allows the user to modify user-defined server roles
`ALTER RESOURCES`	Allows the user to change system resources
`ALTER SERVER STATE`	Allows the user to change server state, including the right to view server state
`ALTER SETTINGS`	Allows the user to change server-level settings
`ALTER TRACE`	Allows the user to modify server trace sessions
`AUTHENTICATE SERVER`	Allows the user to authenticate to this SQL Server
`CONNECT ANY DATABASE`	Allows the user to connect to all databases on the SQL Server
`CONNECT SQL`	Allows the user to connect to the SQL Server
`CONTROL SERVER`	Allows the user to have nearly sysadmin-equivalent rights, which combine multiple permissions
`CREATE ANY DATABASE`	Allows the user to create new databases and restore databases
`CREATE AVAILABILITY GROUP`	Allows the user to create new Availability groups
`CREATE DDL EVENT NOTIFICATION`	Allows the user to create a server DDL trigger
`CREATE ENDPOINT`	Allows the user to create SQL Server endpoints
`CREATE SERVER ROLE`	Allows the user to create user-defined server roles
`CREATE TRACE EVENT NOTIFICATION`	Allows the user to create trace event notifications
`EXTERNAL ACCESS ASSEMBLY`	Allows the user to create assemblies that require external access
`IMPERSONATE ANY LOGIN`	Allows the user to impersonate any login on the SQL Server

SELECT ALL USER SECURABLES	Allows the user to view all data in all databases, where the user can connect to
SHUTDOWN	Allows the user to shut down a SQL Server instance via the TSQL command
UNSAFE ASSEMBLY	Allows the user to create assemblies that require unsafe access
VIEW ANY DATABASE	Allows the user to view the definition of any database
VIEW ANY DEFINITION	Allows the user to view the definition on any object on the SQL Server instance, including the VIEW ANY DATABASE permission
VIEW SERVER STATE	Allows the user to view server state, which is used by Dynamic Management Views and functions

As an example, let's take **Dynamic Management Views** (**DMVs**) where many of them are restricted only to high-privileged users (members of server roles) or users who have a VIEW SERVER STATE permission. To grant such a permission, you can run the following SQL statement:

```
GRANT VIEW SERVER STATE TO [Marek]
```

This will allow one login to query most of the DMVs to troubleshoot and diagnose SQL Server. With many of the permissions, you can use one more option, WITH GRANT OPTION, which will allow the login not only to perform specific actions, but also to grant this action to another login. To remove the permission, we use the keyword REVOKE, which will remove the previously granted permission to the login:

```
REVOKE VIEW SERVER STATE TO [Marek] AS [sa]
```

Bear in mind that the permission may be a part of some server-wide role permission list. Revoking the explicit permission does not necessarily prevent the user from viewing the server state. To do that, you'll need to explicitly deny the permission to the user:

```
DENY VIEW SERVER STATE TO [Marek]
```

To remove the deny permission, you have to use the REVOKE command again in the same way as we did with the GRANT permission option. As you can see, REVOKE clears either a granted or denied permission.

Auditing

SQL Server comes with several options that can be used for the auditing of login events and many more. The first audit option you can see directly in the server properties/security item that you can find with SQL Server Management Studio. There, you can choose what sort of login audit is performed. By default, SQL Server comes with the **Failed logins only** option selected, which may not be enough for many environments where, due to business or security requirements, you have to capture all login attempts.

This audit stores all the information to the SQL Server log, which you can review via Management Studio or, if needed, via any text editor, as the log is a plain text file. On a highly loaded system, this log can generate an enormous amount of information, so you need to consider if this is really the best option to store information about login sessions. This log is also used as an error log, so any error that is logged is then surrounded by many noise messages about successful or failed login events.

SQL Server comes with another audit, which can be utilized. This audit object is available for several versions already (since 2008) and can be used to audit the same failed and successful logons and many more. A great benefit of this audit is the flexibility of the configuration as the specifications for the audit can be either server-wide or database-wide. You can choose if the audit should store the information to a text file or directly to the Windows event logs. Database-level auditing was previously available only in the Enterprise Edition, but since SQL Server 2016 Service Pack 1, it's available in all editions.

Configuring server audit

Audit configuration has several components--two of them are primary audit and audit specifications. Audit is a configuration object where you have to select how to store the captured events, how resilient the audit will be, and so on.

The specification is another object that you have to create, and there you specify what events should be captured:

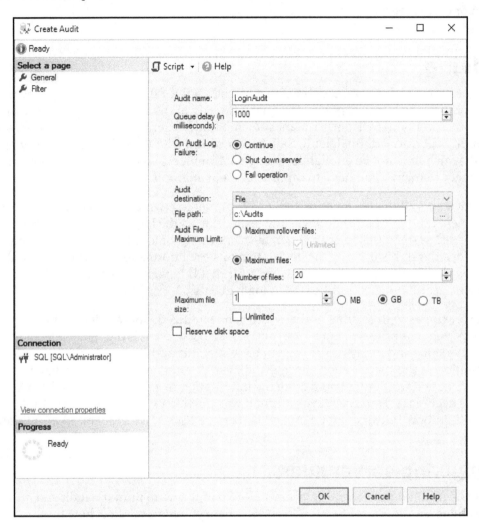

To create the audit on the server, you can use the following TSQL code:

```
CREATE SERVER AUDIT [LoginAudit]
TO FILE ( FILEPATH = N'E:\Audits', MAXSIZE = 1024 MB ,MAX_FILES =
20,RESERVE_DISK_SPACE = OFF )
WITH ( QUEUE_DELAY = 1000 ,ON_FAILURE = CONTINUE )
```

This query will create an object Audit, which will store all the information to text files. These will be located in the E:\Audits folder on your server and can use up to 20 GB of space on your drive--a maximum 20 files with a maximum size of 1 GB each. If such an audit fails to store any event, all operations will continue. Until now, we have only configured the storage for the events, but we haven't configured any events to capture. This is where **server audit specifications** come into the picture.

Server audit specifications

Server audit specifications define what action groups (events grouped by the scope of action) will be tracked by your audit. To configure the audit specifications use a TSQL or GUI.

```
CREATE SERVER AUDIT SPECIFICATION [LogonAuditConfig]
FOR SERVER AUDIT [LogonAudit]
ADD (FAILED_LOGIN_GROUP),
ADD (SUCCESSFUL_LOGIN_GROUP)
```

With this TSQL script, we have configured the audit to collect information about successful and failed login events to a separate file on your SQL Server. You can, of course, add many more action groups to this audit and create more audits on your server. One of my favorite action groups for the auditing is SERVER_ROLE_MEMBER_CHANGE_GROUP, which tracks information about changes in your server roles. You can then see who updated any role membership and when, either adding or dropping a member from the role.

As you can see in the screenshot from SQL Server Management Studio, there are many other useful action groups worth considering for the audit on your server:

Even though this audit is quite lightweight (based on Extended Events, to be discussed in following chapters), you shouldn't just select everything and expect no performance hits on the server. Like everything else in SQL Server, you need to carefully consider which events you should collect. My favorite basic set for security auditing on the server includes just a few action groups and can be configured as follows:

```
CREATE SERVER AUDIT SPECIFICATION [Security audit specifications]
FOR SERVER AUDIT [SecurityAudit]
ADD (SERVER_ROLE_MEMBER_CHANGE_GROUP),
ADD (AUDIT_CHANGE_GROUP),
ADD (SERVER_PERMISSION_CHANGE_GROUP),
ADD (SERVER_PRINCIPAL_CHANGE_GROUP),
ADD (LOGIN_CHANGE_PASSWORD_GROUP)
WITH (STATE = ON)
```

Such a basic set can be always modified, filtered, and tuned to fit your environment needs and requirements. Usually, a compliance and governance team will help you in designing the required collection in larger environments.

Configuring credentials

A credential is an object associated with authentication information required to connect to an external resource. If you need to connect to any external resource outside of SQL Server, you need a proper way of authenticating to the resource. This resource can be, for example, a file share with important XML files to be processed daily on SQL Server. In such cases, a credential object can be used to connect to this file share.

Creating a credential can be done via T-SQL or SSMS; in most cases, it's a Windows account with a proper password. The following code will create a new credential on the server:

```
CREATE CREDENTIAL [WindowsAcct] WITH IDENTITY = N'DOMAIN\ServiceAcct',
SECRET = N'P@ssw0rd'
--you need to specify the password for the Windows account here as a plain
text
```

You can map the credential to any amount of SQL Server logins so that the login has access to external resources. One credential can be used many times, but a SQL login can have only one credential mapped for usage. To map a credential to a SQL Server login, you can use the following TSQL query:

```
ALTER LOGIN [Marek] ADD CREDENTIAL [WindowsAcct]
```

Credentials and proxies in the SQL Server Agent

Credentials are frequently used with SQL Server Agent jobs. When you're configuring SQL Server Agent jobs for any automated task, you have to choose a category of the job step. Several categories allow you to select the security context, which will be used to run the particular part of the scheduled task. There's usually an option visible to run the job step within the context of the SQL Server Agent account, but that is reserved to sysadmin role members only.

If you're not a sysadmin, you need to choose a job proxy, which is in the end mapped to the existing credential. This choice is active for most of the step types, except the Transact-SQL script step, which does not utilize a proxy:

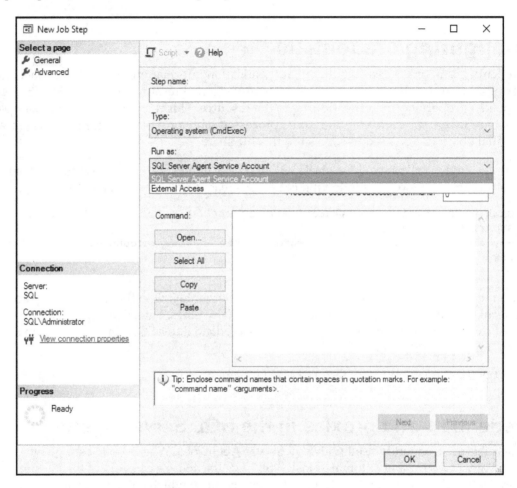

We already know how to create a credential, so now we need to create an agent proxy, which will utilize the credential. We can do this via the SQL Server Management Studio. In this case, it's simpler compared to the TSQL where we would need to use several stored procedures with proper parameter mappings.

In the dialog for creating a new proxy, we need to select a proper subsystem, which will be used by the proxy. With SQL Server 2017, the choices are smaller than with older versions and the available subsystems are as follows:

- Operating System
- PowerShell
- SSAS Query
- SSAS Command
- SSIS Package

The following image gives us a good idea of the different subsystems in SQL Server 2017:

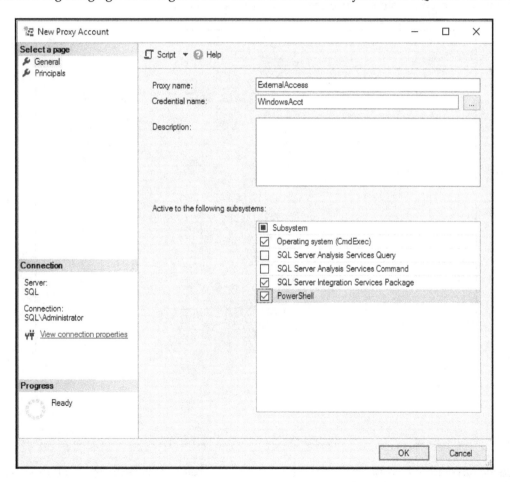

You can configure one proxy for more subsystems, as you can see in the preceding screenshot. Once you create the proxy, you need to configure who can utilize the proxy via the **Principals** tab in the proxy configuration. Yet again, only sysadmin role members have default access to utilize the proxy for the agent jobs. You can add the following principals to the proxy security:

- Server logins
- Server roles
- Roles from MSDB database

To add a new proxy account you can use Management Studio and SQL Server Agent sections, where you can configure the proxies for various subsystems.

Once we have added proper principals (SQL Login **Marek** in this case), such a login can utilize the proxy to run the OS commands from SQL Server Agent jobs.

Encrypting SQL Server data

When you're storing sensitive data on your SQL Server, you may need to encrypt the data to protect the data from accidental misuse. There might be your company's business and technical requirements to encrypt the data or even law requirements to encrypt any sensitive information.

SQL Server has many options on how to protect the data with encryption--depending on the need to protect the data at rest or in transit. The whole encryption ecosystem in SQL Server is quite complex and offers many options:

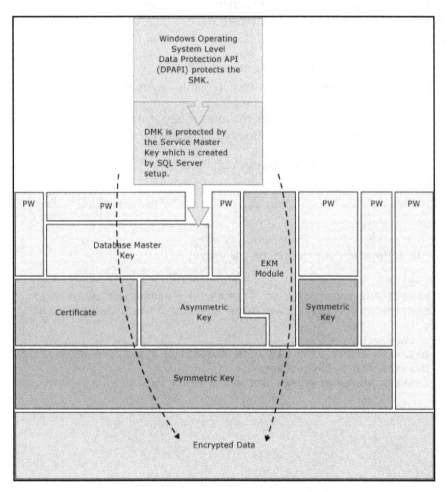

Transparent data encryption

One of the options on how to encrypt the data in the database is transparent data encryption. This feature is available since SQL Server 2008 and works on the I/O level. Both file types--data and log--are encrypted on the disk and SQL Server does the encryption once the data is written to disk and decryption once the data is retrieved from the disk into memory. This encryption works on the page level and does not have an effect on the size of the database.

Data encryption is totally transparent to the application, so you can turn on the encryption for any database and any application. This encryption is symmetric using a **database encryption key** (**DEK**), which is stored in the database boot record and is protected with either one of the following:

- Server certificate created in the master database
- Asymmetric key protected by the extensible key management module

The server certificate is then protected by the master key stored in the master database. To turn on the transparent database encryption, you need to do as follows:

1. Create a master key in the master database.
2. Create a server certificate in the master database.
3. Create a database encryption key protected by the certificate.
4. Turn on the encryption.

You can use the following code to turn on the encryption:

```
USE master;
CREATE MASTER KEY ENCRYPTION BY PASSWORD = 'Pa$$w0rdF0rM4$t3R';
CREATE CERTIFICATE MyServerCert WITH SUBJECT = 'DEK Certificate';

USE AdventureWorks
CREATE DATABASE ENCRYPTION KEY WITH ALGORITHM = AES_128 ENCRYPTION BY
SERVER CERTIFICATE MyServerCert;
ALTER DATABASE AdventureWorks SET ENCRYPTION ON;
```

Database encryption can also be managed via GUI, where, in the **Tasks/Manage Database Encryption** option of the database, you can choose to turn the encryption on and off and configure which certificate should be used to protect the database encryption key and what key length should be used for the database encryption key:

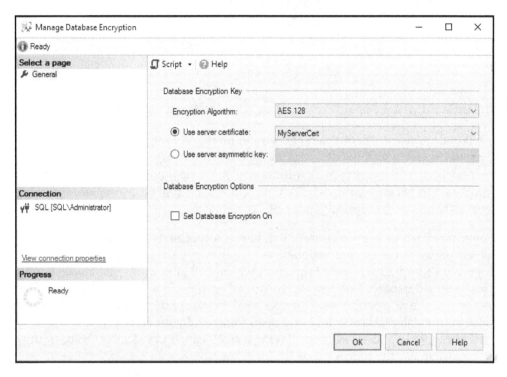

Turning on database encryption may be a complex task, which requires a lot of time. During the transition stage of your database, when the database is getting encrypted, you can use the database for your application with some limitations. You can't modify the database configuration, back up the database, work with snapshots, and so on. To monitor the progress of the encryption, you can use one of the Dynamic Management Views named `sys.dm_database_encryption_keys`:

```
SELECT database_id, encryption_state, key_algorithm, key_length,
percent_complete
FROM sys.dm_database_encryption_keys
```

The result from such a query may be similar to this one on your server:

	database_id	encryption_state	key_algorithm	key_length	percent_complete
1	2	3	AES	256	0
2	5	2	AES	128	34.27872

Query executed successfully.   SQL (14.0 RC2) SQL\Administrator (67) AdventureWorks 00:00:00 2 rows

There are two databases with enabled encryption on this server, one of them is the AdventureWorks for which we did turn on the encryption. The other one is a system database TempDB, which is encrypted automatically. You can monitor the progress with the last column named **percent_complete**. When the database will be encrypted, the column value will be 0 and the **encryption_state** will change to 3.

A very important part of the transparent database encryption is also the certificate management. Once you encrypt the database, you may get a warning that the certificate was not yet backed up. This is very important for any DR situations, otherwise, you'll not be able to restore the database. Not only are the database files on the server encrypted, but backups also use the same encryption. If you need to restore the database to another server or you lose your master database and you need to rebuild your server, you won't be able to restore the encrypted database without having a certificate on the server. To back up your certificate, you can use the following code:

```
USE master
BACKUP CERTIFICATE MyServerCert TO FILE = 'C:\Certificate\MyServerCert.cer'
WITH PRIVATE KEY (FILE = 'C:\Certificate\MyServerCert.pfx', ENCRYPTION BY
PASSWORD = 'Str0ngP@ssw0rd')
```

To create the certificate from these two files, you can use the CREATE CERTIFICATE command with proper parameters:

```
USE master
CREATE CERTIFICATE MyServerCert FROM FILE =
'C:\Certificate\MyServerCert.cer'
WITH PRIVATE KEY (FILE = 'C:\Certificate\MyServerCert.pfx', DECRYPTION BY
PASSWORD = 'Str0ngP@ssw0rd')
```

Always encrypted

SQL Server 2016 has introduced a new way to encrypt the data on SQL Server, which allows the application to encrypt the data and never reveal the encryption keys to the database engine. In this way, not even a sysadmin of SQL Server can read the decrypted values stored in your tables. Unlike the transparent data encryption, which works on the database level, **Always Encrypted** works on the column level. Unlike the regular column-level encryption, **Always Encrypted** allows more types of queries on the data like equality comparisons, joins, group by, and so on:

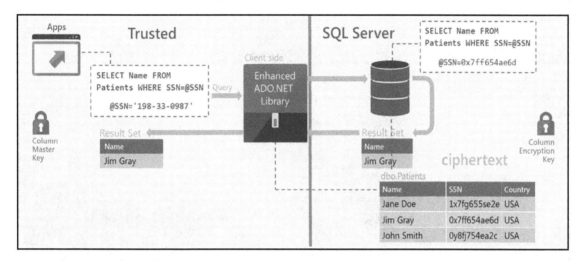

Always Encrypted comes with two flavors of encryption:

- Randomized
- Deterministic

Deterministic encryption always generates the same ciphertext for a given value, whereas randomized does not and is less predictable. This has an impact on the usage of the encrypted data. With randomized encryption, you can't use joins, group by, indexing, or any equality searches.

To encrypt the data with **Always Encrypted**, we go by the following steps:

1. Right-click on the database and go to **tasks/encrypt columns**.
2. Choose the table/column you want to encrypt.
3. Select the encryption type from **Randomized/Deterministic**.
4. Configure the master key configuration.

The master key configuration allows you to select the column master key and the key store. You can store the keys in a **Windows certificate store** or an **Azure Key Vault** service. If you're using the **Windows certificate store**, you can configure whether to use the local user or local computer store for the certificate:

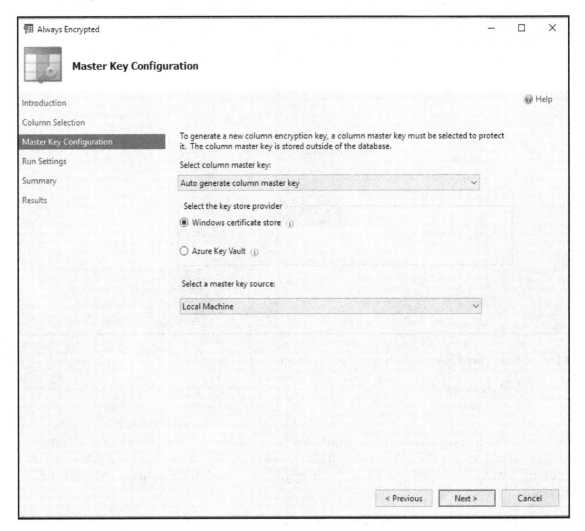

Once this is turned on, it will automatically encrypt the content of the selected columns, which will be encrypted with the selected keys.

Summary

Security is a very important part of your SQL Server deployment and, in this chapter, we have seen many options that you can use to secure your SQL Server environment. You are making important choices already during the setup of your environment where you configure the service accounts and authentication. Once you have SQL Server up and running, you have to configure SQL Server logins for your groups and accounts, which provide them proper access to the SQL Server.

It's important to understand the difference between authentication and authorization. Just because you can log in to the SQL Server does not give you the rights to change configuration, access data, or perform any data changes. There are many configuration items which require sysadmin role membership and there's a frequent push from application teams and application DBAs to be part of this restricted server role, but you should limit the members of the sysadmin role as much as possible. The same can be said for the security admin role, which has very high privileges on the system.

In the next chapter, we will look into the backup and restore operations for SQL Server, which are an important part of the whole DR strategy.

5
Disaster Recovery Options

High availability and disaster recovery are important solutions of an enterprise strategy for data availability. SQL Server has several different features available for implementing high availability and disaster recovery scenarios, which will help you increase the availability metric of your SQL Server environment and your applications that are using the data stored on SQL Server.

High availability and disaster recovery are frequently mixed up together, as many people think these are the same. Be mindful that they are not. Even if you have a solution for high availability in place, it does not mean that you can recover from a disaster or that you have some disaster recovery plan.

In this chapter, we'll explore the disaster recovery basics to understand the common terms in high availability and disaster recovery and we will discuss what SQL Server has to offer regarding the HA/DR options.

The following topics will be covered in this chapter:

- Disaster recovery basics
- SQL Server options for high availability and disaster recovery
- Configuring replication on SQL Server
- Database mirroring
- Log shipping

Disaster recovery basics

Disaster recovery (DR) is a set of tools, policies, and procedures, which help us during the recovery of your systems after a disastrous event. Disaster recovery is just a subset of a more complex discipline called business continuity planning, where more variables come in place and you expect more sophisticated plans on how to recover the business operations. With careful planning, you can minimize the effects of the disaster, because you have to keep in mind that it's nearly impossible to completely avoid disasters.

 The main goal of a disaster recovery plan is to minimize the downtime of our service and to minimize the data loss. To measure these objectives, we use special metrics: Recovery Point and Time Objectives.

Recovery Time Objective (RTO) is the maximum time that you can use to recover the system. This time includes your efforts to fix the problem without starting the disaster recovery procedures, the recovery itself, proper testing after the disaster recovery, and the communication to the stakeholders. Once a disaster strikes, clocks are started to measure the disaster recovery actions and the **Recovery Time Actual** (RTA) metric is calculated. If you manage to recover the system within the Recovery Time Objective, which means that *RTA < RTO*, then you have met the metrics with a proper combination of the plan and your ability to restore the system.

Recovery Point Objective (RPO) is the maximum tolerable period for acceptable data loss. This defines how much data can be lost due to disaster. This closely relates to our backups, which were discussed in `Chapter 3`, *Backup and Recovery*. The Recovery Point Objective has an impact on your implementation of backups, because you plan for a recovery strategy that has specific requirements for your backups. If you can avoid to lose one day of work, you can properly plan your backup types and the frequency of the backups that you need to take.

The following image is an illustration of the very concepts that we discussed in the preceding paragraph:

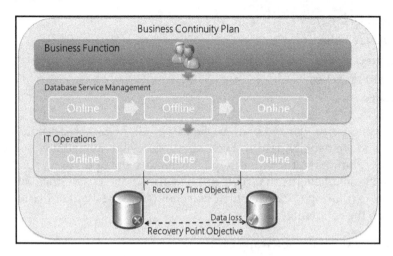

When we talk about system availability, we usually use a percentage of the availability time. This availability is a calculated uptime in a given year or month (any date metric that you need) and is usually compared to a following table of "9s".

Availability also expresses a tolerable downtime in a given time frame so that the system still meets the availability metric. In the following table, we'll see some basic availability options with tolerable downtime a year and a day:

Availability %	Downtime a year	Downtime a day
90%	36.5 days	2.4 hours
98%	7.3 days	28.8 minutes
99%	3.65 days	14.4 minutes
99.9%	8.76 hours	1.44 minutes
99.99%	52.56 minutes	8.64 seconds
99.999%	5.26 minutes	less than 1 second

This tolerable downtime consists of the unplanned downtime and can be caused by many factors:

- Natural Disasters
- Hardware failures
- Human errors (accidental deletes, code breakdowns, and so on)
- Security breaches
- Malware

For these, we can have a mitigation plan in place that will help us reduce the downtime to a tolerable range, and we usually deploy a combination of high availability solutions and disaster recovery solutions so that we can quickly restore the operations. On the other hand, there's a reasonable set of events that require a downtime on your service due to the maintenance and regular operations, which does not affect the availability on your system. These can include the following:

- New releases of the software
- Operating system patching
- SQL Server patching
- Database maintenance and upgrades

Our goal is to have the database online as much as possible, but there will be times when the database will be offline and, from the perspective of the management and operation, we're talking about several keywords such as uptime, downtime, time to repair, and time between failures, as you can see in the following image:

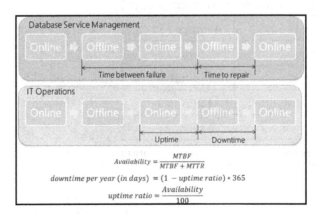

It's really critical not only to have a plan for disaster recovery, but also to practice the disaster recovery itself. Many companies follow the procedure of proper disaster recovery plan testing with different types of exercise where each and every aspect of the disaster recovery is carefully evaluated by teams who are familiar with the tools and procedures for a real disaster event. This exercise may have different scope and frequency, as listed in the following points:

- Tabletop exercises usually involve only a small number of people and focus on a specific aspect of the DR plan. This would be a DBA team drill to recover a single SQL Server or a small set of servers with simulated outage.
- Medium-sized exercises will involve several teams to practice team communication and interaction.
- Complex exercises usually simulate larger events such as data center loss, where a new virtual data center is built and all new servers and services are provisioned by the involved teams.

Such exercises should be run on a periodic basis so that all the teams and team personnel are up to speed with the disaster recovery plans.

SQL Server options for high availability and disaster recovery

SQL Server has many features that you can put in place to implement a HA/DR solution that will fit your needs. These features include the following:

- Always On Failover Cluster
- Always On Availability Groups
- Database mirroring
- Log shipping
- Replication

In many cases, you will combine more of the features together, as your high availability and disaster recovery needs will overlap. HA/DR does not have to be limited to just one single feature. In complex scenarios, you'll plan for a primary high availability solution and secondary high availability solution that will work as your disaster recovery solution at the same time.

Always On Failover Cluster

An **Always On Failover Cluster (FCI)** is an instance-level protection mechanism, which is based on top of a **Windows Failover Cluster Feature** (**WFCS**). SQL Server instance will be installed across multiple WFCS nodes, where it will appear in the network as a single computer.

All the resources that belong to one SQL Server instance (disk, network, names) can be owned by one node of the cluster and, during any planned or unplanned event like a failure of any server component, these can be moved to another node in the cluster to preserve operations and minimize downtime, as shown in the following image:

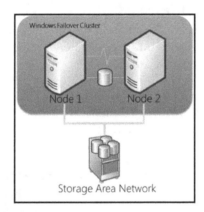

Always On Availability Groups

Always On Availability Groups were introduced with SQL Server 2012 to bring a database-level protection to the SQL Server. As with the Always On Failover Cluster, Availability Groups utilize the Windows Failover Cluster feature, but in this case, single SQL Server is not installed as a clustered instance but runs independently on several nodes. These nodes can be configured as Always On Availability Group nodes to host a database, which will be synchronized among the hosts. The replica can be either synchronous or asynchronous, so Always On Availability Groups are a good fit either as a solution for one data center or even distant data centers to keep your data safe. With new SQL Server versions, Always On Availability Groups were enhanced and provide many features for database high availability and disaster recovery scenarios. You can refer to the following image for a better understanding:

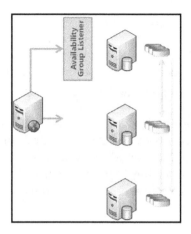

Database mirroring

Database mirroring is an older HA/DR feature available in SQL Server, which provides database-level protection. Mirroring allows synchronizing the databases between two servers, where you can include one more server as a witness server as a failover quorum.

Unlike the previous two features, database mirroring does not require any special setup such as Failover Cluster and the configuration can be achieved via SSMS using a wizard available via database properties. Once a transaction occurs on the primary node, it's copied to the second node to the mirrored database. With proper configuration, database mirroring can provide failover options for high availability with automatic client redirection.

Database mirroring is not preferred solution for HA/DR, since it's marked as a deprecated feature from SQL Server 2012 and is replaced by Basic Availability Groups on current versions.

Log shipping

Log shipping configuration, as the name suggests, is a mechanism to keep a database in sync by copying the logs to the remote server. Log shipping, unlike mirroring, is not copying each single transaction, but copies the transactions in batches via transaction log backup on the primary node and log restore on the secondary node. Unlike all previously mentioned features, log shipping does not provide an automatic failover option, so it's considered more as a disaster recovery option than a high availability one.

Log shipping operates on regular intervals where three jobs have to run:

- Backup job to backup the transaction log on the primary system
- Copy job to copy the backups to the secondary system
- Restore job to restore the transaction log backup on the secondary system

Log shipping supports multiple standby databases, which is quite an advantage compared to database mirroring. One more advantage is the standby configuration for log shipping, which allows read-only access to the secondary database. This is mainly used for many reporting scenarios, where the reporting applications use read-only access and such configuration allows performance offload to the secondary system.

Replication

Replication is a feature for data movement from one server to another that allows many different scenarios and topologies.

> Replication uses a model of publisher/subscriber, where the `Publisher` is the server offering the content via a replication article and subscribers are getting the data.

The configuration is more complex compared to mirroring and log shipping features, but allows you much more variety in the configuration for security, performance, and topology.

Replication has many benefits and a few of them are as follows:

- Works on the object level (whereas other features work on database or instance level)
- Allows megre replication, where more servers synchronize data between each other
- Allows bi-directional synchronization of data
- Allows other than SQL Server partners (Oracle, for example)

There are several different replication types that can be used with SQL Server, and you can choose them based on the needs for HA/DR options and the data availability requirements on the secondary servers. These options include the following:

- Snapshot replication
- Transactional replication

- Peer-to-peer replication
- Merge replication

Configuring replication on SQL Server

In this part of the chapter, we will focus on SQL Server replication in detail and we'll see how to configure replication for a database between different servers. Like with many other features, the configuration can be done with SQL Server Management Studio (GUI) or with T-SQL code, which sometimes provides greater flexibility. Be aware that replication is one of the features that you can configure immediately during installation to be available on your system. In case you haven't installed the feature, you can always add replication to the existing SQL Server instance:

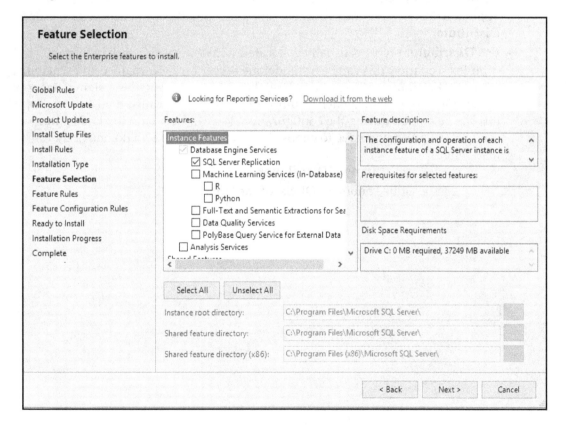

Replication topology includes several roles for servers and offers various scenarios. The primary roles we will work with are as follows:

- **Subscriber**
- Publisher
- **Distributor**

Let's read a little about each of the roles:

- Publisher is the primary server in the replication topology, which hosts the source data. On the Publisher server, we need to create a replication Publication, which is a unit for replication containing one or more articles that are distributed to the **Subscriber** servers.
- **Subscriber** is the server that stores the replica and receives updates from the original data. Between the subscriber and publisher, there's one more role called **Distributor**.
- The **Distributor** server is usually collocated with Publisher, but in more complex scenarios, this can be a standalone server for performance and scalability reasons. **Distributor** utilizes a database that appears among the system databases in the SQL Server Management Studio, which is usually called distribution, but this can be altered during the configuration. We can start with the **Distributor** configuration and you have to choose if your SQL Server will do one of the following:
    - Act as its own **Distributor**
    - Utilize another SQL Server as **Distributor**

Once you finish the configuration, you will have configured the following:

- **Distributor database**
- Replication `snapshot` folder
- Distribution profile
- Assigned a distributor for your `Publisher`

You can then check the **Distributor** properties for your SQL Server by right-clicking on **Replication** and choosing **Distributor** Properties:

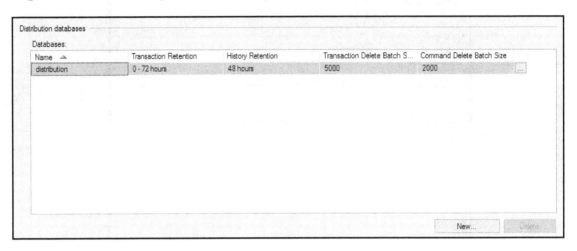

Creating a Publication

Publication is a unit for data replication. You can create a `Publication` via SSMS if you go to the replication/local **Publications** menu item and right-click on **Local Publication**. Here, you can select a **New Publication** item, which will start a wizard for you. This wizard will guide you through the whole publication configuration. The first choice that you have to make is what sort of replication publication you want to create:

- Snapshot
- Transactional
- Peer-to-peer

- Merge

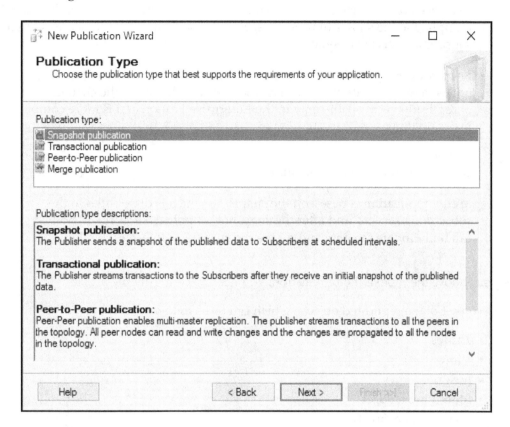

Let's read a little about each type of replication:

- **Snapshot publication** will create a snapshot of your data, which will be periodically transferred to the subscribing servers. Snapshot will include the data as it is present on the `Publisher` at the time of the snapshot creation. Until you create a new snapshot and distribute the snapshot to the subscribing servers again, those will not receive any updates by default.

- **Transactional replication** will be based on the snapshot publication (it can be also based on the backup in more complex types of setup) and, after the snapshot is applied to the subscribing servers, each transaction will be copied to keep the subscribing servers in sync.

- **Peer-to-peer replication** allows multi-master data synchronization, where all the nodes in the replication can update the data and distribute the changes. This type of replication is available only in the Enterprise Edition and is more complex to maintain due to

  higher
  chance of conflict on the data updates.

- **Merge replication** is based on the snapshot, which is distributed to the subscribing servers, and after the snapshot is applied, subscriber and `Publisher` can both update the data and merge the changes between each other.

Once you choose the type of the publication, you need to configure the article.

Articles consist of the replicated objects, which can be as follows:

- **Tables**
- **Views**
- **Indexed views**
- **Stored procedures**
- **User defined functions**

When you are configuring the **Articles**, you can use both horizontal and vertical filtering, which means that you can choose which columns on a table or view and which rows should be replicated.

As can be seen from the following figure, if you don't use any filters, all table columns and rows will be added to the publication for replication by default:

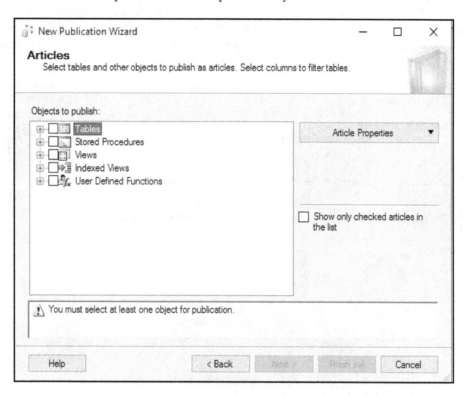

Once you have selected the objects that you would like to publish, you have to configure the schedule for the snapshot creation. You have two options:

- Create the snapshot immediately
- Schedule the snapshot creation

If you are working with a small database or small amount of objects to publish, you can create the snapshot immediately, as with a small size, it won't put much load on your server. However, if you're planning to create a snapshot for a large database with a large amount of objects, you may need to postpone the snapshot creation after the business hours or to some time window when your server is less loaded. This is recommended due to the load on the IO subsystem caused by generating the snapshot.

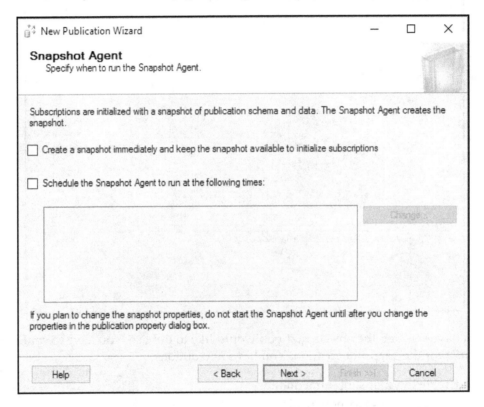

After you configure the schedule, you have to configure the **Snapshot Agent Security**, where you need to set up credentials for **Snapshot Agent** and configure how the agent will connect to the `Publisher` to get the data for the snapshot. You can either use the SQL Server Agent account or configure your own account for the connection and agent credentials:

If you would like to use the T-SQL scripts to create the publication for snapshot replication, you can use the following code, assuming that you have the `AdventureWorks` database available on your SQL Server.

You can download sample databases for the MS SQL Server at `https://github.com/Microsoft/sql-server-samples/tree/master/samples/databases/adventure-works`, where you can find the `AdventureWorks` database, the `WideWorldImporters` database, and samples for analysis, reporting, and integration services. There are also specific databases for data warehouse scenarios, which may be helpful for your learning purposes. Such databases should be deployed only to test/dev servers and it's a good practice never to put those on production systems.

The following code can be used to enable replication:

```
use [AdventureWorks]
exec sp_replicationdboption @dbname = N'AdventureWorks',
    @optname = N'publish',
    @value = N'true'
GO

exec sp_addpublication @publication = N'AWorks - Test',
  @description = N'Snapshot publication of database ''AdventureWorks'' from
Publisher ''SQL''.',
  @sync_method = N'native',
  @snapshot_in_defaultfolder = N'true',
  @repl_freq = N'snapshot',
  @status = N'active',
  @independent_agent = N'true'
GO

exec sp_addpublication_snapshot @publication = N'AWorks - Employee',
@frequency_type = 1

use [AdventureWorks]
exec sp_addarticle @publication = N'AWorks - Employee',
    @article = N'Employee',
    @source_owner = N'HumanResources',
    @source_object = N'Employee',
    @destination_table = N'Employee',
    @destination_owner = N'HumanResources',
    @schema_option = 0x000000000803509D
GO
```

In this way, we have created a snapshot for one single table from the `AdventureWorks` database named `HumanResources.Employee`, which is now available as a publication. Once we have the publication in place, we can configure the subscription.

Configuring the subscription

We can subscribe to existing publications again via the GUI or the T-SQL scripts. You need to know the server name where you host your publications so that you can connect to the proper `Publisher`. Once you are connected to the `Publisher`, you can select the publication that you want to subscribe to:

Subscriptions can be configured in two ways:

- Push subscription
- Pull subscription

The difference in these two is where the **Distributor** agent will run. With push subscription, the **Distributor** agent will run on the **Distributor** server (usually collocated with Publisher), whereas the pull subscription configuration uses **Subscribers** to run the agents. This has a performance impact for larger environments, but for simple configurations, it's fine to run the distribution agents on the **Distributor** server. Once you have selected the publication, you need to configure the **Subscribers**, mainly the server names and the subscription databases. Subscription databases can exist already and the publication will add data to the existing database, or the dialog will let you create a new database for your subscription:

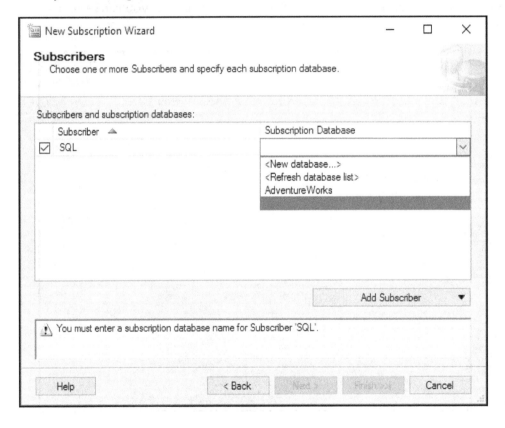

Last but not least, you have to configure the security profiles for your **Distribution Agent security** and, as with **Snapshot Agent**, you can use a separate account or impersonate the account used by SQL Server Agent service:

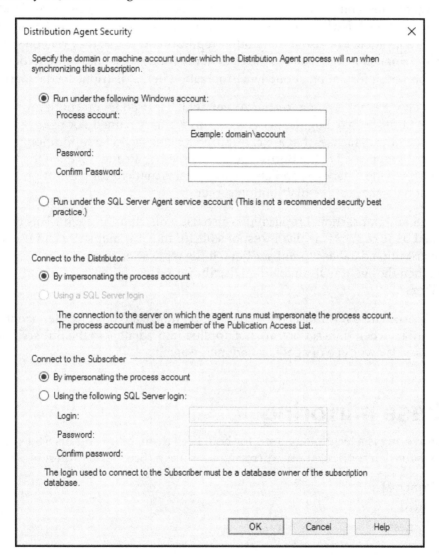

Once you finish the configuration dialog, you will have a subscription active for your publication with snapshot replication.

Replication agents

So far we have seen a **Snapshot Agent**, which we configured for the snapshot replication. **Snapshot Agent** runs a binary named `snapshot.exe` and usually runs on the **Distributor** server. In many cases, **Distributor** and `Publisher` are the same. This agent is not only used for snapshot replication, but also for any other replication types as they rely on snapshot in the beginning. **Snapshot Agent** stores the data in the configured `snapshot` folder and captures important information about synchronization in the distribution database.

Another important agent is a Log Reader Agent, which is used if you configure the replication as transactional. Log Reader Agent runs a binary named `logread.exe` and it's used to check all the databases that are configured for transactional replication. Transactions are replicated to the **Subscribers** is by the Log Reader Agent, which reads the transaction logs of the databases, and any change that is marked for replication is copied to the distribution database at the distribution server.

Both snapshot and transactional replications also use a distribution agent. This agent runs a binary named `distrib.exe`, which is responsible for moving snapshots and transactions from the distribution database to **Subscribers**. If the replication is configured as push replication, then the agent will run on the **Distributor** server; in the case of pull, it will run on **Subscribers**.

More complex scenarios for transactional replication utilize a Queue Reader agent, which is used in situations when transactions are not applied immediately to the **Subscribers**. Merge replication uses its own type of agent, called merge agent.

Database mirroring

Database mirroring is a technology used for both high availability and disaster recovery, which allows for rich configuration. Mirroring uses up to three server roles:

- Principal
- Mirror
- Witness

The principal server holds the database that is mirrored. This database has to be configured with Full Recovery model in order to participate in the mirroring configuration. The mirror server holds a mirrored copy of the database, but unlike replication or log shipping, this database is not available for user access. The witness server can be configured in case you would like to utilize automatic failover of the mirrored database between the principal and mirror server due to unavailability of the principal.

Database mirroring operates in three modes. Each mode has its advantages and disadvantages and it's important to understand these in order to choose the right mode for your setup. These modes are as follows:

- High performance
- High safety without automatic failover
- High safety with automatic failover

High-performance mode requires the Enterprise Edition of SQL Server, whereas the other two modes can work with the Standard Edition as well. High-performance mode uses asynchronous processing, which means that transaction is committed on the principal server first, then on the mirror without any delays. The other two modes use synchronous processing, so the transaction has to be committed on the mirror and the principal in order for the application to continue. Due to the two commits--one on principal and one on the mirror server--high safety modes are not used on slower networks because they can cause slower application performance.

The automatic failover can occur only with Witness server configuration. The witness server is connected to both partners--principal and mirror servers--and can operate with minimum resources and lower editions such as Express.

To prepare for the mirroring, you need to have the database on both servers. To do this, you need to take database backup and log backup and restore both to the mirror server. You can use GUI or TSQL scripts to perform the backups and restore the database to the operational state using recovery option.

Configuring database mirroring

To configure mirroring, you need to take several steps. A lot of important information about mirroring of your database can be found in the mirroring item in the database properties.

First, you need to configure the security, where you will define your principal, witness, and mirror servers including their port numbers. These port numbers will be used in creating endpoints on each SQL Server, which will be used for mirroring sessions, as can be seen from the following image:

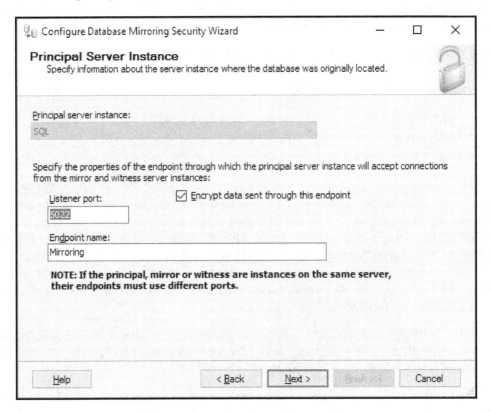

Once you have configured the security, you can start the mirroring for the selected database via the **Start Mirroring** button in the dialog:

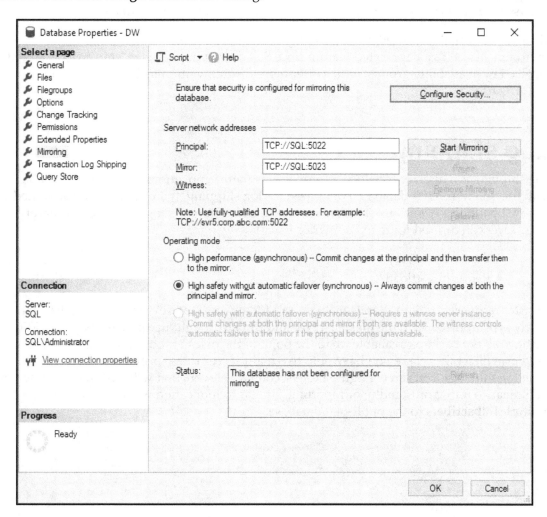

As you can see, the high safety with automatic failover option is not available, as the configuration for the witness server was skipped. Once the mirroring is operational, you can use the **Failover** button to switch the roles of the mirror and principal servers.

Mirroring is usually not used on new deployments and runs mostly on legacy environments as it's a deprecated feature since SQL Server 2012. Today, mirroring is largely replaced by availability groups, which offer more flexibility, monitoring options, and performance.

Log shipping

Log shipping is a disaster recovery technology, as there is no automatic failover available with this solution. With database configured for log shipping, there are several automated jobs that periodically back up the transaction log and restore the log to a different server. This server can be used for many scenarios like:

- Disaster recovery
- Reporting offload

Disaster recovery configuration is mainly used for a warm standby server, which has data nearly synchronized with the master server and can be brought up quite quickly providing we have all the backups available up to the point of the disaster. Log shipping has quite a simple architecture, where you have only two main server roles--primary and secondary. With log shipping, you can configure more secondary servers that will host the database for DR scenarios for warm standby or reporting, similar to replication where you can have multiple **Subscribers** to the published database.

To start with the log shipping configuration, you have to open the **Database Properties** and go to the menu item for **Transaction Log Shipping**:

You need to enable the database as the primary database in the **Transaction Log Shipping** configuration and configure the backup job. This backup job requires a configuration of the following:

- Network path where the backups will be stored
- Job schedule--frequency of the backups
- Backup file retention--how long to keep the backups
- Compression settings

- Alert threshold to notify the DBA if backups don't run

Once you have configured the job, you can add the instances that will be used as secondary servers in the log shipping configuration. You can configure the initial database load option, which will take a fresh backup of the database and restore the database to the secondary server.

If you have done all the initialization steps manually, you can skip this option using a setting, **Secondary database Setting** is initialized. On the copy file tab, you have to configure the copy job settings, mainly the frequency of how often the copy job copies the backups from the primary server to the secondary server. The third tab will allow you to choose the restore options for the database. There are two restoring options that you can use:

- No recovery
- Standby

Then no recovery option will keep your database in the restoring mode and will not accessible to your users. Database will be used only by the log shipping feature on the secondary server to restore the logs periodically. If you would like to work with the database on the secondary server, then this is actually possible if you use the standby mode, which allows read-only access to the databases. This is particularly useful for any offloading for reporting applications, which mostly use read-only access to data.

A screenshot with the option of choosing between the choices is shown here:

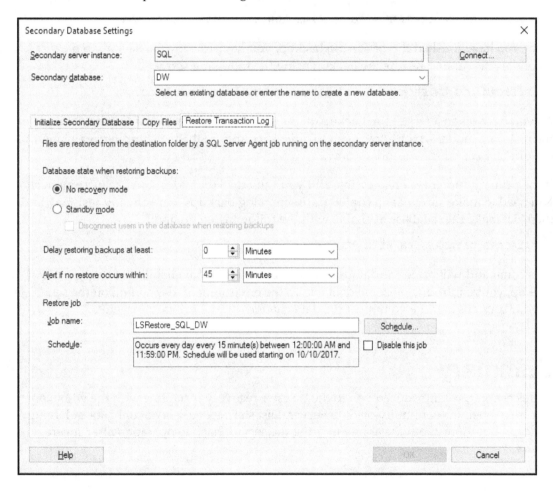

Switching log shipping roles

Servers in the log shipping configuration can be utilized for disaster recovery, but this process is mostly manual. To switch the primary and secondary servers, you need to copy all the available backups to the secondary server. If this is a planned role switch, then you need to take a `tail-log` backup on the primary database:

```
USE master
GO
BACKUP LOG DW TO DISK = 'c:\backups\DW.trn' WITH NORECOVERY
```

Once you have finished the `tail-log` backup, you have to copy the backup to the secondary server and restore the backup using the following script:

```
RESTORE LOG DW FROM DISK = 'c:\backups\DW.trn' WITH RECOVERY
```

As you have taken a `tail-log` backup on the primary server, this has left the database in the restoring mode, which allows you to quickly configure the log shipping again and make the primary server the secondary now.

If the primary server is not accessible and you can't take the `tail-log` backup anymore, you need to make sure that all copied transaction log backups were already restored, and then just make the database available with the following command:

```
RESTORE DATABASE DW WITH RECOVERY
```

This command will bring the database online, but due to unavailability of the `tail-log` backup, you're introducing some data loss to the environment, depending on the schedule of your backups and the volume of the data changes on the primary server.

Summary

In this chapter, we introduced you to the disaster recovery discipline with the whole big picture of business continuity on SQL Server. Disaster recovery is not only about having backups, but more about the ability to bring the service back to operation after severe failures.

We have seen several options that can be used to implement part of disaster recovery on SQL Server--log shipping, replication, and mirroring. All three features are still in use today, although mirroring is being retired in many environments and replaced with the more flexible Availability Groups, which will be discussed in another chapter.

In the next chapter, we'll focus on indexing strategies and introduce various index types that you can use to optimize the performance of your SQL Server environment.

6
Indexing and Performance

Maintaining and troubleshooting Microsoft SQL Server's performance is a very wide set of tasks depending on several factors handled by administrators as well as by developers, sometimes independently and sometimes in conjunction. There's a strong need for cooperation of these two roles working with SQL Server, hence even if this book is taking SQL Server topics from an administrator's point of view, we will go through some development tips and trick briefly to show some cases of performance lags.

In this chapter, we will pay attention to the following topics:

- **Performance monitoring overview**: The first section defines what the performance is and enumerates prerequisites that should be fulfilled for successful monitoring and tuning. Also, top-level overview of monitoring procedures will be explained.
- **Tools for monitoring performance**: This section, describes how to use tools as well as how to read and interpret results measured by the tools.
- **Indexes and maintenance**: This section will explain how different kinds of indexes work and how to think about their usage. From an administrator's perspective, how to diagnose their usefulness and health.

Performance monitoring overview

How to define performance? We could say that it is basically a response time for a request. While monitoring and tuning the performance, we must not just measure the response time but we need to monitor many factors affecting the performance. What's more, we need to find out the rot cause of why the system slows down. Based on previous experience it's good to consider the following points:

- **Amount of requests**: Just a benchmark value affecting the level of concurrency on data and CPUs used by requests.
- **Space affected by the request**: How much data is moved between hard disk and memory? Is this amount of data necessary for request fulfillment or could it be reduced?
- **Request types**: Is the instance of SQL Server being asked more for a lot of smaller random I/O operations or is it being asked more for long scanning operations such as aggregation queries?
- **Request difficulty**: Are certain requests simple (just reading data from one table) or are they complex (many `JOIN` operators, complicated conditions, and so on)?

As an extra consideration, we should know if other concurrent services such as reporting services or antivirus programs are sharing server's resources with a monitored SQL Server instance.

When monitoring and troubleshooting performance, we have two perspectives on how to do it. The first and mostly recommended approach is to know the normal behavior of the operating system and SQL Server. Having such knowledge, we can detect anomalies and address the reason. Then we could find a proper solution for the issue. So the first approach of monitoring is to establish a **performance baseline**.

The performance baseline is a set of measures showing the normal performance behavior of the system in certain areas such as CPU or memory utilization as well as changes to this behavior over time. When any sudden issue occurs, the performance baseline helps us address the problem quickly and accurately. Using a performance baseline is a proactive approach to performance monitoring because we can prevent serious performance issues before they occur.

We can establish the performance baseline on our own using tools such as performance monitor or Extended Events, but a very good and effective tool is Data Collection. All mentioned tools will be described in the following sections.

The second perspective is to react on situations when the SQL Server stops responding in meaningful times. This approach is reactive; the operating system and SQL Server are not monitored regularly and administrator just reacts to sudden failures or unacceptable delays in response reported by users. This way of working seems to be ineffective, but we need to know how to start performance troubleshooting in such sudden situations.

We will also consider which role the person who monitors performance plays. In our book, we pay attention to the administrator's point of view, but developers also have to tune their physical data structures and query performance. From a developer's perspective, we could talk about the bottom-to-up way of monitoring. Developer starts to create physical database schema consisting of tables, constraints, and indexes (we will discuss more about indexes in *Indexes and maintenance* section) and he continues to write procedural objects such as views or stored procedures. All those procedural objects and ad hoc queries should be tuned before they are published to production.

Against the developer's point of view, from an administrator's perspective, we could talk about up-to-bottom monitoring and performance tuning, because, as it was described in `Chapter 1`, *Setting up SQL Server*, and `Chapter 2`, *Keeping Your SQL Server Environment Healthy*, efficient working with SQL Server starts with proper operating system preparation for SQL Server's installation and continues with correct installation and configuration on SQL Server instance. Instance provisioning is not the last action taken by administrators but this is the point when DBA starts to maintain SQL Server and also monitor and troubleshoot SQL Server's performance.

In the next section, we will go through tools for monitoring SQL Server's performance mostly in the way of the up-to-bottom approach.

Tools for monitoring performance

SQL Server's toolset is very rich and, when monitoring, we need to know which tool or tools we have to use to address performance issues and how to interpret the results measured by any certain tool. In this section, we will go through all native SQL Server tools that help us monitor the performance of SQL Server.

Activity Monitor

Activity Monitor is a fast and relatively simple tool incorporated within Management Studio. It could be used for a fast overview of current activities running on the instance. As seen in the following screenshot, **Activity Monitor** is accessible from the popup menu called by right-clicking in **Object Explorer** at instance level:

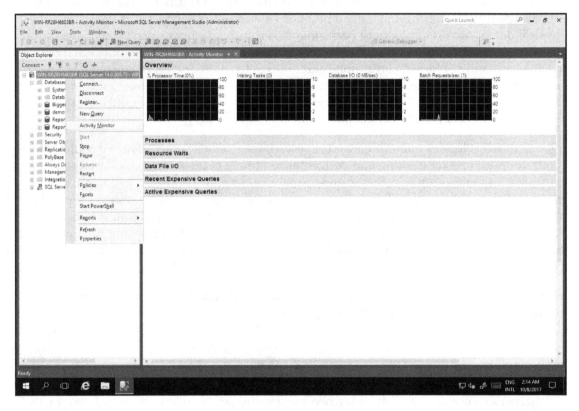

The Activity Monitor window

In the preceding image, the **Activity Monitor** is already opened and divided into six sections:

- **Overview**
- **Processes**
- **Resource Waits**
- **Data File I/O**

- **Recent Expensive Queries**
- **Active Expensive Queries**

Overview

The **Overview** section provides quick information about the current CPU effort consumed by the instance of SQL Server, current amount of tasks waiting for any resource, total amount of current physical data movement between physical disk and buffer cache, and, in the last diagram, current number of new requests coming to the instance. These diagrams are refreshed every 10 seconds by default but it's possible to right-click on any diagram and change the refresh interval. Information provided by the **Overview** section of **Activity Monitor** is just about the current state of the instance; it does not provide comprehensive and detailed monitoring data.

Section processes

Let's go on to the next section called **Processes**. As seen in the following screenshot, this section provides a grid with all sessions currently established against the instance of SQL Server and their current state:

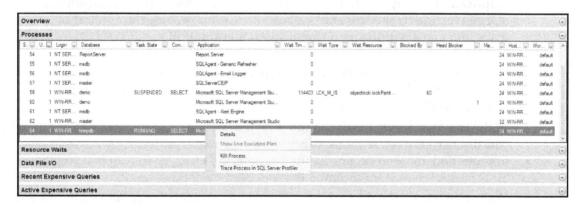

Let's describe columns in the grid. When opening the **Processes** section, columns are shrunk but we can spread them.

For better orientation, positions of columns are also added:

- **Session ID**: It's a unique identifier of the session, also known as **SPID**. We can use the SPID when using the `kill` statement to interrupt the session when needed.
- **User process flag**: In **Activity Monitor**, it's prefiltered to 1--only user sessions are shown. Clicking on the column name, filters can be added or changed on every column. It's very similar to filters, for example, in Microsoft Excel.
- **Login name**: It's the login context of a given session.
- **Database**: It's the database context of the session.
- **Task state**: The task state could be:
    - **Empty**: Session exists but has no actual request to the instance
    - **RUNNING**: The session's request is currently processed by SQL Server (in the preceding image, the only running request is for SPID **64**, which is the **Activity Monitor** itself)
    - **SUSPENDED**: Task is waiting for some resources blocked by another session, for example, we could see session **58** suspended
- **Current type of command**: It's not command text itself but just the type of command such as **SELECT, ROLLBACK,** and so on.
- **Application**: The application name is optionally written in connection strings. SQL Server and its services and applications always provide the application name, but in many third-party applications, the application name is not provided.
- **Wait time**: It's the time in milliseconds spent by the blocked session when waiting for the blocked resource. It's other than zero in rows with blocked sessions (SPID **58** in our case).
- **Wait type**: SQL Server needs to protect its resources as it needs to control concurrency between sessions. When some resource is protected by a certain type of protection, the wait occurs. In our example, the **LCK_M_IS** wait is set on the SPID 58. It's the wait for incompatible lock held by another session.
- **Wait resource**: It's the description of the object on which the incompatible lock is set by another session.
- **Blocked by**: It's probably one of the most important columns. It says which session is the blocker of the current session. Take a look at the preceding image and we'll see that the SPID **58** is blocked by SPID 60.

- **Head blocker**: This column contains bit flag 1 when the session is the one which holds resources and is not waiting for another blocker. We can see in the image that the blocking SPID **60** is not blocked by any other session, hence it's the head blocker. When the blocking time becomes unacceptable for the user, we can resolve the blocking conflict by killing the head blocker process.
- **Memory usage**: This shows how much memory in KB is consumed currently by the session.
- **Host name**: This is actually the name of the SQL Server instance.
- **Workload group**: SQL Server supports a fair usage policy feature called **Resource Governor**. The Resource Governor sets **workload groups**--named resource pools. Every session is assigned to the workload group and the name is seen in the **Processes** section. (Resource Governor is beyond the scope of our book.)

When use is moving mouse pointer over a column header in every section of *Activity Monitor*, tooltip appears with an information about source DMV for the column.

With this section, we can do more than just look at what's working now. When you right-click on a certain session, a popup menu appears with these options:

- **Details**: This shows a dialog with command text (last executed or currently running)
- **Show Live Execution Plan**: This shows execution plan of the query currently running. (more about execution plans later in this chapter)
- **Kill Process**: When some process is being the head blocker, it can be disconnected by this option (or the `kill` statement can be executed, for example, `kill 60`)
- **Trace Process in SQL Server Profiler**: The SQL Server Profiler tool is opened and traces every activity of the session (more about SQL Server Profiler later in this chapter)

SQL Server does not resolve unacceptable blocking waits between sessions: the kill statement is the only handmade way to resolve the conflict by an administrator. Always take a look at the process details before you kill the process. You don't want to be a murderer of some mission-critical business task.

Resource Waits

As noticed in the previous section, SQL Server needs to handle concurrency on resources between sessions. Section **Resource Waits** shows statistics about the most often waits in time. This session does not provide any additional actions but shows for which kind of resources sessions wait:

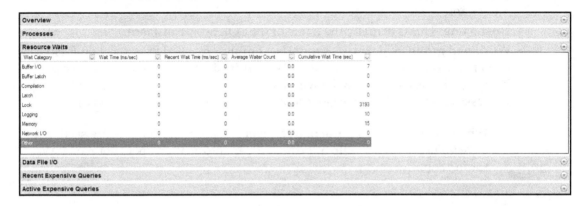

Wait Category	Wait Time (ms/sec)	Recent Wait Time (ms/sec)	Average Waiter Count	Cumulative Wait Time (sec)
Buffer I/O	0	0	0.0	7
Buffer Latch	0	0	0.0	0
Compilation	0	0	0.0	0
Latch	0	0	0.0	0
Lock	0	0	0.0	3193
Logging	0	0	0.0	10
Memory	0	0	0.0	15
Network I/O	0	0	0.0	0
Other	0	0	0.0	0

In the preceding image, a list of the most often recorded wait types issued by the SQL Server instance is displayed. Numbers in columns are self-descriptive, but the first column called **Wait Category** needs some explanation. SQL Server recognizes several hundreds of wait types, not all of them are well documented. We should know several base categories that are common for routine operations of SQL Server.

> The wait itself is never good or bad. It's just a waiting for some resource blocked by another session. But when some type of wait starts to cause performance issues, we need to address the subsystem or the scenario where too many waits occur.

The following table describes the most common wait type categories and probable reasons of these waits:

Wait type category	Short description	Probable cause
Page Latch	Short-time lightweight protection of data page in buffer cache. SQL Server issues this protection on data pages during operation like read or write	For example, non-leaf index pages are defensed by latch to avoid concurrent movements of index pages during operations on indexed data. When page latch contention grows up, the reason could be too many indexes on tables or neglected index maintenance.
Page IO Latch	Short-time lightweight protection of data page when it's being read or written from or to disk	When too many waits of this type occur, too many I/O operations are executed due to small memory or too many different queries and so on. Also, slow disk subsystem can cause this wait.
Latch	Short-time lightweight protection of other resources.	Many types of latches are covered within this wait category. When too many waits are encountered, deeper diagnostics is needed.
Lock	Protection of some part of table (row, data page, extent, and so on) during transactions or SELECT statement.	Too many lock waits are caused by big concurrency of users or wrong controlled transaction. It could also be caused by fragmented data, too many indexes, or out-of-date statistics.
CXPACKET	Wait for dispatcher thread in parallel task.	CXPACKET should be a serious problem mainly in OLTP systems. It means that a parallel task (for example, partition scan) is executed on unevenly distributed data.
LOGBUFFER	Wait for writing to buffer for transaction log records.	Too many small transactions are executed at the same time.

Not every wait automatically causes performance problems. It's very usual that unacceptable waits are a symptom of another problem, which should by found and resolved.

Data File I/O

The **Data File I/O** section shows the current flow of data back and forth from every file of every database. The section is depicted in the following screenshot:

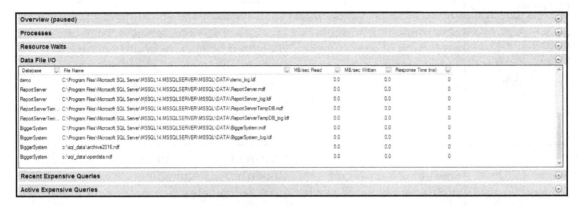

We can check the amount of data and realize how big is the data contention of every database and the duration of time spent by SQL Server waiting for data movement completion. We also could compare the amount of data moved from and to files of a certain database to see if the contention is distributed evenly across more files added to the database.

Recent Expensive Queries and Active Expensive Queries

The last two sections are very similar to each other and both show the list of the most expensive queries with statistical information. The **Recent Expensive Queries** section shows statistics about finished queries and the **Active Expensive Queries** section shows queries actually running.

Both sections are depicted in the following screenshot:

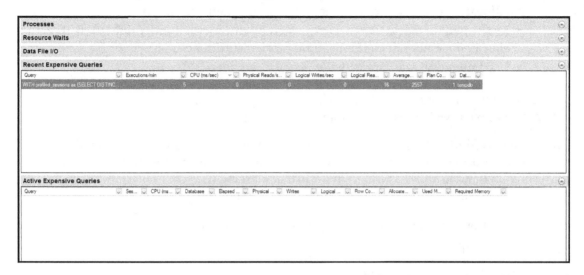

The **Recent Expensive Queries** section shows the following:

- **Number of executions per minute**: How many times the query was executed during a minute
- **Amount of milliseconds spent by the query on CPUs per second**: Ratio of time spent on CPU in every minute
- **Physical reads per second**: Amount of data page reads from a physical disk
- **Logical reads per second**: Amount of logical read operations, which means that the data page is placed into the buffer cache already and it's just used by CPU
- **Logical writes per seconds**: Similar to logical reads, logical writes are operations of modifications of a data page in the buffer cache
- **Average duration of the query**: Average amount of time needed for the number of executions
- **Plan count**: Number of plan versions cached into the procedure cache
- **Database name**: Database context of the query

Data shown by the **Active Expensive Queries** section is similar to the **Recent Expensive Queries** section, but some extra values are provided:

- **Session ID**: The SPID of the requester of the query. It could give a context to the **Processes** section.
- **Elapsed time**: Total time needed for all completed executions of the query.

- **Row count**: Number of rows processed by the query execution.
- **Allocated memory**: Granted memory for the query execution.
- **Requested memory**: Memory requested by the query; if this value is less than the allocated memory, it could mean memory insufficiency.
- **Used memory**: Memory actually used by the query.

In both sections, it is possible to right-click a certain query and, from the popup menu, obtain query text as well as execution plan of the query.

Even though **Activity Monitor** serves as a quick and brief diagnostic tool, it provides a very useful set of information about current SQL Server state and data contention. The only consideration that we have to keep in mind is that all sections except **Overview** and **Processes** show statistical data erased with every restart of the data engine.

In the next section, we will explore some useful performance counters.

Performance monitor

Performance monitor is a commonly known tool delivered within Windows operating systems. It is able to show performance metrics from almost every part of the operating system and from services running on it. We can see live data in the form of diagrams or we can grab the data by so-called **Data Collection Sets**. Data collection sets save values of counters selected by an administrator to a file. The file is then used for offline analysis or for correlation with trace data.

SQL Server and its services install their own performance counters. These counters can be correlated with common operating system counters describing the current performance of subsystems such as physical disks or memory.

 The SQL Server service has 588 counters installed. A complete list of SQL Server's performance counters could be obtained with this query:
```
select distinct object_name, counter_name from
sys.dm_os_performance_counters
```

A detailed list of common performance counters is mentioned in `Chapter 2`, *Keeping your SQL Server Environment Healthy*.

When data is collected by the data collection set, it can be analyzed together with SQL Trace events. This extremely useful feature will be described in the next section.

SQL Server Profiler and SQL Trace

SQL Server Profiler is GUI tool used to create and execute SQL Traces--proprietary SQL Server's server-side event providing feature. In this section, we will show you how to use SQL Server Profiler, SQL Trace, and data collection sets together.

SQL Server Profiler

SQL Server Profiler is a client tool to create and execute **traces**. Trace is a set of events of certain types that the DBA, developer and any other role is interested in. Through SQL Server Profiler, traces could be seen in the form of live data or saved to files or database tables.

 Even though SQL Server Profiler was announced as a deprecated tool (Extended Events should be a successor to SQL Profiler), there is no replacement to open, view, and correlate traced events with performance monitor data.

SQL Profiler could be opened from Management Studio, the **Tools** menu, option--**SQL Server Profiler**. When SQL Server Profiler is opened from Management Studio, the **login** dialog appears directly.

The second option to access SQL Server Profiler is from the start menu of Windows. Using this method causes the SQL Server Profiler to open empty and the user has to use the **New Trace** button to start configuring the trace.

After DBA is logged into a running instance of SQL Server, the following configuration dialog appears:

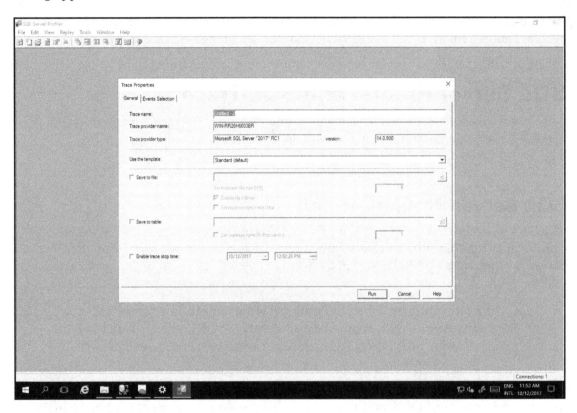

In one instance of SQL Server Profiler, more traces can be defined, hence trace can be named in the **Trace name** textbox for better orientation. The **Trace provider name** is actually the name of the SQL Server instance on which the trace will be created and **Trace provider type** is the version description and version number of the connected instance.

SQL Server Profiler has several predefined templates offering a simpler choice of events. We can also create custom templates or save a defined trace as a custom template for simple reusing. The drop-down control labeled **Use the template** shows all templates (predefined and custom together) and we can select one of them. We can also select the **Blank** template and then we can define our own set of events from scratch.

Checkboxes called **Save to file** and **Save to table** are both optional. If we only need short time monitoring, we will see live data and when we stop the monitoring, data will be lost. We can switch on both channels of saving options together.

When saving to files, more files are often created. This is thanks to the **Enable file rollover** checkbox that causes new file creation every time the actual file reaches the size limit set in the **Set maximum file size (MB)** textbox.

When the **Save to table** option is turned on, a new **login** dialog appears asking us to log on to the instance of SQL Server where the data will be saved. An advantage of saving data to a table is in the ability to query the table by regular SQL queries.

When saving trace data to a database table, use a different SQL Server instance other than the monitored one to avoid circular contention. Files also could be queried through a function called `sys.fn_trace_gettable('c:\myTraces\', 3)` where first parameter is a folder containing `trc` files, and the second is number of files for reading.

The last but very useful setting on the **General** tab of trace configuration is the option to stop trace automatically. SQL Server Profiler is a very resource consuming tool and it's a very common mistake to start tracing by SQL Server Profiler and then leave the session unattended for a longer time.

SQL Server Profiler would consume every available memory and in extreme cases could cause server crash. That's why it's very good practice to switch on the **Enable trace stop time** checkbox and set up meaningful time when the trace will stop.

Even though the stop time is set, never use SQL Server Profiler for long-term monitoring. The threshold time is a couple of hours.

When the **General** tab is configured, we need to get a step ahead and configure events that we are interested in. This is done on the second tab called **Event Selection**:

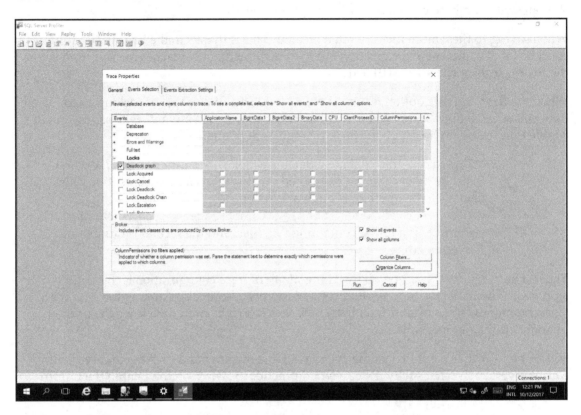

As seen in the preceding image, events are divided into categories for better orientation. Common examples of event categories are as follows:

- **Databases**: Contains events to monitor, for example, file growth operations
- **Errors and Warnings**: Contains events about many kinds of warnings or errors
- **Locks**: Events about different locking situations like deadlocks or lock escalations
- **Performance**: Events providing, for example, execution plans in several formats including XML format used for graphical execution plans rendering in Management Studio
- **Stored Procedures**: Events showing stored procedures execution
- **TSQL**: Events showing executions of ad hoc queries

When a certain event category is collapsed, events are shown and we can select ones we are interested in by clicking the checkbox on the left side of the event. In the preceding image, the **Deadlock Graph** event is selected as an example. The grid of events on the **Event Selection** tab has all possible columns of all possible events listed one by one in alphabetical ordering. However, not every event provides the same data.

As seen in our example with **Deadlock Graph**, almost no columns are selectable because this event type provides a very small set of information. The most important column, in this case, is **TextData**; it contains the graph of SPIDs attending the deadlock, SPID rolled back by SQL Server as a deadlock victim, and resources cross-locked by the attending SPIDs.

Let's take a look at another event type called **SQL:StmtCompleted**. This event type belongs to the category called **TSQL** and shows useful performance data besides the text of ad hoc query captured by the event. The most interesting columns are as follows:

- **TextData**: The text of the query.
- **Duration**: The overall response time.
- **CPU time**: The time spent on CPUs. This time could be bigger than the duration because of parallelism.
- **Reads**: The number of logical data page reads.
- **Writes**: The number of physical data page writes. Very strange when the query is SELECT; it indicates that the SELECT statement is too difficult to be processed and SQL Server needs to save intermediate results in the tempdb database. Such a query is a candidate for optimization probably.

Every event contains many columns but it's a very good thing to select exactly those columns needed for diagnostics. In many cases, for example, user context or database name could be useless, especially when only one user's events is filtered in a certain database. The precise column selection helps maintain saved event data.

In the bottom right corner are two checkboxes called **Show all events** and **Show all columns**. Both are used just to filter a grid to view only selected events and columns. When events and cells are selected, it's very important to filter events just for the needed ones.

The **Column** filters column opens a new dialog window where filters are configured:

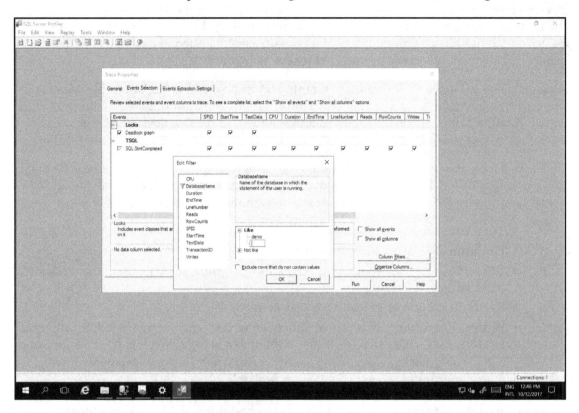

The preceding screenshot shows the filter dialog opened. The column that has to be filtered is selected in the left list and possible comparisons appear in the right tree. The preceding image shows that DatabaseName has to contain value demo added by the user.

When everything is configured correctly and precisely, the **Run** button closes the configuration dialog and SQL Server Profiler does several actions behind the scenes. It generates SQL Trace definition script and executes the script on the monitored instance of SQL Server. SQL Trace on the server side starts event capturing and sends the captured data back to SQL Server Profiler. SQL Server Profiler opens a trace window to show live data and shows events obtained from the SQL Trace. When some awaited event is raised, it's shown in the trace window and it's also saved to the configured storage:

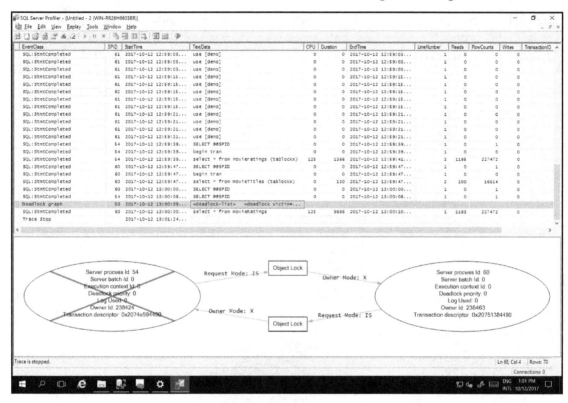

Deadlock graph caught in SQL Profiler

As seen here, the trace window is divided into two parts. The upper part is a grid showing captured events with columns selected during configuration. The bottom part shows details of a selected event from the grid. For text events such as **TSQL:StmtCompleted**, text of the query is shown; our example shows an event called **Deadlock graph**. This event type describes sessions being in conflict, resources locked by incompatible locks, and finally the session that was selected by SQL Server as a deadlock victim whose transaction was rolled back with error 1205 sent back to the client.

Data captured by SQL Profiler could be synchronized with data collected by performance monitor. This is possible when both data sources--performance monitor counters as well as SQL Trace data--are saved into files. In a case when data is captured by SQL Profiler and the trace is stopped, close and reopen the file. When you do this, a new menu option **Import Performance Data** is enabled. The menu option is depicted in the following screenshot:

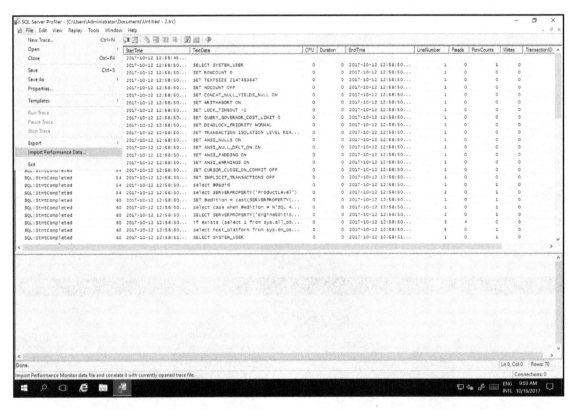

This menu option opens the **Open File** dialog and you need to find the file with extension `.blg`. This is the file used by performance monitor to capture performance data.

Both data sources, trace data and performance data, are synchronized by SQL Profiler and the trace window is divided once again to show grid and detail information from trace in the top part and performance monitor diagrams in the bottom part, as seen in the following screenshot:

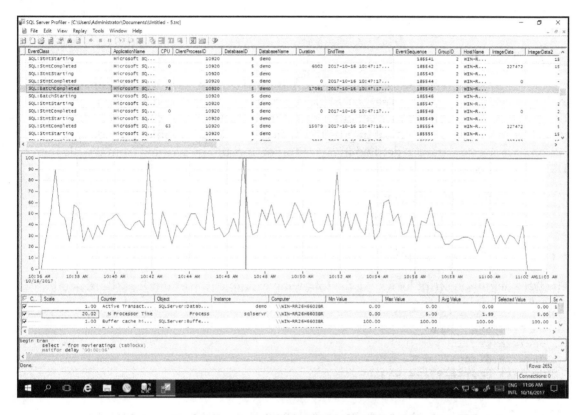

Performance data correlated with caught events in SQL Profiler

Both SQL Trace data and performance monitor data are shown together and it is time-synchronized. When clicking on a certain event in the grid, the vertical red line in the diagram part is moving back and forth synchronously to show the moment in time with current values from performance monitor.

The same synchronous movement occurs when you click on some place in the diagram part; the cursor in the grid is moved on the row that is close to the selected moment. It helps identify poorly performing queries in correlation with data captured by performance monitor.

SQL Profiler is a well-known tool that has a disadvantage in very big resource consumption. When you need to monitor incoming events, you do not need to run SQL Profiler every time, but SQL Profiler helps you generate script for more efficient server-side traditional monitoring called SQL Trace. In the next section, we will explore SQL Trace in more detail.

SQL Trace

SQL Trace is a non-visual server-side tracing feature of SQL Server. SQL Profiler, described in the previous section, serves as a client-side viewer of data captured and provided by SQL Trace. SQL Trace is defined by a set of system-stored procedures. Writing a new trace from scratch is very difficult or almost impossible, which is why SQL Profiler provides a script option. When a new trace is defined in SQL Profiler, it could be scripted from the file menu. The exact procedure is as follows:

1. Define and run a new trace in SQL Profiler.
2. From the **File** menu, choose the **Export, Script trace definition** option and then, **For SQL Server 2005 - 2017.**
3. **Save as** dialog appears and you give a name to your script and save the file.

The trace definition script looks like the following example (the example is shortened for the sake of simplicity):

```
-- Create a Queue
declare @rc int
declare @TraceID int
declare @maxfilesize bigint
set @maxfilesize = 5

-- Please replace the text InsertFileNameHere, with an appropriate
-- ... the description continues

exec @rc = sp_trace_create @TraceID output, 0, N'C:\myTraces\myTrace.trc',
@maxfilesize, NULL
if (@rc != 0) goto error

-- Client side File and Table cannot be scripted

-- Set the events
declare @on bit
set @on = 1
exec sp_trace_setevent @TraceID, 24, 1, @on
exec sp_trace_setevent @TraceID, 24, 9, @on
```

```
exec sp_trace_setevent @TraceID, 24, 2, @on

-- ... many sp_trace_setevent procedure calls were erased here

exec sp_trace_setevent @TraceID, 40, 61, @on
exec sp_trace_setevent @TraceID, 40, 64, @on
exec sp_trace_setevent @TraceID, 40, 66, @on


-- Set the Filters
declare @intfilter int
declare @bigintfilter bigint

exec sp_trace_setfilter @TraceID, 35, 0, 6, N'demo'
-- Set the trace status to start
exec sp_trace_setstatus @TraceID, 1

-- display trace id for future references
select TraceID=@TraceID
goto finish

error:
select ErrorCode=@rc

finish:
go
```

When the trace definition script is saved, it can be used anytime and on every instance of SQL Server. As seen at the end of the script, the script selects a new `TraceID` number. It's an integer identifying the running trace. When the trace is no more needed, simple call `EXEC sp_trace_setstatus <the trace id is placed here>, 0,` which stops the trace. If the `TraceID` is missed, it can be obtained back from the `sys.traces` system view. The command is as follows:

```
select * from sys.traces
```

SQL Trace saves server's resources because the only data provider available when it's running is the so-called file provider. On the other hand, when using SQL Profiler, trace's memory data provider is used to push data back to the SQL Profiler, and it's a much more memory consuming approach.

In the next section, we will pay attention to the successor of SQL Server Profiler called Extended Events.

Extended Events

Extended Events (also called **xEvents** or simply **XE**) are intended for event monitoring. It sounds very similar to the job done by SQL Server Profiler, but xEvents are a modern tool using native eventing features of SQL Server, hence the resource consumption is much less than requirements requested by SQL Server Profiler.

Frugality is not the only advantage of xEvents. Unlike SQL Server Profiler, xEvents can capture events provided by new features such as R Services.

The third big advantage of xEvents is that the definitions are saved into SQL Server's metadata so the configuration of xEvents session made by a DBA is not done repeatedly. Once the xEvents session is created, the session could be started and stopped on demand from Management Studio. Let's take a look at the following screenshot:

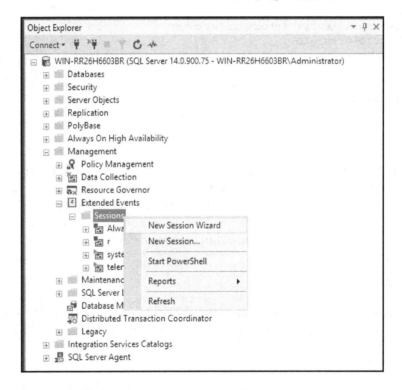

Extended Events definitions are placed in Management Studio under **Management node** in **Object Explorer**. Some system sessions are created during SQL Server installation and could be started and stopped when needed.

When we want to create our own xEvents session definition, we can do it via the wizard, but for better control over preciseness and granularity, it's better to use the second option in the popup menu **New Session...**. When the **New Session...** menu option is selected, a dialog window for the session creation appears, as shown in the following screenshot:

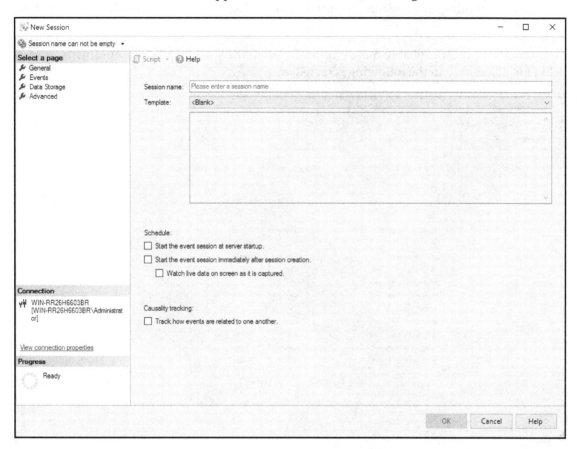

The first tab of the window is the **General** tab. Session must be named in the **Session name** text field and template can also be selected from the **Template** drop-down. Unlike SQL Server Profiler, xEvents provides a more templates. Other controls can be edited later. Session could start every time when SQL Server instance is started if needed. This option is useful for server-level monitoring for later analysis.

When **Start the event session immediately after session creation** is selected, session is saved and started. When the same option is left off, session is just saved but does not start to monitor selected events. When the session is started, live data can be displayed. This option causes that window is opened within Management Studio and DBA can view events how they are coming. The session can run in unattended mode even if the live data window is closed.

The second and most probably most important tab in the session creation window is **Events**. It's shown in the following screenshot:

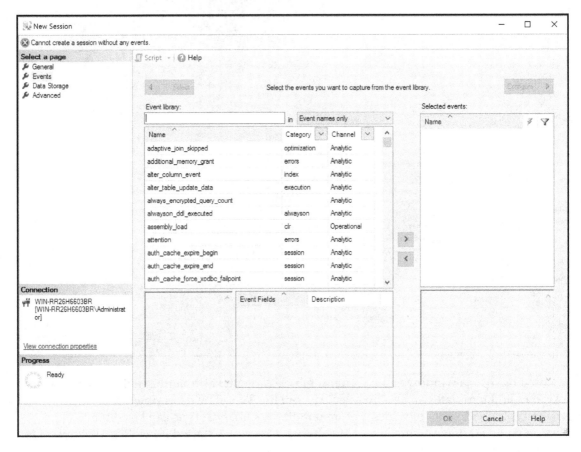

Event selection in Extended Events window

The left list contains every event that would be monitored. It's actually a huge set of possibilities so the empty text field above the list is extremely useful--we can start to type part of event name (for example, `sql`) and the list is filtered. Another option is to filter events by **Category** or by **Channel**. Once the event is found, it can be moved to the right list by double-clicking or by the arrow buttons placed between both lists.

It's very important to refine the configuration of every selected event. An event is selected in the right list, and the **Configure** button is enabled and should be used. The look of the **Events** tab is changed and the new view is depicted in the following screenshot:

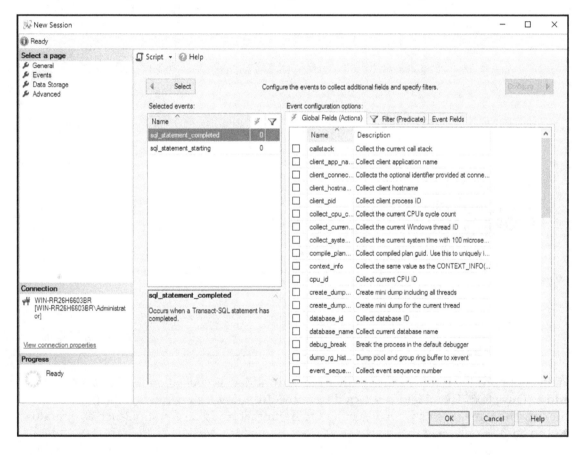

A big difference when comparing xEvents to the SQL Server Profiler is that event fields are not selected by default but have to be selected by an administrator. Fields are divided into common **Global fields** or **Actions** (first tab in the preceding image) and proprietary fields hidden on the **Event fields** tab. It's very usual that event fields are intersecting global fields so decide what fields to capture carefully.

The middle tab called **Filter (Predicate)** is intended for filter definitions. Unlike SQL Server Profiler, every selected event type is filtered separately. It can seem confusing, but it gives the DBA more control over what to filter. The **Filters** tab is shown in the following screenshot:

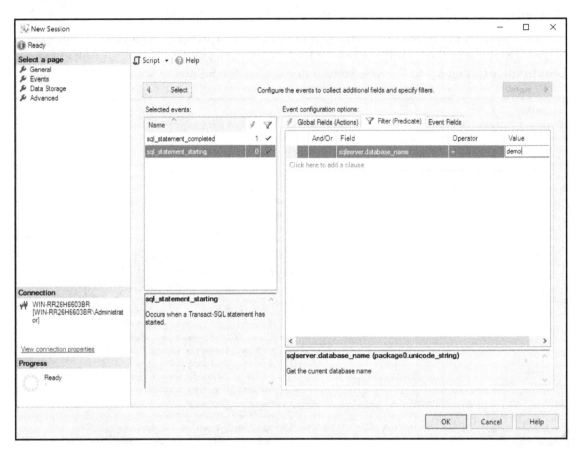

Filter configuration is quite simple--filter rows are added as clicked on the **Click here to add a clause** text. Then **Field** is selected from the drop-down shown when the field is clicked. The same repeats when selecting **Operator** that could be equality, such as operator and so on. The only field that has to be written manually is **Value**.

As events are configured, it could be seen in the form of live data, but they also can be saved. The following image shows the **Data Storage** tab, which is used for the storage configuration:

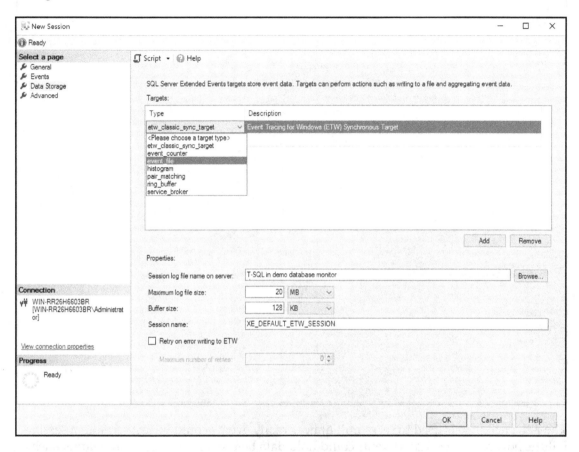

Session data could be stored into more providers. An expanded drop-down shows all of the storage, but the most typical storage targets are as follows:

- **event_file**: A standalone file for event capture.
- **pair_matching**: This storage type allows you to define the starting and ending event establishing the pair. When starting event occurs, it's shown; when matching end event is shown, both events are paired and erased.
- **ring_buffer**: Live data shown to DBA.

The following screenshot shows the **Advanced** tab:

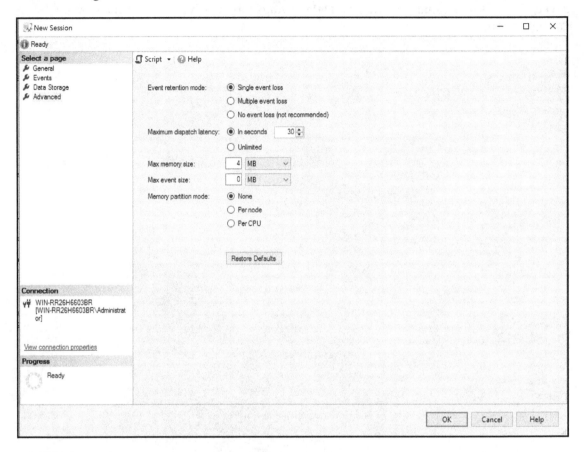

The **Advanced** tab is used to set a limit of how many events could be lost without a session failure, how many seconds xEvents could hold data before they are sent to the target such as live data or event file, and whether to divide memory into partitions according with **NUMA** nodes for event capturing. In the preceding image, settings are left with their default values.

When everything is configured, the session is saved and it's shown in the **Sessions** folder under **Extended Events** node in **Object Explorer**. By right-clicking (see the first image in this section), the session can be started or stopped, exported, or live data can be opened and explored. The live data window is shown in the following screenshot:

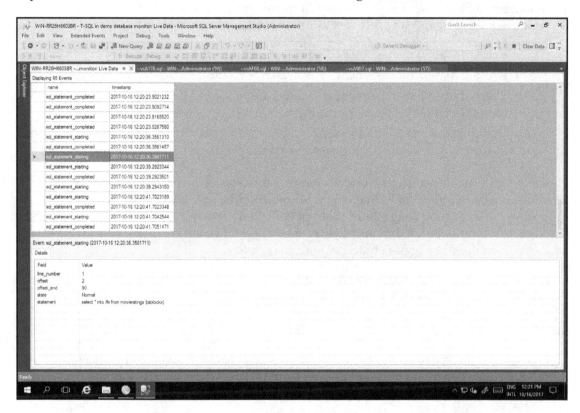

xEvents are a very efficient tool for repeating the monitoring of a wide range of events. Sometimes it looks confusing, but with some practice, it becomes a very good helper when monitoring SQL Server's performance.

Until this moment, we have worked mostly with visual monitoring tools. In the next section, we will explore some source objects providing data to the tools as well as our needs.

Dynamic management

Dynamic management consists of a huge set of views and table-valued functions so it's intended for the querying. Many dynamic management objects are used by other tools such as Management Studio reports or **Activity Monitor**, but we can use them to explore SQL Server ourselves. We can lead with very simple naming conventions:

- Every dynamic management object is placed into the `sys` schema
- Every dynamic management object starts with the `dm_` prefix
- Every dynamic management object has also a second prefix defining subsystem monitored by this object, for example, `sys.dm_db_` or `sys.dm_exec_`
- Dynamic management objects having the `_stats` suffix show data captured from the last SQL Server's startup and are erased every time SQL Server is restarted

The only property not seen in the object's name is the type of the object--is it a view or function? We can profit from Management Studio **Intellisense.** Intellisense is basically a drop-down with naming suggestions that appear when we start typing a query in Management Studio. When dynamic management object's name is written and the object is a function, Intellisense suggests brackets with parameters.

One more advantage is that dynamic management objects have quite long, but self-descriptive names and when we start typing, for example, `select * from sys.coun`, which means nothing itself, Intellisense will advise the `sys.dm_os_performance_counters` view.

> Don't try to remember all the names of dynamic management objects. Be guided by Intellisense, it's more comfortable and also risk of typos is reduced.

Dynamic management objects are divided by subsystems. Let's summarize some of them in the following table:

Dynamic management object prefix	Description	Example
`sys.dm_db_*`	Database statistics such as index state or database file usage	`sys.dm_db_index_usage_stats` `sys.dm_db_file_space_usage`

`sys.dm_exec_*`	Operational information such as sessions, plan cache, and many others	`sys.dm_exec_sessions`
		`sys.dm_exec_requests`
		`sys.dm_exec_cached_plans`

`sys.dm_os_*`	Information bound to operating system, wait statistics, memory state, and so on	`sys.dm_os_performance_counters`
		`sys.dm_os_buffer_descriptors`
		`sys.dm_os_virtual_file_stats`

`sys.dm_tran_*`	Transaction state descriptions	`sys.dm_tran_locks`
`sys.dm_sql_*`	Describes object dependencies (tables used by views and so on)	`sys.dm_sql_referenced_entities` `sys.dm_sql_referencing_entities`

There are many other dynamic management objects defined. Full list can be found on MSDN, but it's not possible to create a list of all of them in those book. For detailed insights, we can use **Object Browser** to explore all objects. Views are kept in every database under **<database name>** | **Views** | **System Views** node, functions are placed in the database master, see **master** | **Programmability** | **Functions** | **System Functions** | **Table-Valued Functions** node in **Object Explorer**.

Dynamic management provides very detailed information about any subsystem of SQL Server. Often it's needed to join more objects to add readability to the results of DMV query. The next section will show an example how to combine more system objects to see what's going on.

How to use dynamic management

Sometimes it's hard to combine system objects, especially dynamic management, together. No simple and unified instructions exist for it, but the next example shows a way of thinking about system queries.

One of the performance issues can be too frequent recompilations of execution plans. We want to have an overview of plan cache content. We want to know which plans are cached and how they are reused. The most simple information is provided by the `sys.dm_exec_cached_plans` view. Let's execute the following script:

```
select * from sys.dm_exec_cached_plans
```

We will see the following result:

	bucketid	refcounts	usecounts	size_in_bytes	memory_object_address	cacheobjtype	objtype	plan_handle	pool_id	parent_plan_handle
1	18419	2	1	81920	0x0000018F90B2E060	Compiled Plan	Proc	0x050006008D5ED731303E1F8C8F01000001000000000000...	2	NULL
2	21020	2	1	204800	0x0000018F89658060	Compiled Plan	Proc	0x050006002DC94956D0361F8C8F01000001000000000000...	2	NULL
3	2269	2	1	57344	0x0000018F89668060	Compiled Plan	Proc	0x05000600F4A45555702F1F8C8F01000001000000000000...	2	NULL
4	3471	2	1	49152	0x0000018F89630060	Compiled Plan	Proc	0x050006004BC4A36310281F8C8F01000001000000000000...	2	NULL
5	38287	2	1	57344	0x0000018F8962E060	Compiled Plan	Proc	0x05000600D9B4DF5550FFA0988F01000001000000000000...	2	NULL
6	13396	2	1	188416	0x0000018F8508A060	Compiled Plan	Proc	0x05000600A329877A90F1A0988F01000001000000000000...	2	NULL
7	17208	2	1	98304	0x0000018F8FC02060	Compiled Plan	Proc	0x050006006B796868F0F7A0988F01000001000000000000...	2	NULL
8	28554	2	1	573440	0x0000018F8FE0C060	Compiled Plan	Proc	0x050004009BA4491230EAA0988F01000001000000000000...	2	NULL
9	11989	2	1	49152	0x0000018F8BAA0060	Compiled Plan	Adhoc	0x060005006F63993560C14E838F01000001000000000000...	2	NULL
10	17452	2	1	49152	0x0000018F8835BC060	Compiled Plan	Adhoc	0x0600060046C9161E5019A1988F01000001000000000000...	2	NULL
11	35630	2	1	40960	0x0000018F8A322060	Compiled Plan	Adhoc	0x060005008E790D27D011A1988F01000001000000000000...	2	NULL
12	38417	2	2	253952	0x0000018F8AC84060	Compiled Plan	Adhoc	0x06000600AACD810E500AA1988F01000001000000000000...	2	NULL
13	32141	2	2	163840	0x0000018F88718060	Compiled Plan	Adhoc	0x060006001BA31F37D002A1988F01000001000000000000...	2	NULL
14	1977	1	2	65536	0x0000018F8A644060	Parse Tree	View	0x0500FF7FEC5CE6D85041648A8F01000001000000000000...	2	NULL
15	281	1	12	49152	0x0000018F844F4060	Parse Tree	View	0x050004007B1DC57350414F848F01000001000000000000...	2	NULL
16	576	1	7	40960	0x0000018F84118060	Parse Tree	View	0x0500FF7F8053E1F5508111843F01000001000000000000...	2	NULL

Such a result is full of almost unreadable and hence useless numbers. Some columns make sense to us, namely the following:

- **usecounts**: How many times the plan was reused
- **size_in_bytes**: This is the size of the plan in memory (bigger plans are scratched later than smaller plans)
- **objtype**: Describes the origin of the plan such as stored procedures (Proc) or ad hoc query call (AdHoc)

The most important column is the plan_handle. It's a unique identifier of the plan kept in the plan cache. When we need to uncover the actual query hidden under this terrible number, we should use the function called sys.dm_exec_sql_text. This function consumes the plan_handle as a parameter and returns the SQL definition of the query.

Let's execute the following query:

```
select
  cp.usecounts
  , cp.size_in_bytes
  , cp.objtype
  , sqltext.dbid
  , sqltext.objectid
  , sqltext.text
from sys.dm_exec_cached_plans as cp
  cross apply sys.dm_exec_sql_text(cp.plan_handle) as sqltext
```

The `CROSS APPLY` operator substitutes a `JOIN` operator when classical `JOIN` is not usable due to the missing join criteria on the function's result set. The join is done through the parameter of the function. A result of the preceding query is much more readable now:

	usecounts	size_in_bytes	objtype	dbid	objectid	text
2	6	57344	Proc	6	1431676148	CREATE PROCEDURE [dbo].[GetAnnouncedKey] @Install...
3	6	49152	Proc	6	1671677003	CREATE PROCEDURE [dbo].[GetAllConfigurationInfo] AS ...
4	6	57344	Proc	6	1440724185	CREATE PROCEDURE [dbo].[GetCurrentProductInfo] AS ...
5	3	573440	Proc	4	306816155	CREATE PROCEDURE sp_sqlagent_get_perf_counters ...
6	1	81920	Proc	6	836198029	CREATE PROCEDURE [dbo].[GetMyRunningJobs] @Com...
7	1	49152	Adhoc	5	NULL	select cp.usecounts , cp.size_in_bytes , cp.objtype , sql...
8	1	188416	Adhoc	1	NULL	SELECT dtb.name AS [Name], dtb.database_id AS [ID], CAS...
9	1	65536	Prepared	1	NULL	(@_msparam_0 nvarchar(4000))SELECT CAST(COLLATION...
10	1	368640	Prepared	1	NULL	(@_msparam_0 nvarchar(4000))SELECT dtb.collation_name ...
11	1	57344	Adhoc	5	NULL	select * from sys.dm_exec_cached_plans as cp cross apply...
12	2	49152	Adhoc	6	NULL	select top 1 NtSecDescState from SecData where NtSecDe...
13	1	40960	Adhoc	5	NULL	select * from movieratings (tablockx)
14	7	253952	Adhoc	6	NULL	declare @BatchID uniqueidentifier ...
15	7	163840	Adhoc	6	NULL	declare @BatchID uniqueidenti...
16	2	24576	View	32767	-852794453	create function sys.fn_helpcollations ( ) returns table as ...
17	4	1236992	View	32767	-213	CREATE VIEW sys.databases AS SELECT d.name, d.id ...
18	3	24576	View	32767	-242583247	CREATE VIEW sys.fulltext_languages AS SELECT lcid, na...
19	3	114688	View	32767	-194	CREATE VIEW sys.syslanguages AS SELECT langid, datef...
20	4	32768	View	32767	-245973352	CREATE FUNCTION sys.dm_exec_sql_text(@handle varbin...
21	4	65536	View	32767	-655991572	create view sys.dm_exec_cached_plans as SELECT b...
22	12	49152	View	4	1942297979	CREATE VIEW sysalerts_performance_counters_view AS ...
23	7	40960	View	32767	-169782400	CREATE VIEW sys.dm_os_performance_counters AS SEL...

As seen in the preceding image, column set was reduced in the `SELECT` clause to provide more readability and now it's much more useful for us. New columns came from the `sys.dm_exec_sql_text` function:

- **dbid**: ID of the database in which the query was executed (pay attention to the ID **32767**--it's the resource db).
- **objectid**: ID of the object saving the query definition (for example, stored procedure). Ad hoc queries do not have **objectid**.
- **text**: The text of the cached plan itself!

We want to have the information a little bit more comfortable. We want to filter database context to the monitored one and we also want to see the database name as well as object name. Let's adjust the query one more time:

```
select
  cp.usecounts
  , cp.size_in_bytes
  , cp.objtype
  , db_name(sqltext.dbid) as dbname
  , sqltext.objectid
  , s.name as schemaname
  , o.name as objname
  , sqltext.text
from sys.dm_exec_cached_plans as cp
  cross apply sys.dm_exec_sql_text(cp.plan_handle) as sqltext
  left join sys.objects as o on o.object_id = sqltext.objectid
  left join sys.schemas as s on s.schema_id = o.schema_id
where sqltext.dbid = db_id('demo')
```

Some new functions and joins were added to the query. Let's describe them:

- db_name(): The metadata function used in the SELECT clause. It's translating the database ID into a name.
- joining sys.objects view: We can use the object_name() function; it's translating the object ID into its name but without the schema name. That's why the sys.objects view (not dynamic view, just catalog view) is added to the SELECT statement.
- joining sys.schemas view: The purpose is the same as when joining sys.objects--we want to know the full object's identifier within the database in a form of <schema>.<object>.

Ad hoc queries are not saved objects, that's why LEFT JOIN operators are used to see ad-hoc query plans and object plans together.

Do we want more? We always want more and the last information extremely useful when analyzing certain query performance is to add a **query plan**. Query plan is a tree containing a set of operators actually needed by SQL Server to fulfill the user's request. Query plan is very desirable for the developer who works on query optimization; for now, let's just capture it. The last dynamic management object used in our example will be a function called sys.dm_exec_query_plan. This function returns the plan described in XML format. The query is shown in the following script example:

```
select
  cp.usecounts
```

```
      , cp.size_in_bytes
      , cp.objtype
      , db_name(sqltext.dbid) as dbname
      , sqltext.objectid
      , s.name as schemaname
      , o.name as objname
      , sqltext.text
      , qplan.query_plan
  from sys.dm_exec_cached_plans as cp
    cross apply sys.dm_exec_sql_text(cp.plan_handle) as sqltext
    cross apply sys.dm_exec_query_plan(cp.plan_handle) as qplan
    left join sys.objects as o on o.object_id = sqltext.objectid
    left join sys.schemas as s on s.schema_id = o.schema_id
  where sqltext.dbid = db_id('demo')
```

One more CROSS APPLY operator is added to join the new function to the query, and a column called query_plan is added to the SELECT clause. The result is depicted in the following image:

	usecounts	size_in_bytes	objtype	dbname	objectid	schemaname	objname	text	query_plan
1	1	49152	Proc	demo	1845581613	NULL	NULL	create proc dbo.procSelectMovieByRating @rating...	\<ShowPlanXML xmlns="http://schemas.microsoft.com...
2	1	16384	Adhoc	demo	NULL	NULL	NULL	SET SHOWPLAN_XML OFF	\<ShowPlanXML xmlns="http://schemas.microsoft.com...
3	1	16384	Adhoc	demo	NULL	NULL	NULL	SET SHOWPLAN_ALL OFF	\<ShowPlanXML xmlns="http://schemas.microsoft.com...
4	1	16384	Adhoc	demo	NULL	NULL	NULL	SET SHOWPLAN_TEXT OFF	\<ShowPlanXML xmlns="http://schemas.microsoft.com...
5	5	368640	Adhoc	demo	NULL	NULL	NULL	SELECT dtb.name AS [Name], dtb.state AS [State] F...	\<ShowPlanXML xmlns="http://schemas.microsoft.com...
6	2	106496	Adhoc	demo	NULL	NULL	NULL	select cp.usecounts , cp.size_in_bytes , cp.objty...	\<ShowPlanXML xmlns="http://schemas.microsoft.com...
7	1	98304	Adhoc	demo	NULL	NULL	NULL	select cp.usecounts , cp.size_in_bytes , cp.objty...	\<ShowPlanXML xmlns="http://schemas.microsoft.com...
8	1	98304	Adhoc	demo	NULL	NULL	NULL	select cp.usecounts , cp.size_in_bytes , cp.objty...	\<ShowPlanXML xmlns="http://schemas.microsoft.com...
9	2	40960	Adhoc	demo	NULL	NULL	NULL	select * from movieratings (tablockx)	\<ShowPlanXML xmlns="http://schemas.microsoft.com...

The right-most column is actually links. When clicked, graphical query plan is opened in a separate window in Management Studio. The plan is shown in the following image:

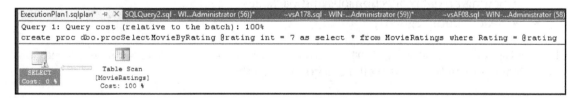

The query plan in the preceding image is very simple and we don't know how to read it now, but we know how to capture it, and we can cooperate with developers to analyze performance bottlenecks and find out corrections.

Until now, we've been working with several more or less complicated tools to monitor and analyze SQL Server's performance from different points of view. It's really hard to join and correlate monitoring results together with such wide monitoring tools. However, it's very good to know these techniques as they are a base for the next monitoring approach called data collection.

Data collection

Detailed observations of SQL Server's performance are needed when the given instance gets into trouble. It's not possible to monitor more than a few instances in this detailed way. That's why Microsoft offers a tool for centralized monitoring of more SQL Servers and the tool is also very useful for proactive monitoring and performance baselining. This section is dedicated to **data collection**. Data collection consists of the following:

- Relational database called **Management Data Warehouse** (**MDW**) hosted on some SQL Server instance
- Jobs reading data from xEvents and dynamic management
- SSIS packages pushing captured data into the MDW
- Reports showing information about several aspects of contention and performance over time

The MDW database could be centralized. In big environments, it's a good practice to place the MDW database on a dedicated SQL Server instance. When working with data collection, we need to do three tasks:

- Setting up the MDW
- Setting up data collection jobs and packages
- Read reports regularly

The first two tasks are done by short wizards in Management Studio; reports are placed within Management Studio as well. Let's go through these tasks.

Setting up MDW

Working with **Data Collection** is quite easy. The following screenshot shows where to find configuration tools for **Data Collection**:

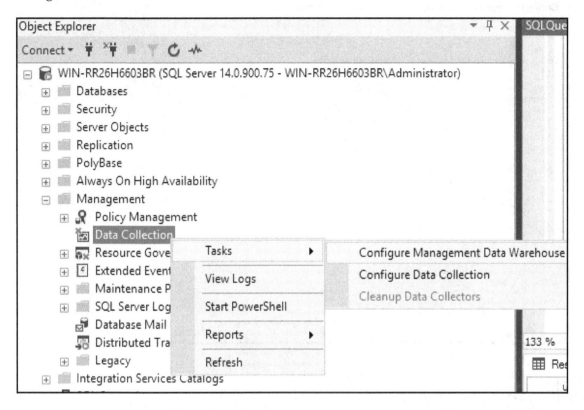

Data Collection is placed in **Object Explorer** under the **Management** node. Right-clicks invoke a popup menu with the **Tasks** option. The first option under **Tasks** is **Configure Management Data Warehouse**. This option is selected when the MDW database has to be created. Using this option opens a wizard and the first step (the **Welcome** step is omitted) has two settings:

- **Server name**: The name of the server on which the MDW database has to be hosted
- **Database name**: When a new MDW has to be created, the **New** button is on the right side of the drop-down (the **New** button opens the database creation window)

The wizard step is shown in the following screenshot:

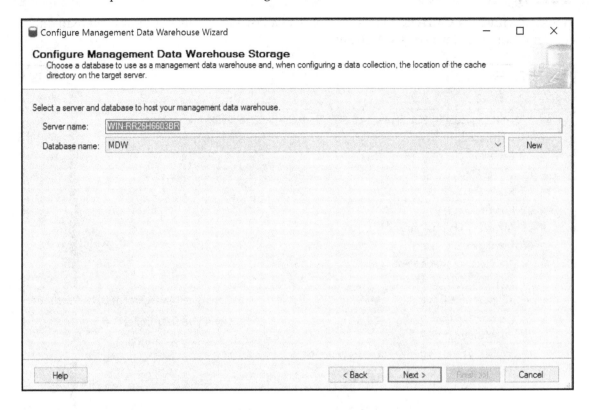

The next step of the wizard is about security. Logins are mapped to the MDW database roles. It enables users without administrative privileges to write data to the MDW database or read it.

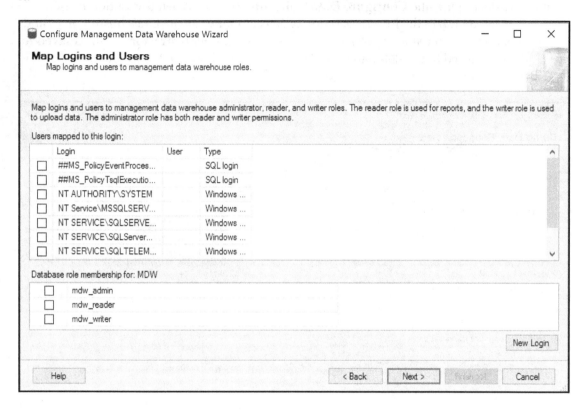

When the wizard is finished, the MDW database is created and logins are mapped to users and database roles.

This task establishes a centralized point for data collection. In the next section, we will enable monitoring of the same instance of SQL Server.

Collecting performance data

Setting up data collection from a certain instance of SQL Server is done via wizard called from the **Tasks** popup--the **Configure Data Collection** option. When this option is used, wizard is opened and, in the first step, tasks for **Server name** (the instance hosting MDW) and **Database name** (actual name of MDW). It also asks for temp **Cache directory**. Data is saved to files and then pushed to the MDW database. The first step is shown in the following screenshot:

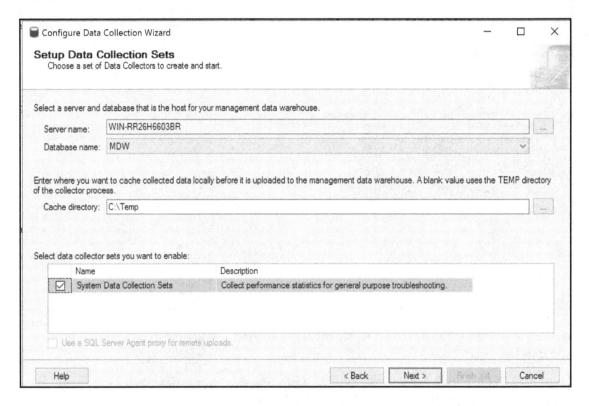

When all questions are answered, the wizard finishes and creates SQL Agent jobs that actually do the work of data capturing.

When this task is finished, we have to wait a day or two before we see some results in the reports.

Viewing data collection reports

The main purpose of data collection is to show overall resource consumption as well as long-term query statistics over time. The information is shown in a very readable graphical form. **Reports** could be invoked from **Object Explorer** by right-clicking on the MDW database in the **Databases** node. The complete path to reports is shown in the following screenshot:

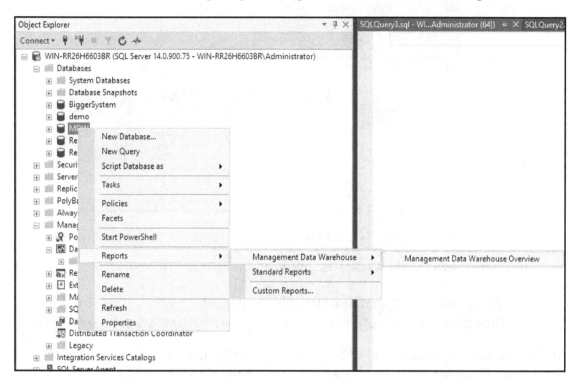

This option opens a report showing a list of all instances of SQL Server monitored by the given MDW:

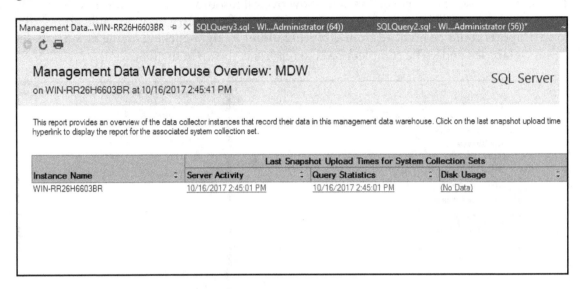

As seen in the preceding image, the overview enables you to click through three sections:

- **Server Activity**: Shows detailed information about disk, memory, CPU, and network usage
- **Query Statistics**: Operational statistics about queries
- **Disk Usage**: Amount of space consumed by every database file of every database

All three detailed reports offer time play control--the ability to set a time range of monitoring. All three reports are very self-descriptive and intuitive, so the best practice is to set up data collection and review reports on your own.

Data collection has one big advantage over tools such as dynamic management: data in MDW is persisted up to two years and not cleared when SQL Server restarts. However, data collection provides server metrics mainly. A similar tool on the database scope is called Query Store. In the next section, we will set it up.

Query Store

Query Store was introduced with SQL Server 2016 because many DBAs and developers missed long-term monitoring of certain database performance. All tools before were able to provide data just until SQL Server instance was not restarted. Query Store provides durable storage created by requests in the database where such monitoring is desired. Important information is that Query Store captures and saves data asynchronously so query performance from user's perspective is not affected.

When configuring Query Store, we will navigate to database properties (right-click on a certain database in **Object Explorer** and choose **Properties** in the popup menu), as shown in the following screenshot:

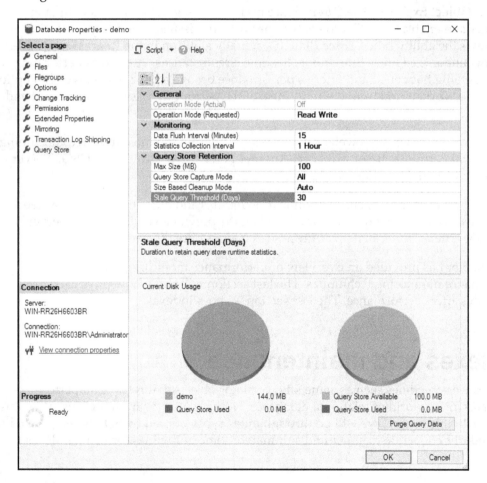

The screenshot shows all settings already filled in with defaults. When switching on Query Store, we have to change the **Operation Mode (Requested)** property to **Read Write**. Other options are **Off** (data is not captured and cannot be explored) and **Read Only** (data is not captured but can be still explored). The **Monitoring** section of the properties says how often data will be saved from cache into the database (the default value is 15 minutes) and how often data will be aggregated for analysis (default is one hour). The last section labeled **Query Store Retention** offers a possibility to set how big will Query Store be and how long time data will be kept before it will be erased in first-in-first-out manner. Once set up, Query Store starts to grab data about queries including costs, statistics, execution plan, and connection settings.

From DBA's perspective, a new node called **Query Store** will appear under the database node in **Object Explorer**. The **Query Store** node offers several windows with query statistics and enables the DBA to analyze performance issues on a query level. One of the features is the ability called **Force Plan**. It's actually a button in the **Regressed Queries** window under the **Query Store** node. In some circumstances, query was performing well but something happened and query's performance becomes poor. The **Force Plan** option serves as a workaround until the root cause of the performance issue is addressed and corrected.

Query Store helps DBAs as well as developers easily find the most resource consuming queries and correct their performance. Another possible scenario is when SQL Server is upgraded from the previous version.

As versions are changing, query optimization metrics and algorithms are enhanced. Sometimes it causes that queries tuned well on the previous version of SQL Server become slow. The Query Store can help address such queries very efficiently.

This chapter has provided an overview of performance monitoring tools and some performance monitoring techniques. The last section will show how physical data structures affect performance. The last section is about indexes.

Indexes and maintenance

Indexes are sometimes seen as some kind of magic objects that resolve all performance problems in the world of relational databases. Nothing is as far from the truth than this opinion. In this section, we will go through index types offered by SQL Server, then discuss how indexes cooperate together and summarize some guidelines for using indexes.

Types of indexes

Sorting in relational databases makes no sense. Even though this statement sounds strange, it comes from the set theory that forms a theoretical base of relational databases. However, sorting is still needed when the database engine has to find out proper records from a table efficiently. When no sorting structure is present, the engine needs to scan over all records to recognize which of them are a candidates for the result of a certain query. An index is a type of object bringing sorting and seeking possibilities over unsorted relational data.

SQL Server provides several types of indexes. The most traditional are B-tree indexes, but columnstore indexes were introduced in SQL Server 2012 and enhanced with every new version of SQL Server. Besides relational indexes, indexes for several not-really-relational data types are present on SQL Server. Their usage is often straightforward so we will pay the most attention to B-trees.

Heap

Heap is a table that has no indexes. Keep in mind that primary key or unique constraints are implemented by B-tree indexes internally, so pure heap is a very rare case of relational data table.

Data pages in heap do not have any particular order, they are not connected by offsets to each other, and records can be placed anywhere in the heap. When SQL Server does tasks over heap, it always need to scan all data pages to retrieve desired ones and work with them.

When SQL Server is inserting a new record into heap, it finds the first data page with sufficient space for the new record and places the inserted record there.

When SQL Server is updating some existing record, two situations can occur:

- Record fits in size into the original data pages and nothing special happens.
- Record is grown after update and it does not fit into the original page, so the record is deleted from the previous data page and is moved to any data page with sufficient space. The original record version is marked as ghost record; SQL Server does not actually erase records.

When a record is deleted from the heap, it is marked as a ghost record. Fragmentation of data occurs rarely and it depends on a number of ghost records.

Heap is not a complicated structure but it is absolutely useless for tables bigger than several rows. As an additional disadvantage, we must say that a table with no constraints is not actually a relational table actually. That's why at least one index is often present.

Non-clustered B-tree index

The B-tree is sometimes interpreted as a binary tree, which is not correct. The *B* leading letter means **balanced tree**. Balanced tree is a tree consisting of root (it's the virtual root page in B-tree indexes) and intermediate nodes (if needed) helping to navigate down to leaf nodes that contain a sorted copy of indexed column(s). The **balanced** term means that the leaf information is accessed in the same level of depth in every section of the tree.

SQL Server enables the creation of up to 499 non-clustered indexes on one table, but this is a theoretical limit in most cases. Each index can have up to 16 columns with sum of byte lengths up to 900 Bytes. One record saved to the index structure is called **index key**.

B-tree indexes could be unique (value or combination of values in index key must never repeat) or duplicated. Unique indexes are often created behind the scenes of unique constraint creation.

Data pages on the same level in an index tree are interconnected by an offset as double-linked lists. In other words, every index page knows its predecessor and successor. It helps SQL Server skip to the next index page quickly and efficiently according to the sorting rule defined by the index.

When a non-clustered index is built on top of a heap, leaf records are created as a copy of values from indexed column(s) and point to data pages in the heap to address the record from which they come.

Let's describe operations done by SQL Server when a non-clustered index is built on a heap. When a read operation is executed, SQL Server resolves if the index is useful for the query. We can notice two general conditions of index usefulness:

- The first column in the index is used in the WHERE clause of the query; it causes that SQL Server will not scan all over the heap but will invoke the index seek operation. The seek is a road from virtual root navigating to proper intermediate index pages (maybe several times, it's about the index's depth) and from intermediate pages to the leaf page containing the key value mentioned in the query.

- The WHERE clause is selective, which means that the ratio of records fulfilling the filter versus amount of records in the table is small. The selectivity is recognized by cardinality estimation, which is a formula computing the estimated number of rows returned by the query. The base of query estimation are index statistics.

When executing a SELECT query containing only columns present in a non-clustered index, SQL Server would use just a leaf level of the index even if no WHERE clause is contained within the query. When no additional columns are needed for the query result, SQL Server scans (or seeks) just the leaf level of the index.

The index scan operation is usually very efficient because less data I/O operations has to be done. We talk about these indexes as covering indexes, because they completely cover query needs. Covering indexes are preferred because they save many I/O operations.

In the opposite case, SQL Server seeks proper index keys and it's lead by pointers to heap data pages to retrieve the rest of records indexed by the non-clustered B-tree. When we want to enhance the covering ability of a non-clustered index, we can add **included columns**. Included columns are not indexed; their values are just added with an index key but the index key itself is still small.

A new record inserted into the heap with a non-clustered column is placed anywhere in the heap but the index key of the new record has to be placed in the correct index page. It could lead to some internal non-clustered index maintenance, mainly **page split**. Page split is an operation causing breakup of the index page to two new ones. It frees space for a new index record when the original index page is too full.

When some record is updated, almost the same two situations can occur:

- The new version of updated record fits back to the original data page so nothing special happened
- The new version of the updated record is bigger and does not fit into the original data page, so the record is moved to a data page with more free space, but a little navigation object called forwarding pointer is created to the original page because it's cheaper for SQL Server than to update index key as well

When a record is deleted, it's marked as a ghost record and pointer from index key is invalidated.

When many forwarding pointers and ghost records are created over time, the table becomes fragmented and has to be defragmented. The same occurs on indexes as index pages are split and reduced. That's why regular maintenance is needed to keep these structures less fragmented.

Clustered B-tree index

The clustered B-tree index seems to be very similar to non-clustered indexes, but there's one big difference. The index key is not copied to its separate storage but the table itself forms the leaf-level of the index. It's obvious that only one clustered index can be created by a table. When a clustered index is created, records in the table are sorted accordingly with the index definition and data pages are ordered in a double-linked list.

When SQL Server performs read on a clustered index, it could use these operations:

- **Clustered index scan**: This is executed when the SELECT statement is issued. The entire table is retrieved.
- **Clustered index seek**: The WHERE condition of the query contains a predicate for the clustered index key.

When SQL Server performs an insert operation on the clustered index, the new record has to be placed in the correct position within the index. It can cause more index splitting operations.

When SQL Server updates a record in a clustered index, these situations might occur:

- The column that is not a clustered index key is updated and record is not grown beyond the data page free space: Nothing special occurs
- The column that is not a clustered index key is updated but record is grown beyond the data page free space: Record must still be placed in the same place, new data page is needed, and index split occurs
- The column that is a clustered index key is updated: the whole record has to be moved to the new position to keep sorting; index split may occur

When SQL Server deletes a record from a clustered index, the record is marked as a ghost record.

Non-clustered and clustered index cooperation

It's usual that a table has more than just one index, but a combination of indexes is often used. When a clustered index exists, leaf-pages of non-clustered indexes do not point to data pages addressing their records, but every non-clustered index key keeps association to a proper clustered index key.

In other words, when some non-clustered index is used in a query that needs, for example, all columns of selected records, non-clustered index key values are found and then SQL Server iterates through those values and searches the rest of the records over the clustered index.

This operation is known as **key lookup** and it works as a loop. Keys found in a non-clustered index are searched one by one in a clustered index. When several records are retrieved, this operation is correct and should not be a performance issue, but when SQL Server reuses the same execution plan with other parameter values in the WHERE clause of the query, it may lead to poor performance. This situation is sometimes called **parameter sniffing**. We can help reduce occurrences of key lookup in several ways but usually it's recommended to cooperate with the developer.

Columnstore indexes

Columnstore indexes were introduced by SQL Server 2012 with many limitations. Most of them are gone now and columnstore indexes became very popular in data warehouse applications. Columnstore index uses segments as a store unit rather than data pages. Columnstore indexes could be both clustered and non-clustered.

When a columnstore index is created, a table is divided into **row groups**--sections containing approximately a million records. Every row group is divided into **segments**. Segment is the storage unit containing data of one column in one row group. Data in segments is strongly compressed. This is a very good approach when many aggregation queries are issued, for example, for reporting purposes or data cube processing.

When creating a non-clustered columnstore index, we create just one. The index cannot contain columns of big data types like nvarchar(max) or special data types such as XML or geography. When a non-clustered columnstore is created, it does not affect data contention flow, because SQL Server executes columnstore index maintenance asynchronously so no locks are requested.

The clustered columnstore index has the same limitation for data types. As all columns are obligatory in columnstore, the presence of mentioned data types can be a roadblock when thinking of it.

The clustered columnstore index can cooperate with non-clustered B-tree indexes and the cooperation is usually very efficient.

Other index types

B-tree as well as columnstore indexes are heavily used in conjunction with classical relational data. However, modern databases often handle bigger and more complicated data types. For some of them, SQL Server offers special indexes:

- **XML indexes for XML data type**: XML indexes are divided into the following:
    - **Primary XML index**: It forms the internal structure of all nodes from XML column. These nodes are associated to a unique clustered index value in the same table.
    - **Secondary XML indexes**: These are index structures sorting paths, values, or attributes of XML nodes stored in primary XML index. Secondary XML indexes are always built on top of the primary XML index.
- **Spatial indexes for geometry and geography data types**: These are spatial index structure dividing every spatial value into three levels of grid to zoom-in the value and to make the process of finding a certain point or object simpler. However, the spatial indexes cannot completely cover all task types executed on spatial data.

Indexing considerations

No exact recipe exists for the indexing, but some considerations and best practices have to be written:

- Poorly normalized database design cannot be saved by indexes. It's a big mistake of many developers.
- The best candidate column for a clustered B-tree index is the one that contains a simple value like integer, and the value grows with every new record.
- When primary key constraint is created with defaults, a clustered unique index is created behind the scenes. It's a good approach when integers (especially with `IDENTITY` property set) are used. It's a very bad approach when `uniqueidentifier` is used as a data type for the primary key.
- It's better not to have a clustered index than to have a bad one.
- In OLTP databases, non-clustered indexes with less columns are often better.
- As the database resolves more data warehouse tasks like aggregated queries, more composed B-tree indexes or columnstore indexes are useful.

- Use `sys.dm_db_index_usage_stats` to check whether your indexes are useful.
- Use `sys.dm_db_index_physical_stats` to check a level of fragmentation.
- Check accuracy of statistics using the `DBCC SHOW_STATISTICS` function.

Summary

Monitoring performance and resolving performance issues should be described in their own book but all information is useful.

In the beginning, several approaches used in performance monitoring were described, namely, the top-to-bottom approach and proactive monitoring.

A lot of information was covered in the *Tools for monitoring performance* section. As seen, Microsoft provides a wide set of tools and techniques to monitor and troubleshoot SQL Server. Most of them are graphical, but it's also recommended to have brief knowledge of non-visual objects like dynamic management views and functions.

The *Indexing and maintenance* section demystified typical index types, their usage by SQL Server in common situations, and also some guidance to indexing was covered.

In the next chapter, we will show what to do when things go wrong. We will use some similar techniques to detect problem causes and find solutions for them.

7
Troubleshooting SQL Server Environment and Internals

Your SQL Server workload and environment may not run with the performance you expect or require, and you'll need to troubleshoot the SQL Server. For a good troubleshooting approach, you need to have a basic understanding of the SQL Server architecture and internals, since SQL Server is a very complex software. There are four major components of the SQL Server architecture:

- SQLOS
- Storage engine
- Query processor
- Protocol layer

In the following image, you can see all these components and their relationship:

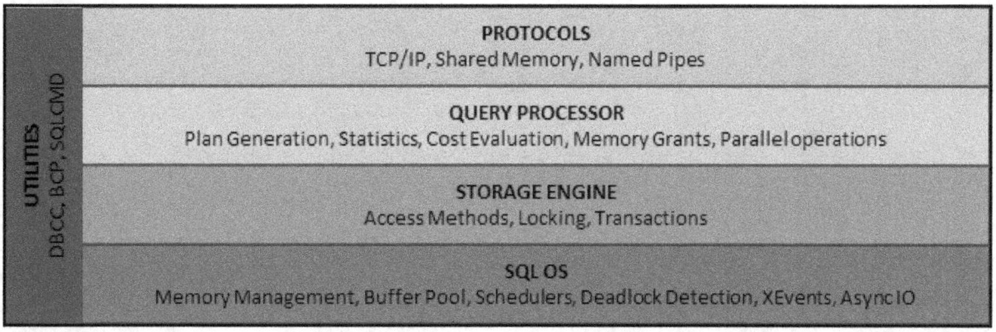

UTILITIES DBCC, BCP, SQLCMD	PROTOCOLS
	TCP/IP, Shared Memory, Named Pipes
	QUERY PROCESSOR
	Plan Generation, Statistics, Cost Evaluation, Memory Grants, Parallel operations
	STORAGE ENGINE
	Access Methods, Locking, Transactions
	SQL OS
	Memory Management, Buffer Pool, Schedulers, Deadlock Detection, XEvents, Async IO

SQL Server protocols

Any application that requires a connection to our SQL Server needs to communicate either over a network or locally on the same server via a protocol layer. SQL Server communication is based on tabular data stream packets, which are encapsulated into a common communication protocol. There are several options available for you, which you can configure in the **SQL Server Configuration Manager** tool. If you expand the **SQL Server Network Configuration**, you'll see the network configuration for your instance:

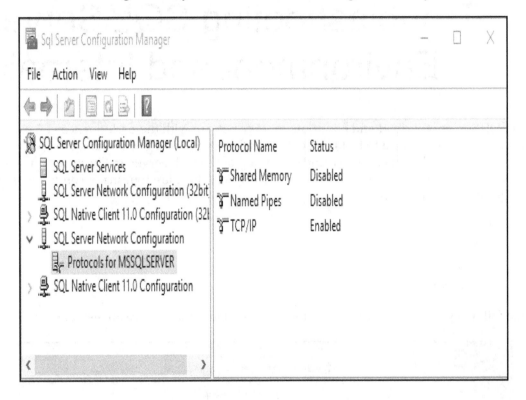

The available protocols are as follows:

- **TCP/IP**: This is the most common choice for SQL Server deployments
- **Shared Memory**: This is the most simple protocol, which can be used only locally and not for remote connections
- **Named Pipes**: This is a protocol developed for LAN connections, and it can work remotely

For most deployments, we need to properly configure the instance **TCP/IP** settings with regards to the available port numbers, which, on the default instance, are set to `TCP/1433`, but on the named instance these are selected randomly. These random port numbers can cause issues with the **Service Principal Name** (**SPN**) registration. SPN is a unique identifier of an SQL Server instance used by Kerberos authentication. To check the registered SPNs, you can use the following command; here `<account>` is the service account used to run your SQL Server services:

```
setspn -l <account>
```

There can be two types of SPNs registered for your SQL Server, which are `MSSQLSvc` for your SQL Server database engine and `MSOLAPDisco.3` for the analysis services. To register the SPN for a named instance, you'll need to know the name of the instance and the port on which the instance is running. Considering that our SQL Server will run with the `CONTOSO\sqlService` account, we can use the following code to register the SPNs:

```
setspn -S MSSQLSvc/sql.contoso.com sqlService
setspn -S MSSQLSvc/sql.contoso.com:1433 sqlService
```

There will be two SPN records registered in the Active Directory—one for the default instance name and one for the defaul port number, `1433`. With a named instance, you'll also need to enter the instance name on the first record.

Through the **SQL Server Configuration Manager**, you can also configure additional properties for the network configuration. You can configure the certificate for your SQL Server, force the encryption, and hide the instance, so the instance is not visible in the local or remote servers in SQL Server Management Studio.

In order to start using SSL/TLS, in fact `TLS1.2`, for your SQL Server, you will have to provide a proper certificate via the configuration manager, as shown in the following screenshot:

Once you select the certificate you also have to modify the Windows OS registry to enable the `TLS1.2` transport protocol encryption. To turn on the TLS1.2 support on the Windows OS, you'll have to modify the following registry entries:

```
[HKEY_LOCAL_MACHINE\SYSTEM\CurrentControlSet\Control\SecurityProviders\SCHA
NNEL\Protocols\TLS 1.2]
[HKEY_LOCAL_MACHINE\SYSTEM\CurrentControlSet\Control\SecurityProviders\SCHA
NNEL\Protocols\TLS 1.2\Client] "DisabledByDefault"=dword:00000000
"Enabled"=dword:00000001
[HKEY_LOCAL_MACHINE\SYSTEM\CurrentControlSet\Control\SecurityProviders\SCHA
NNEL\Protocols\TLS 1.2\Server] "DisabledByDefault"=dword:00000000
"Enabled"=dword:00000001
```

SQL Server 2017 does support `TLS1.2` without any problems, but the older versions require specific updates to be installed. If you enforce `TLS1.2` via the OS registry before you have a proper update in place, your SQL Server may stop working and won't start.

You may find many errors in the errorlog of your SQL Server, which will lead you to the required `TLS1.2` hotfix installation. The common errors that you can find look as follows:

- The server was unable to initialize encryption because of a problem with a security library
- The security library may be missing. Verify that `security.dll` exists on the system
- `TDSSNIClient` initialization failed with error **0x139f**, status code **0x80**. Reason: Unable to initialize SSL support
- The group or resource is not in the correct state to perform the requested operation

Query processor

The query processor is an important layer of architecture, which includes many components. We can split them between query optimization and query execution. Query processor works with the query tree and determines the possible ways of optimization. Many of the complex commands can be optimized with more approaches, and the optimizer can find those, especially for typical DML commands: SELECT, INSERT, UPDATE, DELETE, and MERGE. The query optimizer is based on the following two main inputs:

- **Cost**: This indicates the cost of the plan
- **Cardinality**: This indicates the number of rows being processed

The cardinality metric is used as an input to the cost metric, so the better the cardinality, the better the whole cost of the plan. The cardinality, if it can be determined, is based on histograms of the statistics and index information. Since SQL Server 2014, there has been a new cardinality estimator available, which can be controlled via the following:

- Database compatibility level
- Trace flags
- Database-scoped configuration
- Hints

With the latest SQL Server versions, we can use **Database Scoped Configuration**, which is available for each individual database. When you click on any database and select **Properties/Options**, you can find a scoped configuration like this one:

Database Scoped Configurations	
Legacy Cardinality Estimation	OFF
Legacy Cardinality Estimation For Secondary	PRIMARY
Max DOP	0
Max DOP For Secondary	
Parameter Sniffing	ON
Parameter Sniffing For Secondary	PRIMARY
Query Optimizer Fixes	OFF
Query Optimizer Fixes For Secondary	PRIMARY

In this configuration, you can control interesting behavior for your database, where the first two options are related to the cardinality estimator. As you can see, by default, the legacy estimator is off, and secondary replicas from the availability groups use the same setting as the primary replica. The same settings are also available for three other very important configurations, which previously had to be configured on the server level, instead of the database level. These are as follows:

- Max DOP
- Parameter Sniffing
- Query Optimizer Fixes

The query optimizer is constantly being improved by new updates on the current SQL Server 2017, called only cumulative updates. Any time a new update is installed, by default you can see no fixes of the query optimizer are used by your SQL Server, unless you turn this on for individual databases or globally by using trace flag T4199. The trace flags can be configured via the SQL Server Configuration Manager on the properties of your instance. If you go to the **Startup Parameters** tab, you can add the trace flags to the list.

The other major part of the query processor is the query execution engine. This engine uses the plans generated by the query optimizer and runs them. Running the plan or executing the query can involve many operations on the storage engine and in the memory to return the entire required dataset. To see the query plan, you can use the **SQL Server Management Studio** (**SSMS**) and use one of the following options:

- Include actual execution plan (*Ctrl + M*)
- Include live query statistics
- Display the estimated execution plan (*Ctrl + L*)

There's a considerable difference between the estimated and actual execution plans. The estimated plan is created without executing the query whereas the actual plan is, in fact, the used workflow to perform the query operations. These two plans can differ either in the structure and operators used or in the estimates on the row counts and the size of data being pulled through the plan. Let's see some common plan operators that you can see in the plans.

When we need to pull the data from the tables, we can see several common operators:

- **Table scan**: This retrieves all the rows from a table that does not have a clustered index (heap structure)
- **Clustered index scan**: This retrieves all the rows from a table that have a clustered index
- **Columnstore index scan**: This retrieves all the rows from a columnstore index
- **Clustered index seek**: This retrieves only the rows based on a seek predicate from a clustered index
- **Nonclustered index seek**: This retrieves only the rows based on a seek predicate from a nonclustered index

The following are the typical plan operator icons in the same order as we just listed:

When you capture a query plan, you can see such an operator being used, as shown in the following screenshot:

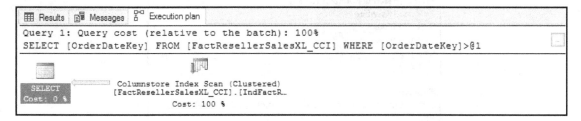

With such a query, you can see that the columnstore index was used to retrieve all the data required by the query. When you show the execution plan, you can move your mouse over any operator to display the details about the operator: the cost of the IO and CPU, the number of rows, and other information. The important attributes for us to watch during any troubleshooting action are as follows:

- The actual number of rows versus the estimated number of rows
- The number of executions
- Whether parallelism is used
- Whether any warnings are displayed

The following screenshot shows **Columnstore Index Scan (Clustered)**:

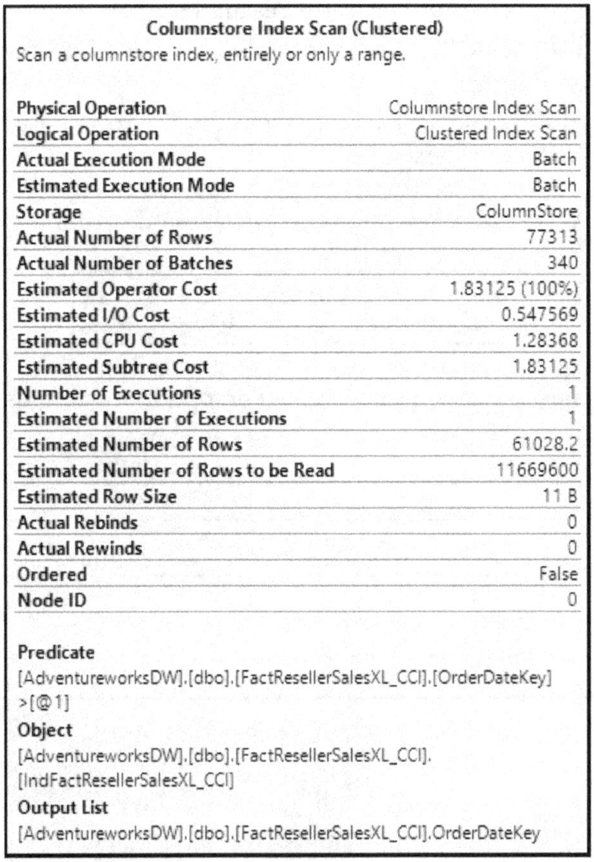

Columnstore Index Scan (Clustered)	
Scan a columnstore index, entirely or only a range.	
Physical Operation	Columnstore Index Scan
Logical Operation	Clustered Index Scan
Actual Execution Mode	Batch
Estimated Execution Mode	Batch
Storage	ColumnStore
Actual Number of Rows	77313
Actual Number of Batches	340
Estimated Operator Cost	1.83125 (100%)
Estimated I/O Cost	0.547569
Estimated CPU Cost	1.28368
Estimated Subtree Cost	1.83125
Number of Executions	1
Estimated Number of Executions	1
Estimated Number of Rows	61028.2
Estimated Number of Rows to be Read	11669600
Estimated Row Size	11 B
Actual Rebinds	0
Actual Rewinds	0
Ordered	False
Node ID	0

Predicate
[AdventureworksDW].[dbo].[FactResellerSalesXL_CCI].[OrderDateKey]
>[@1]
Object
[AdventureworksDW].[dbo].[FactResellerSalesXL_CCI].
[IndFactResellerSalesXL_CCI]
Output List
[AdventureworksDW].[dbo].[FactResellerSalesXL_CCI].OrderDateKey

The displayed plans can be much more complex, and the whole plan revision is important, object by object, to spot any issues and warnings. If any warning is automatically detected by the SQL Server engine, it is displayed on the operator with a small yellow warning sign, as shown in the following image. If you then hover your mouse over the operator, you can find the entire warning:

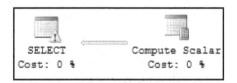

Let's move on to the other category of operators, which are usually displayed with nested lookup join:

- **Key lookup**: This is a lookup on a table with a clustered index
- **RID lookup**: This is a lookup on a heap

The nested lookup join is used for many join operations, where for a row in the outer table, the SQL looks for rows in the inner table and returns them. The other types of join can include the following

- **Merge join**: This algorithm is the most efficient way of joining two very large sets of data, which are both sorted on the join key
- **Hash match**: This type of operator is used when the scenario doesn't fit in any of the other join types. Hash match is often used when the tables are not properly sorted or if there are no indexes

The full operator reference can be found at `https://docs.microsoft.com/en-us/sql/relational-databases/showplan-logical-and-physical-operators-reference`, which lists all the logical and physical operators alphabetically.

The storage engine layer

The storage engine layer is responsible for all access to your data stored in the database and has three major components:

- Access methods
- Transaction and locking

Access methods are used to get the data out of the data and index pages, which are delivered as a resultant set of your SQL Server operation. The access methods then split deeper between operations on rows and indexes, which are responsible for maintaining the data in the row and index pages. There are several types of pages available with the SQL Server. The user data is stored in the data pages, row-overflow pages, or LOB pages (used for large objects). If there are indexes used, the index rows are stored on the index pages (and on the row-overflow and LOB pages too). Then, the SQL Server uses several allocation maps to keep track of the used/free space in the data files; these pages are as follows:

- **PFS**: This page keeps a bitmap of usage of the pages in the data file
- **GAM**: The **Global Allocation Map** (**GAM**) page keeps track of the extents that have been allocated for uniform extents
- **SGAM**: The **Shared Global Allocation Map** (**SGAM**) keeps track of the extents that are used as mixed extents

A space in the database is managed by objects called extents, which are made of eight contiguous pages. Uniform extents are used by a single object, so all the eight pages that form the extent are used for the same object. Here, the mixed extents can be shared by several different objects.

The transaction component is important for handling the transactions. Transaction is a unit of work in SQL Server, where all the commands in the transaction are handled as a unit and must be successfully finished as a whole. All the transactions must follow the **Atomic, Consistency, Isolation, Durability** (**ACID**) rules:

- **Atomic**: Each transaction is handled as all or nothing.
- **Consistency**: The transaction cannot harm the system, in a way, of any logical inconsistency. All the constraints and rules must be followed.
- **Isolation**: This separates the one transaction from another by locking or row versioning. There are several different isolation levels available in the SQL Server, which have an impact on the locking, versioning, and the overall transaction isolation.
- **Durability**: Once a transaction is committed, it is persisted.

Performance monitoring and tuning

Performance monitoring and tuning is a crucial part of your database administration skill set so as to keep the performance and stability of your server great, and to be able to find and fix the possible issues. The overall system performance can decrease over time; your system may work with more data or even become totally unresponsive. In such cases, you need the skills and tools to find the issue to bring the server back to normal as fast as possible. We can use several tools on the operating system layer and, then, inside the SQL Server to verify the performance and the possible root cause of the issue.

The first tool that we can use is the performance monitor, which is available on your Windows Server:

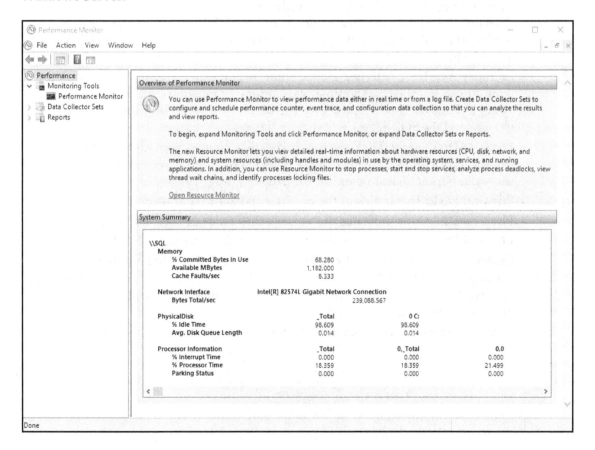

Performance monitor can be used to track important SQL Server counters, which can be very helpful in evaluating the SQL Server Performance. To add a counter, simply right-click on the monitoring screen in the *Performance monitoring and tuning* section and use the **Add Counters** item. If the SQL Server instance that you're monitoring is a default instance, you will find all the performance objects listed as SQL Server. If your instance is named, then the performance objects will be listed as MSSQL$InstanceName in the list of performance objects. We can split the important counters to watch between the system counters for the whole server and specific SQL Server counters.

The list of system counters to watch include the following:

- **Processor(_Total)\% Processor Time**: This is a counter to display the CPU load. Constant high values should be investigated to verify whether the current load does not exceed the performance limits of your HW or VM server, or if your workload is not running with proper indexes and statistics, and is generating *bad* query plans.
- **Memory\Available MBytes**: This counter displays the available memory on the operating system. There should always be enough memory for the operating system. If this counter drops below 64 MB, it will send a notification of *low memory* and the SQL Server will reduce the memory usage.
- **Physical Disk—Avg. Disk sec/Read**: This disk counter provides the average latency information for your storage system; be careful if your storage is made of several different disks to monitor the proper storage system.
- **Physical Disk**: This indicates the average disk writes per second.
- **Physical Disk**: This indicates the average disk reads per second.
- **Physical Disk**: This indicates the number of disk writes per second.
- **System—Processor Queue Length**: This counter displays the number of threads waiting on a system CPU. If the counter is above *0*, this means that there are more requests than the CPU can handle, and if the counter is constantly above 0, this may signal performance issues.
- **Network interface**: This indicates the total number of bytes per second.

Once you have added all these system counters, you can see the values real time or you can configure a data collection, which will run for a specified selected time and periodically collect the information:

LogicalDisk	G:
Avg. Disk Bytes/Read	57,344.000
Avg. Disk Bytes/Write	5,120.000
Disk Reads/sec	2.026
Disk Writes/sec	4.053
Memory	
Available MBytes	1,987.000
Processor	_Total
% Processor Time	15.609
Processor Information	_Total
% Processor Time	15.609
System	
Processor Queue Length	0.000

With SQL Server-specific counters, we can dig deeper into the CPU, memory, and storage utilization to see what the SQL Server is doing and how the SQL Server is utilizing the subsystems.

SQL Server memory monitoring and troubleshooting

Important counters to watch for SQL Server memory utilization include counters from the SQL Server: Buffer Manager performance object and from SQL Server:Memory Manager:

- **SQLServer-Buffer Manager—buffer cache hit ratio**: This counter displays the ratio of how often the SQL Server can find the proper data in the cache when a query returns such data. If the data is not found in the cache, it has to be read from the disk. The higher the counter, the better the overall performance, since the memory access is usually faster compared to the disk subsystem.
- **SQLServer-Buffer Manager—page life expectancy**: This counter can measure how long a page can stay in the memory in seconds. The longer a page can stay in the memory, the less likely it will be for the SQL Server to need to access the disk in order to get the data into the memory again.

- **SQL Server-Memory Manager—total server memory (KB)**: This is the amount of memory the server has committed using the memory manager.
- **SQL Server-Memory Manager—target server memory (KB)**: This is the ideal amount of memory the server can consume. On a stable system, the target and total should be equal unless you face a memory pressure. Once the memory is utilized after the warm-up of your server, these two counters should not drop significantly, which would be another indication of system-level memory pressure, where the SQL Server memory manager has to deallocate memory.
- **SQL Server-Memory Manager—memory grants pending**: This counter displays the total number of SQL Server processes that are waiting to be granted memory from the memory manager.

To check the performance counters, you can also use a T-SQL query, where you can query the sys.dm_os_performance_counters DMV:

```
SELECT [counter_name] as [Counter Name], [cntr_value]/1024 as [Server
Memory (MB)]
FROM sys.dm_os_performance_counters
WHERE
    [object_name] LIKE '%Memory Manager%'
    AND [counter_name] IN ('Total Server Memory (KB)', 'Target Server
Memory (KB)')
```

This query will return two values—one for target memory and one for total memory. These two should be close to each other on a warmed up system. Another query you can use is to get the information from a DMV named sys.dm_0s_sys_memory:

```
SELECT total_physical_memory_kb/1024/1024 AS [Physical Memory (GB)],
       available_physical_memory_kb/1024/1024 AS [Available Memory (GB)],
       system_memory_state_desc AS [System Memory State]
FROM sys.dm_os_sys_memory WITH (NOLOCK) OPTION (RECOMPILE)
```

This query will display the available physical memory and the total physical memory of your server with several possible memory states:

- Available physical memory is high (this is a state you would like to see on your system, indicating there is no lack of memory)
- Physical memory usage is steady
- Available physical memory is getting low
- Available physical memory is low

The memory grants can be verified with a T-SQL query:

```
SELECT [object_name] as [Object name] , cntr_value AS [Memory Grants
Pending]
FROM sys.dm_os_performance_counters WITH (NOLOCK)
WHERE
    [object_name] LIKE N'%Memory Manager%'
    AND counter_name = N'Memory Grants Pending' OPTION (RECOMPILE);
```

If you face memory issues, there are several steps you can take for improvements:

- Check and configure your SQL Server max memory usage
- Add more RAM to your server; the limit for Standard Edition is 128 GB and there is no limit for SQL Server with Enterprise
- Use **Lock Pages** in Memory
- Optimize your queries

SQL Server storage monitoring and troubleshooting

The important counters to watch for SQL Server storage utilization would include counters from the SQL Server:Access Methods performance object:

- **SQL Server-Access Methods—Full Scans/sec**: This counter displays the number of full scans per second, which can be either table or full-index scans
- **SQL Server-Access Methods—Index Searches/sec**: This counter displays the number of searches in the index per second
- **SQL Server-Access Methods—Forwarded Records/sec**: This counter displays the number of forwarded records per second

Monitoring the disk system is crucial, since your disk is used as a storage for the following:

- Data files
- Log files
- tempDB database
- Page file
- Backup files

To verify the disk latency and IOPS metric of your drives, you can use the Performance monitor, or the T-SQL commands, which will query the `sys.dm_os_volume_stats` and `sys.dm_io_virtual_file_stats` DMF. Simple code to start with would be a T-SQL script utilizing the DMF to check the space available within the database files:

```
SELECT f.database_id, f.file_id, volume_mount_point, total_bytes,
available_bytes
FROM sys.master_files AS f
CROSS APPLY sys.dm_os_volume_stats(f.database_id, f.file_id);
```

To check the I/O file stats with the second provided DMF, you can use a T-SQL code for checking the information about `tempDB` data files:

```
SELECT * FROM sys.dm_io_virtual_file_stats (NULL, NULL) vfs
join sys.master_files mf on mf.database_id = vfs.database_id and mf.file_id
= vfs.file_id
WHERE mf.database_id = 2 and mf.type = 0
```

To measure the disk performance, we can use a tool named `DiskSpeed`, which is a replacement for older SQLIO tool, which was used for a long time.

 DiskSpeed is an external utility, which is not available on the operating system by default. This tool can be downloaded from GitHub or the Technet Gallery at `https://github.com/microsoft/diskspd`.

The following example runs a test for 15 seconds using a single thread to drive 100 percent random 64 KB reads at a depth of 15 overlapped (outstanding) I/Os to a regular file:

```
DiskSpd –d300 –F1 –w0 –r –b64k –o15 d:\datafile.dat
```

Troubleshooting wait statistics

In Chapter 6, *Indexing and Performance,* we have seen several wait types in the Activity Monitor tool. We can use the whole Wait Statistics approach for a thorough understanding of the SQL Server workload and undertake performance troubleshooting based on the collected data. Wait Statistics are based on the fact that, any time a request has to wait for a resource, the SQL Server tracks this information, and we can use this information for further analysis.

When we consider any user process, it can include several threads. A thread is a single unit of execution on SQL Server, where SQLOS controls the thread scheduling instead of relying on the operating system layer. Each processor core has it's own scheduler component responsible for executing such threads. To see the available schedulers in your SQL Server, you can use the following query:

```
SELECT * FROM sys.dm_os_schedulers
```

Such code will return all the schedulers in your SQL Server; some will be displayed as **visible online** and some as **hidden online**. The hidden ones are for internal system tasks while the visible ones are used by user tasks running on the SQL Server. There is one more scheduler, which is displayed as **Visible Online** (**DAC**). This one is used for dedicated administration connection, which comes in handy when the SQL Server stops responding. To use a dedicated admin connection, you can modify your SSMS connection to use the DAC, or you can use a switch with the `sqlcmd.exe` utility, to connect to the DAC. To connect to the default instance with DAC on your server, you can use the following command:

```
sqlcmd.exe -E -A
```

Each thread can be in three possible states:

- `running`: This indicates that the thread is running on the processor
- `suspended`: This indicates that the thread is waiting for a resource on a waiter list
- `runnable`: This indicates that the thread is waiting for execution on a runnable queue

Each running thread runs until it has to wait for a resource to become available or until it has exhausted the CPU time for a running thread, which is set to 4 ms. This 4 ms time can be visible in the output of the previous query to `sys.dm_os_schedulers` and is called a quantum. When a thread requires any resource, it is moved away from the processor to a waiter list, where the thread waits for the resource to become available. Once the resource is available, the thread is notified about the resource availability and moves to the bottom of the runnable queue.

Any waiting thread can be found via the following code, which will display the waiting threads and the resource they are waiting for:

```
SELECT * FROM sys.dm_os_waiting_tasks
```

The threads then transition between the execution at the CPU, waiter list, and runnable queue. There is a special case when a thread does not need to wait for any resource and has already run for 4 ms on the CPU, then the thread will be moved directly to the runnable queue instead of the waiter list.

In the following image, we can see the thread states and the objects where the thread resides:

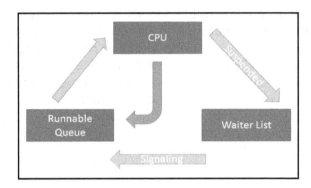

When the thread is waiting on the waiter list, we can talk about a resource wait time. When the thread is waiting on the runnable queue to get on the CPU for execution, we can talk about the signal time. The total wait time is, then, the sum of the signal and resource wait times. You can find the ratio of the signal to resource wait times with the following script:

```
Select signalWaitTimeMs=sum(signal_wait_time_ms)
    ,'%signal waits' = cast(100.0 * sum(signal_wait_time_ms) / sum
(wait_time_ms) as numeric(20,2))
    ,resourceWaitTimeMs=sum(wait_time_ms - signal_wait_time_ms)
    ,'%resource waits'= cast(100.0 * sum(wait_time_ms -
signal_wait_time_ms) / sum (wait_time_ms) as numeric(20,2))
from sys.dm_os_wait_stats
```

When the ratio goes over 30 percent for the signal waits, then there will be a serious CPU pressure and your processor(s) will have a hard time handling all the incoming requests from the threads.

The following query can then grab the wait statistics and display the most frequent wait types, which were recorded through the thread executions, or actually during the time the threads were waiting on the waiter list for any particular resource:

```
WITH [Waits] AS
    (SELECT
        [wait_type],
        [wait_time_ms] / 1000.0 AS [WaitS],
```

```
        ([wait_time_ms] - [signal_wait_time_ms]) / 1000.0 AS [ResourceS],
        [signal_wait_time_ms] / 1000.0 AS [SignalS],
        [waiting_tasks_count] AS [WaitCount],
        100.0 * [wait_time_ms] / SUM ([wait_time_ms]) OVER() AS
[Percentage],
        ROW_NUMBER() OVER(ORDER BY [wait_time_ms] DESC) AS [RowNum]
    FROM sys.dm_os_wait_stats
    WHERE [wait_type] NOT IN (
        N'BROKER_EVENTHANDLER',
        N'BROKER_RECEIVE_WAITFOR',
        N'BROKER_TASK_STOP',
        N'BROKER_TO_FLUSH',
        N'BROKER_TRANSMITTER',
        N'CHECKPOINT_QUEUE',
        N'CHKPT',
        N'CLR_AUTO_EVENT',
        N'CLR_MANUAL_EVENT',
        N'CLR_SEMAPHORE',
        N'DIRTY_PAGE_POLL',
        N'DISPATCHER_QUEUE_SEMAPHORE',
        N'EXECSYNC',
        N'FSAGENT',
        N'FT_IFTS_SCHEDULER_IDLE_WAIT',
        N'FT_IFTSHC_MUTEX',
        N'HADR_CLUSAPI_CALL',
        N'HADR_FILESTREAM_IOMGR_IOCOMPLETION',
        N'HADR_LOGCAPTURE_WAIT',
        N'HADR_NOTIFICATION_DEQUEUE',
        N'HADR_TIMER_TASK',
        N'HADR_WORK_QUEUE',
        N'KSOURCE_WAKEUP',
        N'LAZYWRITER_SLEEP',
        N'LOGMGR_QUEUE',
        N'MEMORY_ALLOCATION_EXT',
        N'ONDEMAND_TASK_QUEUE',
        N'PREEMPTIVE_XE_GETTARGETSTATE',
        N'PWAIT_ALL_COMPONENTS_INITIALIZED',
        N'PWAIT_DIRECTLOGCONSUMER_GETNEXT',
        N'QDS_PERSIST_TASK_MAIN_LOOP_SLEEP',
        N'QDS_ASYNC_QUEUE',
        N'QDS_CLEANUP_STALE_QUERIES_TASK_MAIN_LOOP_SLEEP',
        N'QDS_SHUTDOWN_QUEUE',
        N'REDO_THREAD_PENDING_WORK',
        N'REQUEST_FOR_DEADLOCK_SEARCH',
        N'RESOURCE_QUEUE',
        N'SERVER_IDLE_CHECK',
        N'SLEEP_BPOOL_FLUSH',
        N'SLEEP_DBSTARTUP',
```

```
            N'SLEEP_DCOMSTARTUP',
            N'SLEEP_MASTERDBREADY',
            N'SLEEP_MASTERMDREADY',
            N'SLEEP_MASTERUPGRADED',
            N'SLEEP_MSDBSTARTUP',
            N'SLEEP_SYSTEMTASK',
            N'SLEEP_TASK',
            N'SLEEP_TEMPDBSTARTUP',
            N'SNI_HTTP_ACCEPT',
            N'SP_SERVER_DIAGNOSTICS_SLEEP',
            N'SQLTRACE_BUFFER_FLUSH',
            N'SQLTRACE_INCREMENTAL_FLUSH_SLEEP',
            N'SQLTRACE_WAIT_ENTRIES',
            N'WAIT_FOR_RESULTS',
            N'WAITFOR',
            N'WAITFOR_TASKSHUTDOWN',
            N'WAIT_XTP_RECOVERY',
            N'WAIT_XTP_HOST_WAIT',
            N'WAIT_XTP_OFFLINE_CKPT_NEW_LOG',
            N'WAIT_XTP_CKPT_CLOSE',
            N'XE_DISPATCHER_JOIN',
            N'XE_DISPATCHER_WAIT',
            N'XE_TIMER_EVENT'
            )
    AND [waiting_tasks_count] > 0
    )
SELECT
    MAX ([W1].[wait_type]) AS [WaitType],
    CAST (MAX ([W1].[WaitS]) AS DECIMAL (16,2)) AS [Wait_S],
    CAST (MAX ([W1].[ResourceS]) AS DECIMAL (16,2)) AS [Resource_S],
    CAST (MAX ([W1].[SignalS]) AS DECIMAL (16,2)) AS [Signal_S],
    MAX ([W1].[WaitCount]) AS [WaitCount],
    CAST (MAX ([W1].[Percentage]) AS DECIMAL (5,2)) AS [Percentage],
    CAST ((MAX ([W1].[WaitS]) / MAX ([W1].[WaitCount])) AS DECIMAL (16,4))
AS [AvgWait_S],
    CAST ((MAX ([W1].[ResourceS]) / MAX ([W1].[WaitCount])) AS DECIMAL
(16,4)) AS [AvgRes_S],
    CAST ((MAX ([W1].[SignalS]) / MAX ([W1].[WaitCount])) AS DECIMAL
(16,4)) AS [AvgSig_S]
FROM [Waits] AS [W1]
INNER JOIN [Waits] AS [W2] ON [W2].[RowNum] <= [W1].[RowNum]
GROUP BY [W1].[RowNum]
HAVING SUM ([W2].[Percentage]) - MAX( [W1].[Percentage] ) < 95
GO
```

This code is available on the *whitepaper*, published by SQLSkills, named *SQL Server Performance Tuning Using Wait Statistics* by Erin Stellato and Jonathan Kehayias, which then refers the URL on SQLSkills and uses the full query by Paul Randal available at `https://www.sqlskills.com/blogs/paul/wait-statistics-or-please-tell-me-where-it-hurts/`.

Some of the typical wait types were already described in `Chapter 6`, *Indexing and Performance*, in the *Resource Waits* section. We'll just build on top of those to further explain some of the typical wait stats you can see.

PAGEIOLATCH

The `PAGEIOLATCH` wait type is used when the thread is waiting for a page to be read into the buffer pool from the disk. This wait type comes with two main forms:

- `PAGEIOLATCH_SH` : This page will be read from the disk
- `PAGEIOLATCH_EX` : This page will be modified

You may quickly assume that the storage has to be the problem, but that may not be the case. Like any other wait, they need to be considered in correlation with other wait types and other counters available to correctly find the root cause of the slow SQL Server operations. The page may be read into the buffer pool, because it was previously removed due to memory pressure and is needed again. So, you may also investigate the following:

- **Buffer Manager**: Page life expectancy
- **Buffer Manager**: Buffer cache hit ratio

Also, you need to consider the following as a possible factor to the `PAGEIOLATCH` wait types:

- Large scans versus seeks on the indexes
- Implicit conversions
- Inundated statistics
- Missing indexes

PAGELATCH

This wait type is quite frequently misplaced with PAGEIOLATCH but PAGELATCH is used for pages already present in the memory. The thread waits for the access to such a page again with possible PAGELATCH_SH and PAGELATCH_EX wait types.

A pretty common situation with this wait type is a tempDB contention, where you need to analyze what page is being waited for and what type of query is actually waiting for such a resource. As a solution to the tempDB, contention you can do the following:

- Add more tempDB data files
- Use traceflags 1118 and 1117 for tempDB on systems older than SQL Server 2016

CXPACKET

This wait type is encountered when any thread is running in parallel. The CXPACKET wait type itself does not mean that there is really any problem on the SQL Server. But if such a wait type is accumulated very quickly, it may be a signal of skewed statistics, which require an update or a parallel scan on the table where proper indexes are missing.

The option for parallelism is controlled via MAX DOP setting, which can be configured on the following:

- The server level
- The database level
- A query level with a hint

Summary

In this chapter, we saw some basic performance tuning tips and SQL Server internals, which are essential to the understanding of troubleshooting. The SQL Server consists of several different layers, where it has it's own operating system inside, which is responsible for many tasks and is a subject for several DMVs, which we saw for troubleshooting. We can then check many of the performance counters, which closely relate to the storage and query processor layers to see how SQL Server is working and if there is any pressure on any of the subsystems such as CPU, memory, disk, or network.

Going further with the SQL Server analysis, we introduced the Wait Statistics troubleshooting methodology and possible DMVs to use to get more insight on the problems occurring in the SQL Server. At the end of the chapter, we extended the information about several wait types, which were previously introduced in Chapter 6, *Indexing and Performance*.

In the next chapter, we will see what possible approaches we can use to upgrade, migrate, and consolidate the SQL Server workload. There are several options available, so we'll discuss their benefits, their advantages and disadvantages, and typical usage scenarios.

8
Migration and Upgrade

Although this book is about SQL Server 2017, you're not always working with the latest versions and editions of SQL Server. You may be surprised how diverse versions of SQL Server are still in production and you will face a task of upgrading and migrating the server configuration and the content to the new server running the latest version of SQL Server. Each new version of SQL Server brings out many new features that are not available in the older versions and they may be very useful for your environment to bring better performance, stability, and many other factors to your application.

 Migration of SQL Server is also usually bound to new hardware for the server or a virtual machine with the latest operating system using new features, so you can actually upgrade the whole platform, not just SQL Server.

We will be covering the following topics in the chapter:

- Understanding why migration is necessary
- Planning the upgrade
- Performing the upgrade
- Migration from other platforms

Why migration is necessary

An important reason to upgrade is the support for SQL Server. Once the mainstream support for SQL Server ends, there will be no more service packs and cumulative updates bringing new features to the old versions.

As you can see from the following table, just three SQL Server versions are supported as of now (Fall 2017). And those are SQL Server 2014, SQL Server 2016, and the current SQL Server 2017:

SQL Server version	Release date	End of mainstream support
SQL Server 2000	Nov 2000	4/8/2008
SQL Server 2005	Jan 2006	4/12/2011
SQL Server 2008	Nov 2008	1/14/2014
SQL Server 2008 R2	Jul 2010	1/14/2014
SQL Server 2012	May 2012	7/11/2017
SQL Server 2014	June 2014	7/9/2019
SQL Server 2016	June 2016	10/12/2021
SQL Server 2017	Sept 2017	10/11/2022

Although many of the older versions are not supported anymore, it does not mean those are not used in production environments. This table does not list all the SQL Server versions there are even older systems, which can be used today, but those fell out of support a very long time ago. Also note that SQL Server 2008 and SQL Server 2oo8 R2 share the end date for mainstream support, although those two are separate products released in different years.

In the following table, you can find the support dates for the operating system, where the common Windows Server 2012 and Windows Server 2012 R2 will reach the end of the mainstream support next year:

Windows Server version	End of mainstream support
Windows Server 2003 R2	7/13/2010
Windows Server 2008 with SP2	1/13/2015
Windows Server 2008 R2 with SP1	1/13/2015
Windows Server 2012	1/9/2018
Windows Server 2012 R2	1/9/2018
Windows Server 2016	1/11/2022

Upgrading your SQL Server and the operating system can bring you many new features that can work together to achieve better performance and availability for your environment.

Planning the upgrade

Upgrading a complex infrastructure is not an easy task and it should not be executed without any preparation. Careful planning of the required steps will help you eliminate possible issues to the minimum and the upgrade will run smoothly. Through the versions of SQL Server, there have been many changes, so it's worth exploring your options while planning the new installation also from the perspective of the available edition.

While upgrading the SQL Server from older versions, you also have to understand the changes in the licensing for SQL Server where SQL Server 2008 R2 and older used the per-processor licensing model or user CAL licensing model. Starting with SQL Server 2012, Microsoft has moved to core-based licensing, where you need to have a license for each CPU core used on your operating system.

SQL Server licensing is a very complex topic, which goes beyond the scope of the book. There are many minor details that have influence on the SQL Server licensing, starting with the platform—physical server or a virtual one, and many others. For more information about licensing, you can visit the Microsoft website at `https://www.microsoft.com/en-us/sql-server/sql-server-2017-pricing` where you can find the SQL Server licensing datasheet, which is a great start for you.

From the edition perspective, there are two very important aspects you need to consider during upgrade—hardware limits and feature limits. SQL Server is usually deployed with two major editions—Standard and Enterprise. Enterprise has more features, offers more scalability, high availability, security, and so on. With SQL Server 2016 Service Pack 1, many Enterprise features were made available also for the Standard Edition, which may allow you to upgrade to a lower edition while keeping the application working with all the required features. For the choice of the edition, you also have to consider the hardware limits for CPU/cores and memory, which have a huge impact on the overall server performance.

SQL Server Standard Edition supports up to 128 GB RAM (for SQL Server 2016 and 2017, older versions had lower limits) and can use up to four CPU slots and 24 cores. This is mainly important with current servers, which can have many more CPU cores than the Standard Edition limit and those can't be used for the SQL Server workload.

 All the differences between editions are outlined at the online documentation available here https://docs.microsoft.com/en-us/sql/sql-server/editions-and-compon ents-of-sql-server-2017#Cross-BoxScaleLimits

The following is a list of features that are now available in the Standard Edition after SQL Server 2016 SP1:

- Change data capture
- Database snapshot
- Columnstore index
- Partitioning
- Data compression
- InMemory OLTP
- Always encrypted
- PolyBase
- Fine grained auditing

Quite a standard practice is to have a production and development server for an application, and we aim to have those two, so we're not surprised in production after deploying the new code. Since SQL Server 2014, we can use the SQL Server Developer Edition for free, which is an ideal candidate for the development/test servers.

 The only limitation for the Developer Edition is that it can't be used in production. You have to keep in mind that the Developer Edition is similar to the Enterprise Edition, so if your production environment is based on the SQL Server Standard Edition, you need to watch closely on what features to use, so they can be used on the Standard Edition.

Upgrade scenarios

As a part of the planning phase, you have to carefully consider the upgrade path for your environment. There are three main types of upgrades which you can take the following:

- In-place upgrade
- Rolling upgrade
- Side-by-side migration

SQL Server in-place upgrade

In this scenario, the SQL Server setup upgrades your existing SQL Server installation. In a case where you have more SQL Server instances on the same server you have to choose a specific instance to upgrade. There are advantages and disadvantages to this upgrade path.

The main advantages are:

- It's easy and fast
- It does not require new hardware or new virtual machine
- It does not require extra storage
- The operating system is not upgraded

But the disadvantages are there too, and these include a longer required downtime compared to a side-by-side type of upgrade. Another big disadvantage is the more complex rollback, if one is required. And last but not least, in-place upgrade is not supported for all scenarios of deployed SQL Server services.

An in-place upgrade is mostly used for non-production systems, where a downtime is acceptable. During the upgrade there will be a limited time when the SQL Server services will be stopped and upgraded to a newer version during which it is unavailable to end users.

You can use the in-place upgrade to upgrade from SQL Server 2008 to SQL Server 2016:

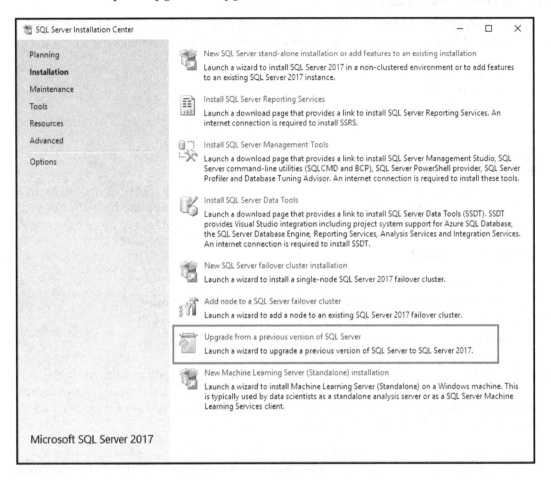

Side-by-side migration

The side-by-side upgrade path is more complex compared to the in-place upgrade type, but it offers you more control over the overall process. In this type of upgrade, you will have two SQL Servers running and you will move the objects from one server to another. This will allow you a lot of space for testing, where two SQL Servers—the original and the new/upgraded one—can be evaluated from the application teams to resolve any possible issues. The original server will be intact and you will need to install a fresh new SQL Server with many choices:

- New hardware
- New virtual machine
- New SQL Server instance (least recommended option)

With new hardware or virtual machine, you can also have the benefit of installing the SQL Server on the latest operating system, which is not covered by the in-place upgrade. The in-place upgrade is only to upgrade the SQL Server version, so the Windows operating system has to be handled usually by the Windows admin team of your company. Having the option of using the latest and greatest Windows operating system and new hardware or virtual machine can also bring you many performance benefits with newer and faster CPUs, more RAM, different storage options, and much more.

When you're using the side-by-side migration you have to consider that many objects won't be part of the databases, which you will eventually restore to the new system. There are many system objects stored in master or MSDB databases, which require special attention, otherwise, your new SQL Server won't work as you may expect. Those objects include:

- SQL Server logins
- SQL Server certificates
- SQL Server principals
- Linked servers
- SQL Server jobs and other SQL agent-related objects (proxies, operators, alerts)
- SQL Server server-level triggers
- SQL Server SSIS packages stored in MSDB

Login information is essential so your DBA team, application team, and the application itself can log in to the SQL Server. These logins are stored in the `master` database and can be copied to the new SQL Server in several ways. One of them would be a use of a stored procedure `sp_help_revlogin`.

 Stored procedure `sp_help_revlogin` is an old procedure available from Microsoft, which is not installed to the SQL Server by default. The source code is available at `http://bit.ly/2m5pwUY`. You can grab the code from the site, run the code on your SQL Server, and then just use the procedure to generate the required T-SQL code for recreating logins from scratch on the new system.

To export the logins via this stored procedure, simply run the following T-SQL code after you have successfully created all the required objects:

```
EXEC sp_help_revlogin
```

This stored procedure will generate the T-SQL code needed to recreate all the logins which exist on the current SQL Server. The output also includes specific system logins and certificates, service accounts, and much more, which you may skip and focus only on the logins required for the application team. The output may look as follows:

```
-- Login: SQL\SQLAdmins
CREATE LOGIN [SQL\SQLAdmins] FROM WINDOWS WITH DEFAULT_DATABASE = [master]

-- Login: WebAppAcct
CREATE LOGIN [WebAppAcct] WITH PASSWORD =
0x0200FB0844C8CE6803535BB339EC378F40AF5AD003D64EF3748D3568AE49CA2D3436C102B
5F7EA44729F6ED16D3CF16DF1F4BA74C6D47D0789AEF2915C6773B677E7FB0AC6DC HASHED,
    SID = 0x968A6D6212D4634D9CF7C3E10FFAEC84,
    DEFAULT_DATABASE = [master],
    CHECK_POLICY = ON,
    CHECK_EXPIRATION = ON
```

In the example output, you can see two types of logins—Windows login and SQL login. SQL logins use passwords, which are not provided in a clear text, but with hash values, and they also come with SID, which is important for login to user mapping in your user databases. In this way, database users will be correctly mapped to SQL Server loging once you bring the databases from the old server to the new one.

 Another option would be the use of the PowerShell, where you can find a module named dbatools at https://dbatools.io/download/ This PowerShell module is not default to SQL Server, but offers various interesting commands to use with your SQL Server not only for migration, but also for the common operation. The Export-DbaLogin command will generate similar output compared to the sp_help_revlogin stored procedure, but with a little bit more info and code control blocks.

For more complex projects you can use SQL Server data tools for Visual Studio, or data tools for short. Data tools provide you a development platform for your database and business intelligence development. The most important projects for data tools are:

- Integration services package project
- Analysis services projects
- Reporting Services report project

To transfer logins from one server to another you can use integration services package and use one of the tasks named **Transfer Login Task Editor**. This task offers simple configuration requiring:

- Source server
- Destination server
- Login list to migrate
- If to copy SIDs

Once you define the task parameters, you can run the package and it will copy the required logins from the old server to the new server as the following screenshot shows:

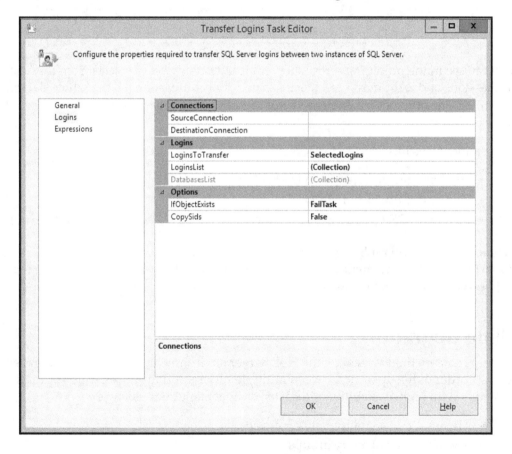

Using the SQL Server integration services can be very useful for larger scenarios, because there are more types of objects that can be transferred with the side-by-side upgrade path. As we mentioned earlier, there are more system-specific objects that you will need to copy from the old server to the new one and many of these can be handled by SQL Server SSIS, as can be seen from the following screenshot:

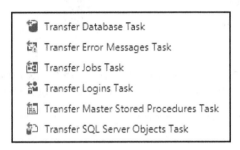

As you can see in the preceding screenshot, you can transfer many objects from the MSDB database—jobs and error messages, master stored procedures, or even the whole databases. Using SSIS is one of the possible methods for transfer the databases from the old server to the new one.

Other possible ways include:

- Restoring the database from the backup
- Using attach/detach methods
- Using any DR option—replication, mirroring, log shipping, availability groups

The choice of the option for bringing the database to the new server will be dependent on many factors and those are mainly the size of the database, the requirement to keep the new and old server in sync, and the availability of the storage.

Rolling upgrade

Rolling upgrade method is used on the SQL Server environment, where you need to keep the correct order of the upgrade between multiple servers and instances. This approach is used mainly with high availability or disaster recovery solutions, such as:

- Always-On availability failover cluster
- Always-On availability groups
- Mirroring

- Log shipping
- Replication

Rolling upgrade is also used with several services such as reporting Service if scale-out deployment for high availability and load balancing is used.

Upgrading the SQL Server if more servers are used for high availability and disaster recovery usually starts with the passive node of the installed solution. Depending on the solution, you will have to perform manual failover and then continue with the unupgraded node of the solution. The only part where SQL Server automatically determines if the failover should occur is the upgrade of the failover cluster. If more than a half of the nodes were upgraded to the new version, SQL Server will automatically failover the SQL services to an upgraded node.

 The full upgrade scenario for HA/DR solutions is out of the scope of this book and you can find more information at books online on the link `https://docs.microsoft.com/en-us/sql/database-engine/availability-groups/windows/upgrading-always-on-availability-group-replica-instances` for availability groups.

Pre-upgrade checks

Regardless of the chosen upgrade path, in-place or side-by-side, you need to check if your database can be upgraded to new version. SQL Server 2017 comes with a tool Data Migration Assistant that can be used to verify if there are any blockers to your upgrade and verify if all the databases don't include any features that would prevent the migration to the new SQL Server 2017.

Data Migration Assistant

Let's see what the **Data Migration Assistant** looks like:

The **Data Migration Assistant** has to be configured to connect to your SQL Server instance and you'll need to select the databases for evaluation. This evaluation will examine the objects in the databases, compatibility levels, and other parameters for the SQL Server 2017 and will produce a report for you.

Data Migration Assistant can be used to evaluate the migration towards:

- New SQL Server
- Azure SQL database
- Azure SQL Server on a VM

The discovered issues are split into several categories based on the impact of your application during the upgrade:

- Breaking changes
- Behavior changes
- Deprecated features

You can also use the **Discover New Features** option, which will evaluate the existing database and recommend new features based on the difference between the source SQL Server version and SQL Server 2017. These recommendations will be split into the following categories:

- Performance—InMemory OLTP and Columnstore Index
- Security—Always encrypted, transparent data encryption, dynamic data masking, and so on
- Storage

We can see what discover new features looks like:

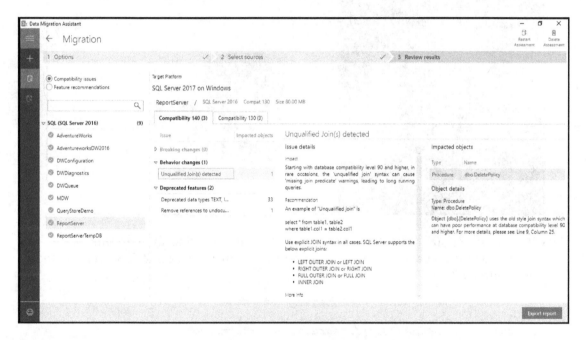

As you can see in the preceding screenshot, the evaluation of the existing databases was ok, but the **Data Migration Assistant** was able to detect several deprecated features and behavior changes, which you should carefully examine before you proceed with the upgrade. These can have performance, security, and stability impacts for your environment.

The **Data Migration Assistant** can be used not only to perform assessment, but also for the migration itself. In that case, you'll create a different type of project and you have to configure what databases and logins you would such as to migrate to the new environment, as seen in the following screenshot:

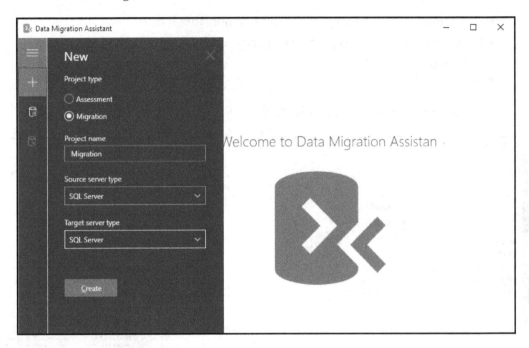

Data Migration Assistant can also be used from the command line, but currently, only assessment mode is available. To run the assessment against the local SQL Server, use the following command:

```
DmaCmd.exe /AssessmentName="MigrationAssessment"
/AssessmentDatabases="Server=SQL;Initial
Catalog=AdventureWorks2016;Integrated Security=true"
/AssessmentEvaluateCompatibilityIssues /AssessmentOverwriteResult
/AssessmentResultJson="C:\MigrationAssessments\AWReport.json"
```

This command will run the assessment with SQL Server named SQL for a database called AdventureWorks2016 and store the output in a local file.

SQL Server system configuration checker

The SQL Server setup uses the system configuration checker to perform basic checks if there are any blockers for your upgrade. You can either run the system configuration checker as a standalone task from the installation media, or it will run automatically as part of the SQL Server installation, once you install a new instance or upgrade the existing one.

The SQL server setup looks as follows:

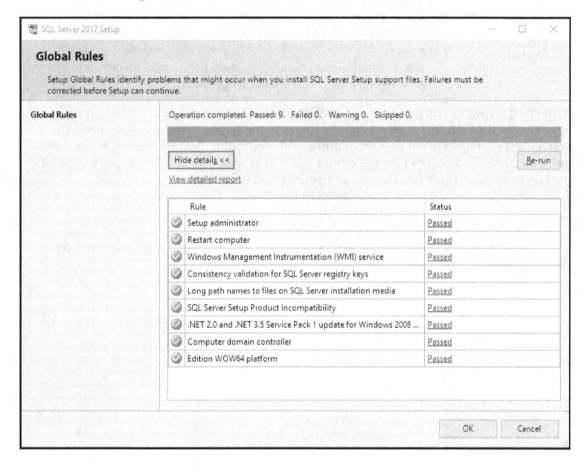

Performing the upgrade

Once you have finished the planning phase and all preparations it's time to perform the upgrade/migration of your SQL Server environment. For the scenario used in this chapter, we'll upgrade an existing SQL Server 2016 to SQL Server 2017. One thing you also need to carefully consider is the edition upgrade path, which you need to follow.

 We will be upgrading Enterprise Edition and the Edition will stay the same after the upgrade. You can, however, upgrade between editions. You can find the whole edition and version upgrade matrix on Microsoft's website at https://docs.microsoft.com/en-us/sql/database-engine/ install-windows/supported-version-and-edition-upgrades where you can see what versions and editions can be upgraded.

In the next steps, we will consider the in-place upgrade of the SQL Server first. Once we have started the SQL Server setup and the upgrade the setup program has to check the system and prerequisites so we can continue with upgrading the SQL Server. If you have more instances, you will be presented with a choice of which instance to upgrade. One of the choices is to upgrade just the shared features, and those include:

- SQL Server integration services
- Master data services
- SQL Server Management Studio (although SSMS is a separate download, it's still listed as a shared feature)

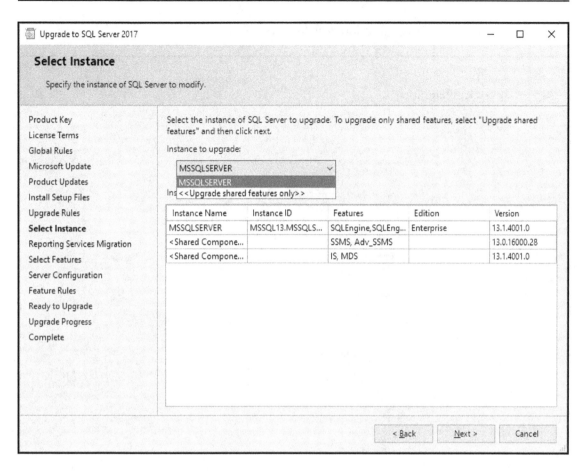

One of the services that were formerly included in SQL Server installation is now a separate download, and during the upgrade, it will be uninstalled. What you need to do is outlined in the setup window:

- Back up your report server databases
- Back up your report server encryption key
- Install new Reporting Services
- Migrate the reports

The **Reporting Services Migration** looks as follows:

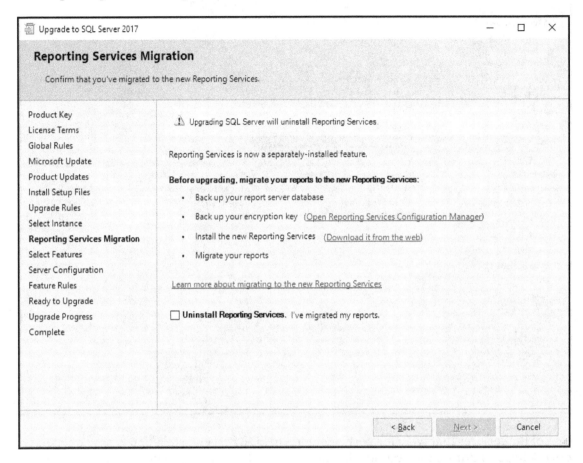

Once you go through all the remaining pages of the setup dialog, then the setup program will start the upgrade of your SQL Server. It's then just a measure of time, depending on the performance of your system and how long it will take to finish the upgrade. After the upgrade you need to verify the services and connectivity to your SQL Server. If all the services are running correctly and you can connect to the SQL Server, you need to also check all the applications using your SQL Server to verify that the upgrade went fine.

You can also check the `log` file, which is generated during the upgrade for any possible issues if any of the services do not upgrade correctly:

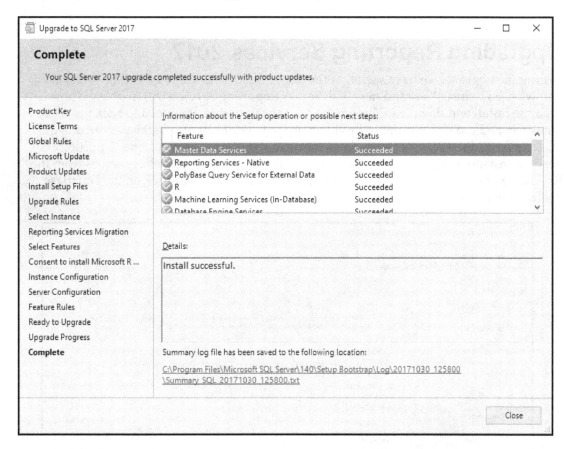

Once you start the Management Studio on the upgraded SQL it will check for the upgrade and let you install the latest version of the SQL Server Management Studio, which is now a separate tool from SQL Server installation.

To finish the upgrade, you will need to perform several additional steps:

- You need to check your maintenance plans and take backups of your databases
- You should check the integrity of the databases with the DBCC command
- Evaluate the compatibility level of the databases and raise to the highest level with performance checks in mind
- Install the latest updates that were not included in the installation media (cumulative updates)

- Rebuild indexes and update statistics
- Repopulate full-text catalogs

Upgrading Reporting Services 2017

During the upgrade, we have seen that the Reporting Services service will be uninstalled and we need to install a brand new SQL Server Reporting Services 2017, which is now a separate install and download. Before we can start with that, you need to back up your databases and the key in order to be able to migrate your reports. Databases are on your SQL Server and if you're not sure about the names, in the case of multiple Reporting Services instances, you can check the database server name and database names from the **Reporting Services Configuration Manager** tool, where you can click on the **Database** configuration page, as can be seen in the following screenshot:

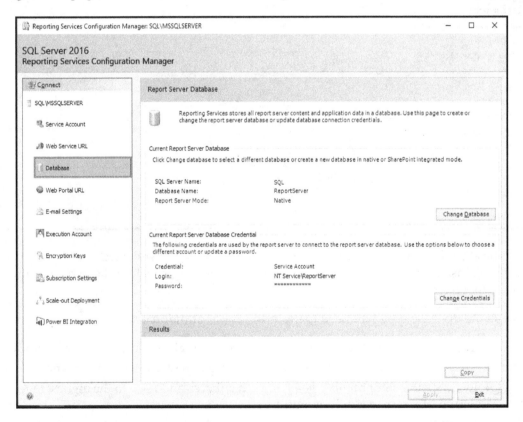

To back up the key, you need to switch to the **Encryption Keys** page of the configuration to find several buttons available to you. The most important one for us in this step is the **Backup** button, which is used to back up the key. This Reporting Services key is used to encrypt sensitive data in your datasets, connections, and subscriptions.

If this key is lost, you can wipe out all the sensitive info with the **Delete** button and all the connections will need to be reconfigured:

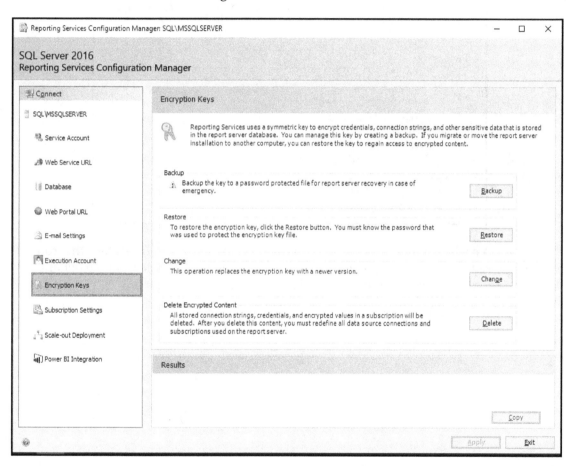

While you're performing the backup of the key, you need to provide the location where to store the key on the filesystem and also the password to protect the key.

You need to keep this password safe and available for the future restore of the key:

You can also use the command line to back up the key, to have a scheduled task that can back up the key on a regular basis. This command will back up the key from the default Reporting Services instance and protect the key with the value P@ssw0rd:

```
rskeymgmt -e -f c:\backup\ssrskey.snk -p P@ssw0rd
```

When you have the full backup of the databases and your keys, you can install your new **Install SQL Server Reporting Services**. The installation files are not present directly on SQL Server 2017 installation, but there's a link provided in the setup tool, which opens a web page where you can download the binaries needed to install the new Reporting Services:

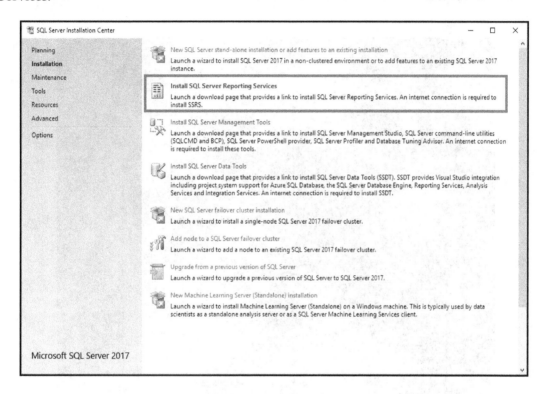

Once you start the installation, you'll be presented with several dialog choices. The first one is to **Install Reporting Services**. In the next one you need to select the edition that you're about to install. Developer, Express, and Evaluation don't require any serial number, but the remaining editions do. Once you select the location to install the Reporting Services, you can just hit the **Install** button, as shown in the following screenshot, and the installation will start:

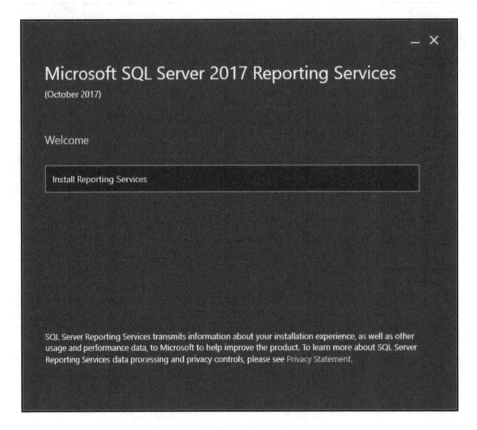

Once Reporting Services is installed, you need to perform the configuration of the server. Just hit the **Configure report server** button and the **Reporting Services Configuration Manager** tool will open, similar to the one where we did performed the key backup. This time it's a version for SQL Server 2017.

For the configuration we will focus only on key aspects needed for successful upgrade, and not the full Reporting Services configuration:

You need to configure the following items in Reporting Services:

- **Web Service URL**
- **Web Portal URL**
- **Database**
- **Encryption Keys**

We have backed up the databases on the old system, so you need to restore the backups to your new SQL Server. When you configure the databases you will use the **Change Database** button to open up a dialog to attach existing databases from your SQL Server.

You need to select the correct database name to attach:

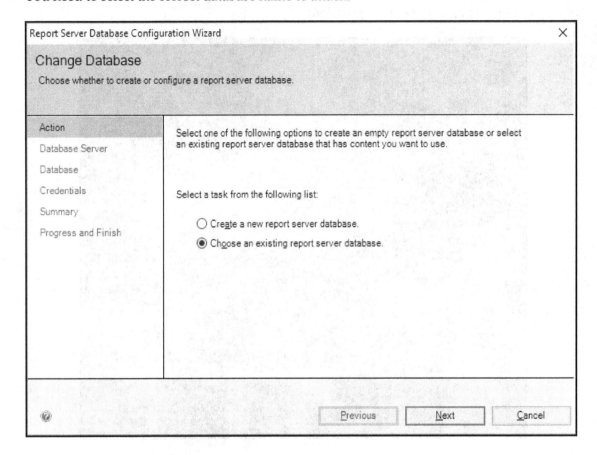

Once we have the database available, you need to configure two URLs used for Web Service and Web Portal. If you don't want to make any customization to the configuration, you can navigate to the correct pages in the **Reporting Services Configuration Manager** and just hit the **Apply** button on those two configuration pages—**Web Service URL** and **Web Portal URL**, as seen in the following screenshot:

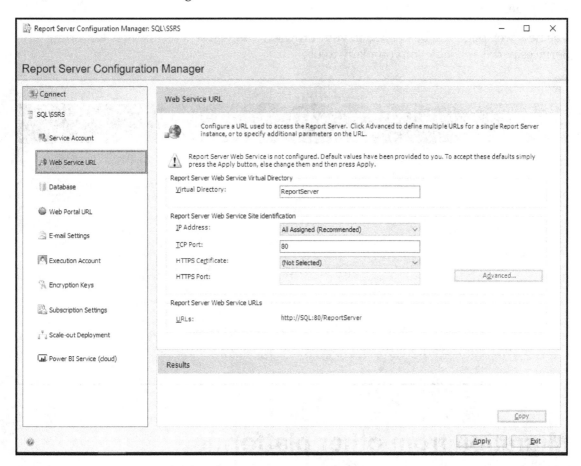

If both URLs have been configured the last item remaining is to restore the key from the backup. I hope you have the password available, since you'll need to provide the password used during the backup of the key. On the **Encryption Keys** page, you can use the **Restore** button and provide the file with the key and password. If all these items were configured you can navigate to the URL of the web portal, which you can find on the **Web Portal URL** page.

The new web page will be opened in your browser, and you will see the new Reporting Services portal available for you ready to use:

Migration from other platforms

SQL Server migration projects don't necessarily include only SQL Server as a primary data source, but there are many other platforms where you may choose to upgrade to SQL Server. You can use **SQL Server Migration Assistant** (**SSMA**), which is available for several DMBS systems:

- SSMA for access
- SSMA for DB2
- SSMA for Oracle

- SSMA for SAP ASE
- SSMA for MySQL

SSMA is able to create a project for a number of target versions of SQL Server, where SQL Server 2017 is included with both platforms—Linux and Windows operating systems. The other targets available are:

- SQL Server 2008/2008 R2
- SQL Server 2012
- SQL Server 2014
- SQL Server 2016
- SQL Server 2017 Windows/Linux
- Azure SQL database
- Azure SQL Data Warehouse

If you would like to use the tool for the migration, you need to have drivers for correct DBMS systems in place. For access migration, you need Microsoft access runtime, which you can download from Microsoft's website. The tool can open the download link for you:

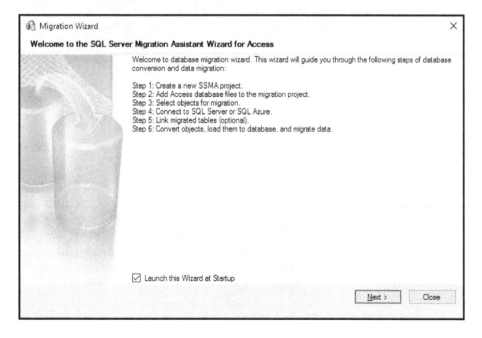

There's a lot of planning and testing required for platform migration due to type conversions, query differences, performance objects, and many other possible issues. SSMA can be a useful start for such analysis, where you can evaluate possible migration blockers and start resolving them one by one.

Migration example from MS Access

We can use SSMA for MS Access to convert data stored in the `Access` database to the SQL Server. And there are several possible options for us. With SSMA you can evaluate all existing objects in the `Access` database, configure the type mapping between SQL Server and Microsoft Access, and migrate the content of the `Access` to a new SQL Server database:

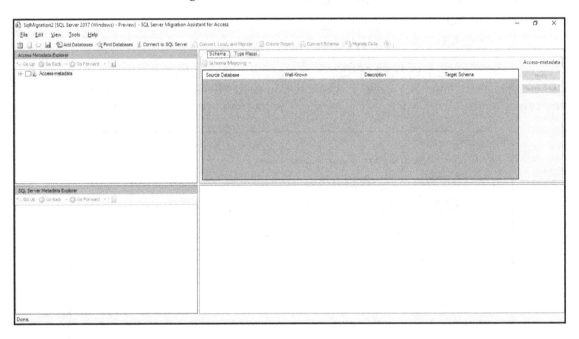

To open the `Access` database you can use the **Add Database** button to open the Access database file and to explore existing objects - tables, views, queries, and so on. To connect to your SQL Server use the **Connect to SQL Server** button, where you need to enter your instance name and database name, where you will import the data:

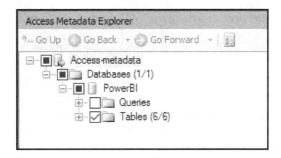

Once you have connected to all the systems, you can evaluate the data and use any of the possible tasks:

- Convert, load, and migrate
- Create report
- Convert schema
- Migrate data

With `Access` you have an option to use linked tables, which will allow your application to connect to `Access`, and the data will be already stored in SQL Server when you finish all the migration steps, including the configuration of the application connection information.

Summary

Upgrade and migration are important phases in the SQL Server operation lifecycle. Each path has its own advantages and disadvantages. As we went through the chapter, you saw that careful planning of such a task is crucial, since there are numerous considerations for the new platform.

In-place upgrade offers you the option to utilize the current hardware of the virtual environment, allowing you to quickly upgrade your SQL Server to new versions. However, this option has more complex rollback if your upgrade fails. With side-by-side migration, you can really use the benefits of the new hardware platform, modern CPUs, and the latest operating system, which will allow you to build the SQL Server again and then you just need to migrate the data between the old and new SQL Server. There are again numerous options for you, where the most common would be backup and attach/detach methods. There are many tools that can be used to plan the upgrade—especially SQL Server Data Migration Assistant and SSMA.

SSMA is used to migrate not only to the latest SQL Server 2017, but also to older SQL Server platforms and Azure SQL database, since this tool is used for migration from other supported DBMS systems.

In the following chapter, we will explore SQL Server automation capabilities. Automation is very important today since the size of environments we manage is growing and you may like to eliminate the manual steps in the repeated tasks. These components for automation can also be used for SQL Server monitoring, so we'll explore the alerting system and other monitoring capabilities of SQL Server.

9
Automation - Using Tools to Manage and Monitor SQL Server 2017

A lot of administrator tasks are executed in a regular manner and it's inconceivable to run these tasks manually. SQL Server offers a dedicated service called SQL Server Agent helping us automate many common tasks. Along with this service, a very helpful tool called **maintenance plan** was developed to support regular tasks that should be run against each database.

In this chapter, we will cover the following topics:

- **Using SQL Server Agent**: We need to know what SQL Server Agent is and how to set up this service from reliability and security perspectives; we also want to be informed when things are going wrong, which means the need of database mail setup as well
- **Maintenance plans**: This powerful tool helps administrators when they are considering which tasks are needed to maintain healthy databases protected against data loss and performance degradation; a relatively simple wizard covers very complicated tasks
- **SQL Server Agent objects**: SQL Server Agent holds definitions for jobs, operators, and alerts; we will see the benefit of their usage and how to create them

Using SQL Server Agent

SQL Server Agent is a **Windows service** serving mainly as a provider for the **automation of regular tasks**. Tasks that can be automated are not only administrative ones, but also other tasks supporting the operation of information systems. For example, data movements like ETL processes, migration tasks, integration package runs, and so on and so forth. Having SQL Server Agent running for all time is also a prerequisite for some features offered by other SQL Server services, for example, data collection or reporting services unattended report executions or subscriptions.

SQL Server Agent service is installed within the SQL Server setup without an option to skip its installation. Actually, every edition except Express Edition of SQL Server has SQL Server Agent installed.

When we want to start using SQL Server Agent, we need to perform several simple tasks described in following sections.

SQL Server Agent service setup

First setup task is to check service startup mode of SQL Server Agent after installation. The check is done in **Sql Server Configuration Manager**. The procedure is very simple and it's described step by step with images showing what to find and where to find it:

1. Start **Sql Server Configuration Manager** and, in the left pane, click on **SQL Server Services**.
2. In the right pane, a list of services already installed appears, as shown in the following screenshot:

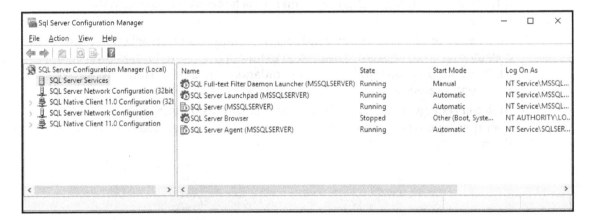

3. In the right pane, right-click on the **SQL Server Agent** row (instance name--**SQL Server (MSSQLSERVER)** in our screenshot) and select **Properties**. Modal dialog (depicted in the following screenshot) is opened and we will go through it:

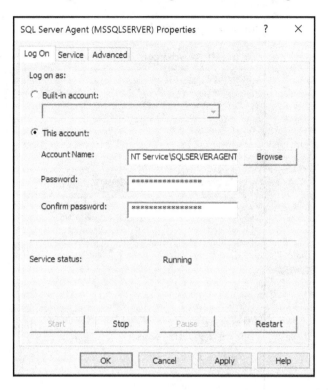

4. In the **Log On** tab, we can change the service login and password. The choice of the right login depends on several factors and will be described after this procedure description.

5. The most important tab is the second tab with the caption, **Service**. In this tab, we must ensure that SQL Server Agent has **Automatic** start mode set. If not, just switch the option to automatic:

6. When this setting is checked, click on **OK** and close **Sql Server Configuration Manager**.

The security context of SQL Server Agent is crucial for the correct execution of all jobs. The best service accounts recommended by Microsoft are managed service accounts for domain environment or virtual service accounts for infrastructure without a domain.

As a second choice, we could use a regular domain account with start as a service permission, but we must consider the group policy object and the possible need of a regular password change.

The account that is used should not have any elevated permissions. When set during installation, SQL Server setup sets necessary permissions on it; otherwise, we could suffer problems with SQL Server Agent running. More about security is provided in `Chapter 4`, *Securing Your SQL Server*.

Setting up SQL Server Agent Properties

Next, setup tasks are done in Management Studio in the **Properties** window of SQL Server Agent service:

1. Open Management Studio and connect to the SQL Server instance.
2. In object explorer is a node called **SQL Server Agent**. Right-click on it and choose **Properties**:

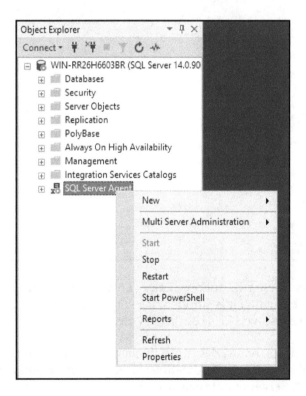

3. The **Properties** window will be opened and we have to check several options. When the **Properties** window is open, we can go through six pages. In the first page called **General**, we should switch on checkboxes as it's shown on following image:

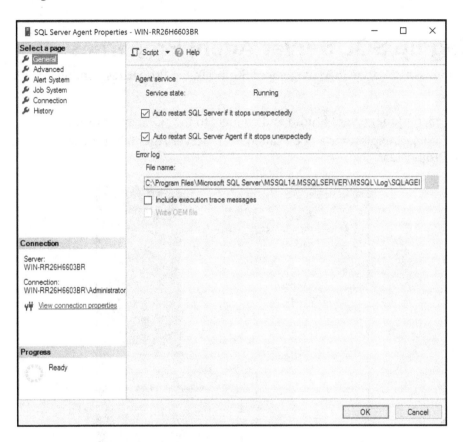

4. Switching on these two options mainly ensures that SQL Server Agent will attempt to start when it is stopped. It's very rarely noticed but formerly SQL Server Agent resolved jobs conflicts by restarting itself.

The second page contains **Advanced** settings. In fact, advanced settings has two independent parts. The upper part is sometimes used for centralized management of SQL Servers. It's called **SQL Server event forwarding**.

Event forwarding is a feature providing ability to forward error messages from certain SQL Server instances to another server to establish a central point of diagnostics. A positive of this feature is the ability to make one clear and comfortable place for SQL Server management, but as a concern we must consider a moment when the central server collecting error log data is inaccessible. Jobs and other tasks will not be affected by the inaccessibility, however.

The lower part of **Advanced** SQL Server Agent settings is used to determine what it means when SQL Server's CPUs are idle. As seen in the following screenshot, by default CPU is idle when it comes below 10 percent of effort for at least 10 minutes. However, we can adjust these settings as needed. For example, when some concurrent service runs on the same server and we know that CPU's effort never goes under 20 percent. The **Define idle CPU condition** needs to be switched on checkbox first and then we can adjust the rest of the settings. The **Advanced** page is shown in the following screenshot:

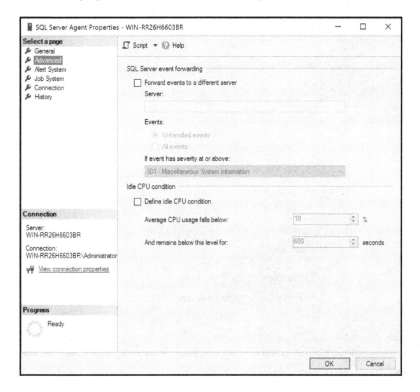

The next **Alert System** page in the **SQL Server Agent Properties** window is seen in the next screenshot. It has more parts but for common administration, just the two parts marked in red are important. The big part in the middle of the window is obsolete as pagers are used less and less:

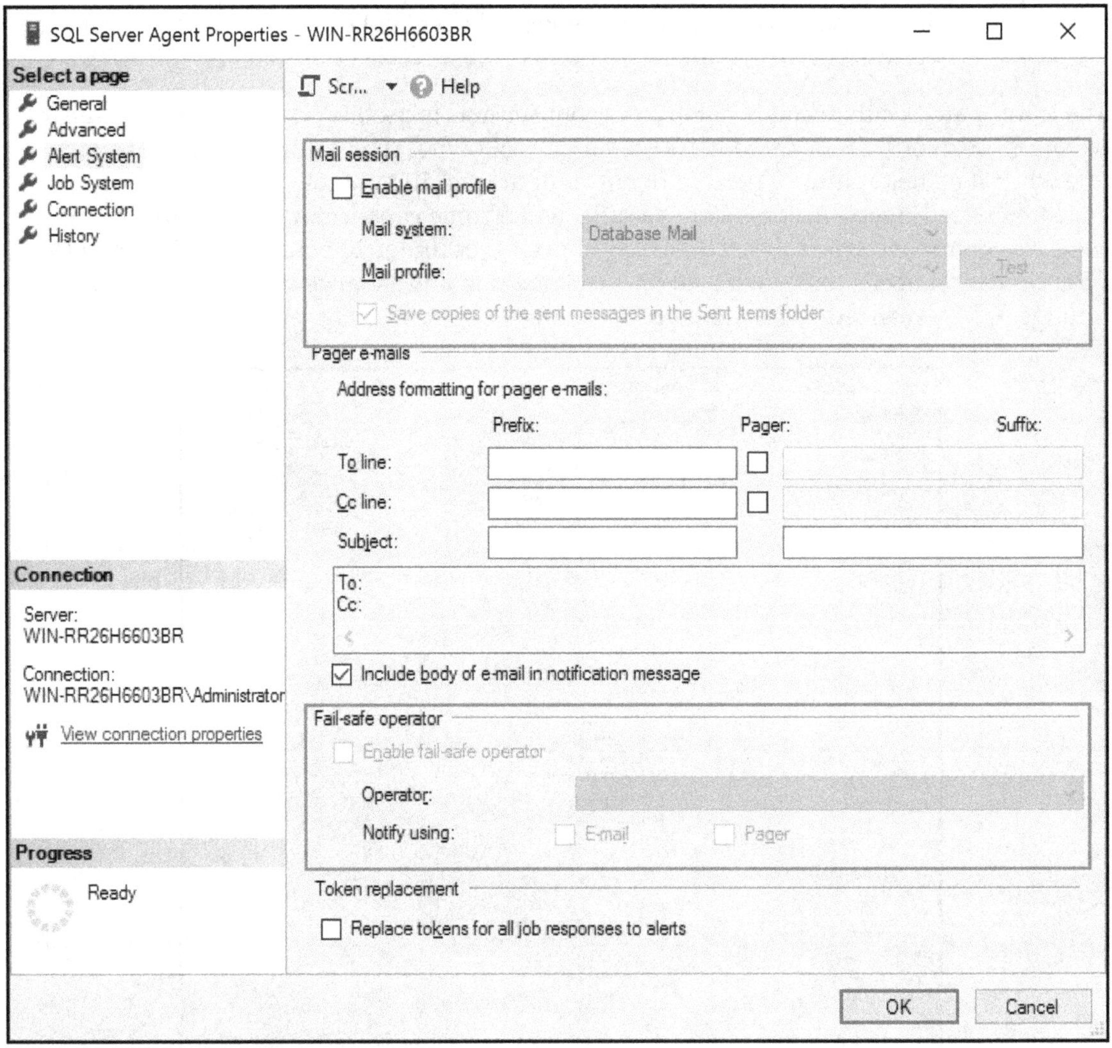

It's highly useful and also recommended to use an alerting system. It greatly helps administrators to stay informed about everything that might happen on SQL Server (for example, more serious errors, failed jobs, and so on). For the correct settings of the alert system, we need to configure the **Database mail** profile for SQL Server Agent first, which will be described in the next section. When the **Database mail** profile has been created, it should be used in the first setting of the preceding screen. The **Enable mail profile** checkbox is enabled, the **Mail system** drop-down is filled with the **Database mail** value (it's now the only possible value; the second value called **SQL Mail** was marked as deprecated several versions of SQL Server ago and now it's gone), and if some **Mail profile** were already configured, their names appear in the drop-down called **Mail profile**.

The second red box is about **Fail-safe operator**. The fail-safe operator is a regular operator defined on SQL Server Agent (see *Operators* section) but it has one extra behavior. When SQL Server Agent is started, the **Fail-safe operator** definition is cached to be ready in case the regular operator is not accessible, for example, due to some serious problem with the msdb database. To set the **Fail-safe operator**, the first step is to create a regular operator. Then, when the **Enable fail-safe operator** checkbox is switched on, operator names are seen in the **Operator** drop-down.

The last interesting tab in the **SQL Server Agent Properties** window is the tab to set job history retention. Every step of every job writes its result in the msdb database. The history table has, by default, a maximum of 1000 records in total, and a maximum of 100 records per job. When the 1000 limit is reached, maximum records per job is reduced.

This default setting can be changed, as shown in the following screenshot (the screenshot shows default values):

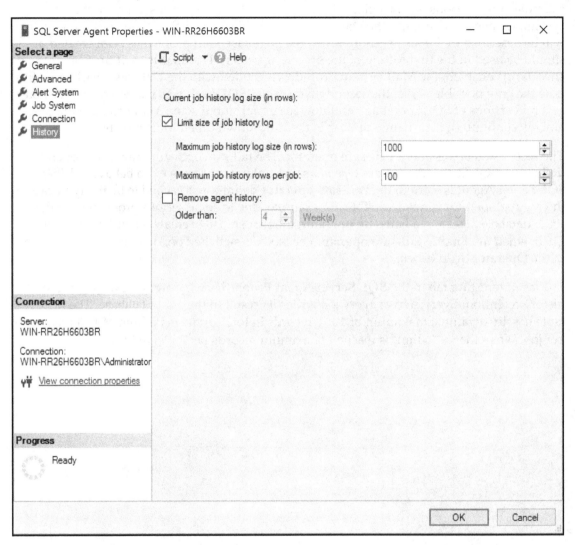

If both checkboxes are turned off, history will last in the `msdb` database up to its limit. We can also keep history measured by the amount of rows. A relatively new but very useful option is to turn off the **Limit size of job history log** checkbox but switch on **Remove agent history** and set up the time limit. By default, the retention period is four weeks. It's quite enough because it covers histories for a month of regular automation.

Database mail setup

`Database Mail` is a component of SQL Server providing email features for any desired task. The main purpose is to be informed by SQL Server or SQL Server Agent when anything happens that needs the administrator's attention. When the `Database Mail` is set up, administrators could be notified in a form of email when job fails, alert occurs, and so on:

1. To set up as well as make changes to `Database Mail` configuration, a wizard incorporated into Management Studio is used. This section is a walk-through of this wizard. It is accessible from Management Studio, node `Management`, as shown in the following image:

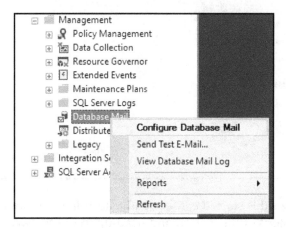

2. When the **Configure Database Mail** option is chosen, the wizard starts and guides us through the configuration process.

3. The first step after the welcome page is a signpost for what to do next. When the wizard is running for the first time, the first option is selected as follows:

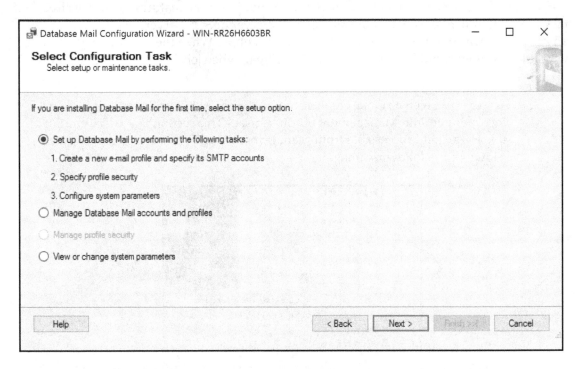

When the wizard is started consequently, additional options on the first step just skip several steps of the wizard and head up to the step with the desired part of settings. During the first pass, we will visit all of them.

4. When the **Next** button is clicked during the first pass through the wizard, a question **The Database Mail feature is not available**. **Would you like to enable this feature?** Will appear. This is because `Database Mail` is one of the features disabled on the instance level by default and, answering **Yes** to this question, email configuration can continue. Maybe the feature was enabled previously by calling `exec sp_configure 'Database Mail XPs', 1` for some reason. Then the question in the wizard will not be shown.

`Database Mail` uses profiles. Profile is a secure container for one or more SMTP accounts. When `Database Mail` is used for more purposes than for SQL Server Agent emailing, it's a good practice to create separated `Database Mail` profiles for such tasks due to security isolation. More email accounts assigned to one profile provide an enhanced level of reliability.

5. When the first email account in a certain profile does not work for any reason, the second email account is used for repetitive attempts to send emails and so on. In the wizard's step shown in the following image, profile is named and some SMTP accounts are created:

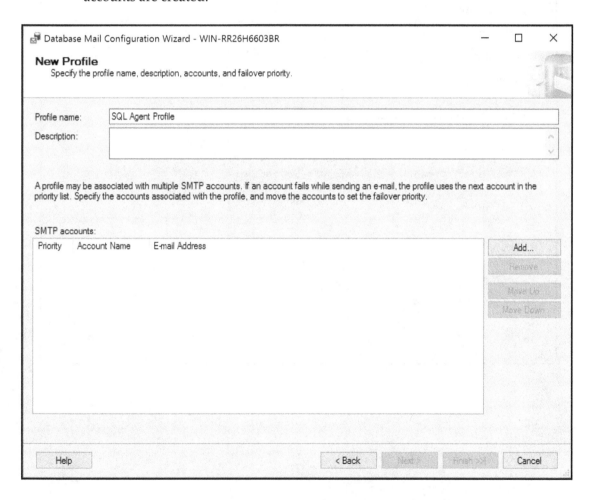

6. The **Profile name** should be filled by any descriptive name (the **SQL Agent Profile** value is written as an example, it's not a default). Then click on the **Add** button and a dialog window appears for valid SMTP configuration:

As seen in the preceding image, SMTP account settings are quite simple, it's very similar to email settings in any other email client. Which fields will be filled with values depends on the actual email server used. Let's go through mandatory fields and options:

- **Account name**: Any descriptive name of an account (for example, *mydomain.com agent email*)
- **E-mail address**: Email address used within this profile as a sender's address (for example, *agent@mydomain.com*)
- **Server name**: Valid name of SMTP server (for example, *smtp.mydomain.com*)
- **This server requires a secure connection (SSL)**: If needed, communication could be secured
- **Port number**: Often TCP port 25 or, if SSL is used, 995
- Authentication options:
    - Windows account
    - Basic authentication (user and password checked by the email server itself)
    - Anonymous access

After adding all the required information to the email account settings dialog, click on **OK**. If needed, additional accounts could be added in the same way. When more accounts are defined, they can be prioritized by clicking on the **Move up** and **Move down** buttons the wizard's step. When email profile and its account's definition is done, we can continue to the next step, which is used to define profile security.

Every profile could be a public or private profile. When the profile is private, it's set for the SQL Server's principal that the profile serves. When the profile is public, every user who has sufficient permissions can send an email by a procedure `sp_send_dbmail` stored in the `msdb` database. When a profile is signed as a default profile, it's used when no explicit profile name is defined as a parameter of the `sp_send_dbmail` procedure.

The wizard's step with profile settings is shown in the following image:

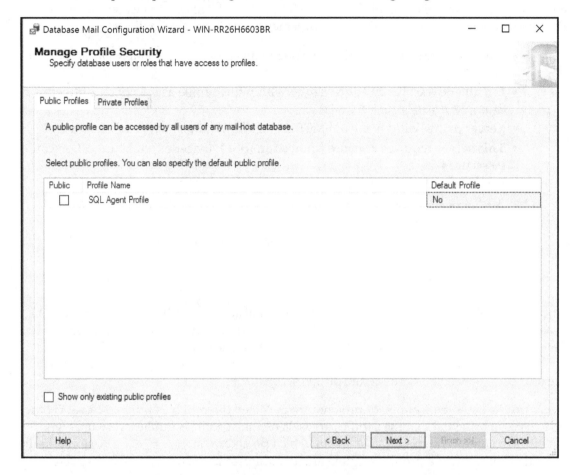

The next and almost last step in the **Database Mail Configuration Wizard** is used to set system parameters. System parameters are common parameters of Database Mail and contain these options:

- **Account retry attempts**: How many times SQL Server tries to send an email when the sending is failed. Default value is 1.
- **Account retry delay** (seconds): How long time SQL Server waits before it tries to send an email again (only more than one retry attempt is set). Default value is 60 seconds.

- **Maximum file size** (bytes): It's not so usual when using `Database Mail` for SQL Server Agent, but in some user mailing scenarios, attachment can be a part of the sent email. This setting restricts maximum attachment size. Default value is 1,000,000 bytes.

- **Prohibited attachment file extensions**: This setting restricts file extensions for attachments. Default values are `.exe`, `.vbs`, `.dll`, `.js`, but could be enhanced by other potentially dangerous extensions such as `.com`, `.bat`, `.ps1`, and so on.

- **Database mail executable minimum lifetime** (seconds): When the first email is sent to queue, the service is started. This setting says how long it will be running (potentially in idle state) before it sleeps. The default value is 600 seconds.

- **Logging level**: This setting says how many messages will be written to the `msdb` database. Default value is **Extended** (errors and warnings are captured), but it can be changed to **Normal** (errors only) or **Verbose** (errors, warnings, and information messages).

A very common practice is that listed settings stay unchanged.

When the wizard is finished, the first email profile is created and we can run the wizard more times to add profiles, or reconfigure existing ones as well as reconfigure all other settings. When the profile intended to email from SQL Server Agent is created, we can go back to the **SQL Server Agent Properties** window and set the `Database Mail` profile as it was described in `Chapter 4`, *Setting up SQL Server Agent properties*.

Now when Database Mail is configured correctly, we can start to set up automation of our regular tasks. In the next section, we will find a very good starting point for automated administration.

Sending emails from SQL Server

To test our `Database Mail` definition or for any user purposes, we can send emails directly from SQL Server using a stored procedure, `sp_send_dbmail`. This procedure is defined in the `msdb` database. The procedure has many parameters, but for basic needs, we can list these:

- `@profile_name`: If not set, default public profile is used to send an email.
- `@recipients`: A list of email addresses (separated by a semicolon (`;`)).
- `@subject`: Some text as in a regular email.
- `@body`: Some text, it's the same as when writing any email.

- @query: Any query returning a result set (for example, SELECT statement). The result of the query will be sent to recipients.

An important question is who is authorized to call the procedure? Administrators, however, are authorized for this, but when we need to authorize regular users without administrator privileges, SQL Server prepares a special database role called **DatabaseMailUserRole** to the msdb database. Users added to this role have permissions to call the procedure.

Let's explore the calling itself:

```
exec msdb..sp_send_dbmail
  @recipients = 'administrator@example.com'
  , @subject = 'Test'
  , @body = 'Hello world'
```

The first thing that we have to consider is that even if the procedure has the sp_ prefix, it's not defined in the master database but in the msdb database; hence, we need to add a database prefix, as seen in the preceding script. Our call used the default public mail profile so the @profile_name parameter is not needed. The rest of the script is obvious and self-descriptive.

What's the result of the execution? It's a message, Mail (Id: 2) queued. It says that the send operation itself is executed asynchronously and doesn't affect the user's waiting for the actual result of the send attempt. If we want to see the result of the sending itself, we can go to the sysmail_sentitems and sysmail_faileditems tables respectively:

```
select * from msdb..sysmail_sentitems
select * from msdb..sysmail_faileditems
```

These two simple SELECT statements show all items queued on user requests and also errors that occurred during email delivery. Both tables have the same column called mailitem_id as a joining key. There are more tables with the sysmail_ prefix in the msdb database but, for testing purposes, the two listed here are sufficient.

The last thing that we have to consider is mail retention policy. As common email clients such as Outlook do not remove emails automatically, the same is with Database Mail. We can find a stored procedure called sysmail_delete_mailitems_sp in the msdb database with the @sent_before parameter and an optional parameter, @sent_status.

We can plan job running, for example, once a week to delete old messages. Example script for this action could look like this:

```
declare @newestDate date = dateadd(week, -4, getdate())
exec msdb..[sysmail_delete_mailitems_sp] @sent_before = @newestDate
```

The preceding script computes the date four weeks before, saves the result into a variable called @newestDate, and then the variable is used as a parameter for the stored procedure. If needed, this code could be copy-pasted as a job definition and used as is.

Maintenance plans

For DBAs who are not so familiar with SQL Server, the best starting point is a tool called **Maintenance Plan**. We can think of the tool as a set of typical regular tasks that should be executed on every database hosted on our SQL Server instance. The Maintenance plan itself can be created manually using **Maintenance plan designer** or **Maintenance plan wizard**, which is very good for our assurance that all the basic tasks needed to keep our database healthy are not missed.

Maintenance plans allow you to create one big sequence of many tasks scheduled together, but it is not desirable for most scenarios. For example, planning full backup and transaction log backups to be executed at the same time makes no sense. That's why a more common approach is to create one maintenance plan divided into **subplans**--units of work containing fewer tasks grouped together by their meaning. Subplans also have separate schedules.

The focus of the next two sections will be as follows:

- Creating a maintenance plan prototype using the maintenance plan wizard
- Editing the prototype using the maintenance plan designer

Maintenance plan wizard

Creation and maintenance of maintenance plans is fully covered in Management Studio. Object explorer in Management Studio contains node **Management** and under this node is subnode called **Maintenance Plans**. This is the point where all previously created maintenance plans are saved and can be edited or executed. For diagnostic purposes also maintenance plan histories are enabled here.

The **Maintenance Plan wizard** to create a new plan is started from the object explorer window in Management Studio, as shown in the following image:

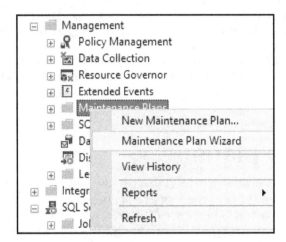

When the wizard is started and the welcome screen is skipped, the first meaningful step appears. In this step, we need to decide the following:

- **Name of the plan**: Some meaningful name, for example, database name daily maintenance
- **Run as**: The user context under which the plan will run
- **Schedule distribution**: This option leads to resolution if every task has its own schedule or the entire plan will be executed at once:
    - Separate schedules for each task
    - Single schedule for the entire plan or no schedule
- **Schedule settings**: When separate schedules are chosen in the previous option, this setting is disabled because a schedule will be set within every task chosen later during the wizard

The first step is seen in the following image:

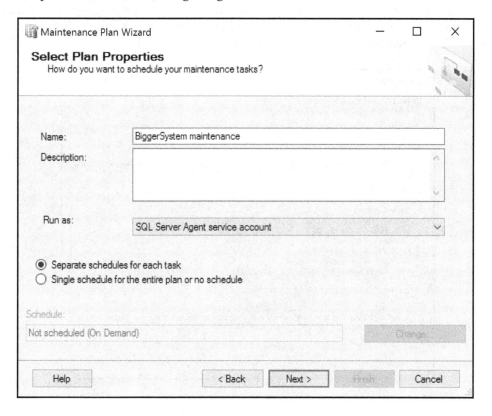

The second step of the wizard contains a list with all typical tasks that need to be executed regularly against every database. This is probably the most important step because this is the point where the DBA will be aware of everything important. The wizard step is shown in the following image and we will explain every task type briefly:

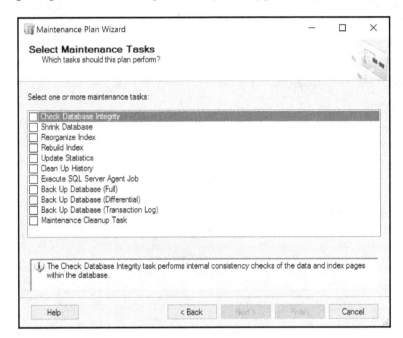

Check database integrity

This task uses the `DBCC CHECKDB()` function. The DBCC shortcut means database consistency checker. There are more DBCC functions on SQL Server, for example, `DBCC SHOW_STATISTICS()` to explore index or column statistics, `DBCC SHRINKFILE()` to return free space from database file back to the operating system, and so on. The `DBCC CHECKDB()` function checks consistency and readability of the database from three perspectives calling three other DBCCs:

- `DBCC CHECKTABLE()`: This function tests the readability of table data pages
- `DBCC CHECKCATALOG()`: This function tests the readability of metadata objects
- `DBCC CHECKALLOC()`: This function tests the logical consistency of allocation units

The DBCC CHECKDB() function can find inconsistent places in the database. When such a situation occurs, an error is raised and the task is failed due to the error. The error could be then seen in the maintenance plan history. When DBCC CHECKDB() fails, DBA needs to immediately resolve the problem from backup. If no suitable backup is available, there is a last and only action possible, but data loss is highly probable. DBCC CHECKDB() has two options to resolve inconsistencies. The first is shown in the following script:

```
DBCC CHECKDB(<database_name>, REPAIR_REBUILD)
```

This option tries to repair inconsistent data pages, but if they are seriously broken, SQL Server cannot repair lost data.

The second option is to call a more aggressive variant:

```
DBCC CHECKDB(<database_name>, REPAIR_ALLOW_DATA_LOSS)
```

When using this option, corrupted data pages are removed from the database forever. Hence, the robust backup strategy is strongly preferred.

Shrink database

This task serves to return free space in data files back to the filesystem. Internally, this task is executed as the DBCC SHRINKDATABASE() function. In production, this task is almost useless because when the database has some free space, it's better for performance and less growth operations occur.

 The only situation to use the Shrink database task is when some bigger data was loaded once to some staging tables to the database, then the data was processed to final structures, and staging tables were dropped. Maybe then the shrink would be executed. However, we can say that everyday shrinking is useless and a disk-intensive operation that should be used rarely.

Reorganize index

Data stored in the database tables is changing by inserting new records as well as updating or deleting existing ones. It leads to a situation when data pages are not full and also not in logical order within extents. We can talk about internal (data pages not full) and external (data pages in extents not in logical order) fragmentation. This state of data leads to decreased performance time over time.

IO controller has its throughput. In a given amount of time, some finite number of data pages could be transferred through the controller. In an optimized case, every data page will be almost full of records, but when internally fragmented, the same amount of data pages will bring much fewer records.

In an ideal situations, index pages containing table or index data are ordered as a double-linked list. When SQL Server scans those data pages, it can be brought in logical order adjusted with the physical order on disk. When external fragmentation occurs, SQL Server is forced to skip back and forth between data pages to follow pointers from one data page to another, because logical order differs from physical order of data pages.

As examples show, it's very important for performance reasons to maintain indexes as well as heaps in a somewhat defragmented state.

The index reorganization compacts just leaf-level on indexes. It's not a long-running process and issues fewer locks, that's why it's more suitable for day-to-day maintenance. The Reorganize index task calls the following statement for every chosen index or table:

```
ALTER INDEX index_name ON table_name WITH REORGANIZE
```

Rebuild index

As described in the previous section, fragmentation causes more data handling and it can lead to degradation of the performance. When fragmentation occurs heavily (typically on more indexed tables with big data contention), we need to rebuild entire index(es) on such tables. When comparing REBUILD with REORGANIZE, we have to consider more effort needed for index rebuild. When SQL Server is not the Enterprise edition, exclusive table locks are issued when rebuilding an index.

The statement executed internally by the Rebuild index task is as follows:

```
ALTER INDEX index_name ON table_name WITH REBUILD
```

Rebuilding is also possible on heaps. Then the statement looks like this:

```
ALTER TABLE some_table_without_clustered_index WITH REBUILD
```

Update statistics

For every index and for some columns, statistics are created automatically or manually. Statistics provide a very important description of data density and distribution for SQL Server's cardinality estimation when optimizing and compiling queries. Statistics, unlike indexes, are not refreshed within every query-modified data. That's why statistics are going out of date, even if SQL Server has an auto-update statistics feature. To maintain up to date statistics is the DBA's responsibility. The simplest way to reach it is to use the update statistics task in the maintenance plan. This task calls two different statements depending on its setting. When update all statistics is set, system stored procedure sp_updatestats is executed. If statistics (or objects) are selected during task configuration, the following statement is called for every selected object:

```
UPDATE STATISTICS statistics_name
```

 When rebuilding index, SQL Server drops and recreates the index entirely. So statistics are recreated and their update makes no sense in this case.

Clean up history

Clean up history is quite a straightforward task. It just deletes records from historical tables in the msdb database. Histories are cleansed, for example, from backup and restore history, maintenance plan history, and so on.

Execute SQL Server Agent job

This task is an empty task prepared to execute manually prepared jobs that cannot be known by SQL Server as a regular administrative task. For example, some ETL processes or refreshing of some test database from production database backup can be used here.

Backup tasks

Backup tasks in maintenance plans cover full, differential and transaction log backup types. All these tasks are described in detail in Chapter 3, *Backup and Recovery*. Let's remember that various scenarios combining different types of backup operations can be established. These backup tasks in maintenance plans are a typical example of the need for several subplans in one plan.

Maintenance cleanup task

This task clears all files created during the execution of a maintenance plan.

All right, now we know which tasks we have to execute regularly; but what about their combination?

As an example, for some OLTP database, we can create combinations given in the following table:

Subplan	Frequency	Task
subplan_1	Weekly, off hours (for example, Sunday)	Check database integrity Backup database (full) Clean up history
subplan_2	Weekly, off hours (for example, Wednesday)	Reorganize index Update statistics
subplan_3	Hourly	Backup database (log)

As mentioned at the start of this section, the wizard is a very good starting point for working with maintenance plans. When executed, a maintenance plan is saved and can be edited later by the designer. The manual work will be described in the next section.

Maintenance plan designer

The maintenance plan wizard hides one very interesting thing: maintenance plan definition is actually a kind of Integration Services package. Creation of a new plan is available as well as the edit feature for existing ones.

The main surface is depicted in the following image and we will go over almost every control to describe how to work with it:

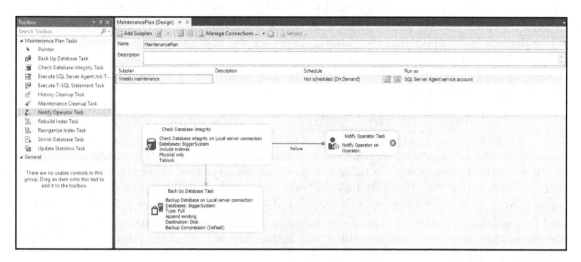

As seen in the preceding image, we can divide the designer into three main components:

- **Toolbox**: The left dockable window with tasks which are selected and moved into the designer's surface
- **Designer header**: The upper part of the designer for subplans and their schedule definition
- **Surface**: The graphical part containing icons of certain tasks joined by arrows

Every maintenance plan has at least one subplan. Every subplan contains a set of tasks that could be executed sequentially or in parallel.

An administrator's first task in the designer is to create proper subplans and define their schedules. A new subplan is created by clicking on the **Add subplan** button. A new subplan is added to the list of subplans. Sorting of subplans in the list does not matter because every subplan has its own schedule. Subplan can be empty but that is not so useful. So we need to add some tasks to it.

The administrator's second task is to define the subplan's content. It's necessary to select the subplan that we want to edit in the list of subplans. Certain tasks are then painted into the surface from the toolbox. If the toolbox is not visible, we can call the **Toolbox** option from the **View** menu in Management Studio (*Ctrl+Atl-X* also exists, but do we remember it?). When the task is dropped onto the surface, it needs some configuration according to its purpose. When the task is not properly configured, a big red sign is visible on it (in the preceding image, we can see it in the notify operator task). Task properties are available by double-clicking on the task.

Tasks need to be executed in some logical order. That's why we can see a green arrow hanging from every task. The arrow is called **precedence constraint**. We have to connect tasks by the arrows. It can be reached when we click the arrow using the mouse and pull it to the next task. Colors of arrows matter. A green arrow says that the next task will be executed only when the preceding task will end with success. Red color says that the consequential task will be executed when its predecessor fails, and black color says that the next task will be executed no matter how its predecessor finishes. To change the precedence constraint's behavior, we have to right-click a certain arrow and, in the popup menu, select the **Success**, **Failure**, or **Completion** option.

The last task is to create the subplan's schedules. It can be reached by clicking on the **calendar** button in the **Schedule** column in the subplan list. A very intuitive dialog appears and we can select the most appropriate time interval to execute the subplan.

When using maintenance plans, a big advantage is that all the basic regular maintenance operations are encapsulated in one big and very well-arranged object and we don't need to explore hundreds of jobs and schedules created one by one. Let's consider that a maintenance plan is just a base, not an advanced technique for full database administration. To refine our maintenance needs, we need to handle smaller objects like operators, jobs, and alerts. In the next chapter, we will describe features covered under these three object types.

SQL Server Agent objects

In previous sections, we described how to establish an environment for automation and **Maintenance Plans** were discussed in detail. However, what's working behind the scenes? How to automate some specific tasks that may be assigned? In this section, we will take a look at three types of objects that actually participate in automation:

- Operators
- Jobs
- Alerts

Operators

One of the first tasks when setting up an automation environment is the enabling of database mail and mail profile creation. Although mail profiles could be used for regular emailing, their main purpose is to use emails for administrator's notifications about job results or when some alert is raised. SQL Server Agent does not notify directly to an email address, it uses a special object called **operator**. Operator is named address defining where to send notifications mainly about job results.

The address of the operator may be as follows:

- **Email address**: Person, more people, or distribution group can be set as an email.
- **Pager email**: Pagers were signed as deprecated on SQL Server 2014 but when needed, they are still possible. This chapter will not pay attention to pagers.

Many administrators ask for SMS notifications, but SQL Server doesn't support cellular phone text messages. If a mobile provider supports some SMS gateway for its customers, the user is usually informed by SMS when a new email comes. This may be a way to be notified by SMS, because SQL Server just needs any valid email address no matter from which email provider. Just add the email address bound to some mobile phone number to the operator's definition and enable SMS notification in your phone provider's email profile.

To define a new operator or edit the existing one is quite simple. Management Studio keeps all definitions operators in object explorer in a folder called **Operators** under the **SQL Server Agent** node. By right-clicking on this folder, a popup menu appears and the first option is **New operator...** Dialog is opened as seen in the following screenshot:

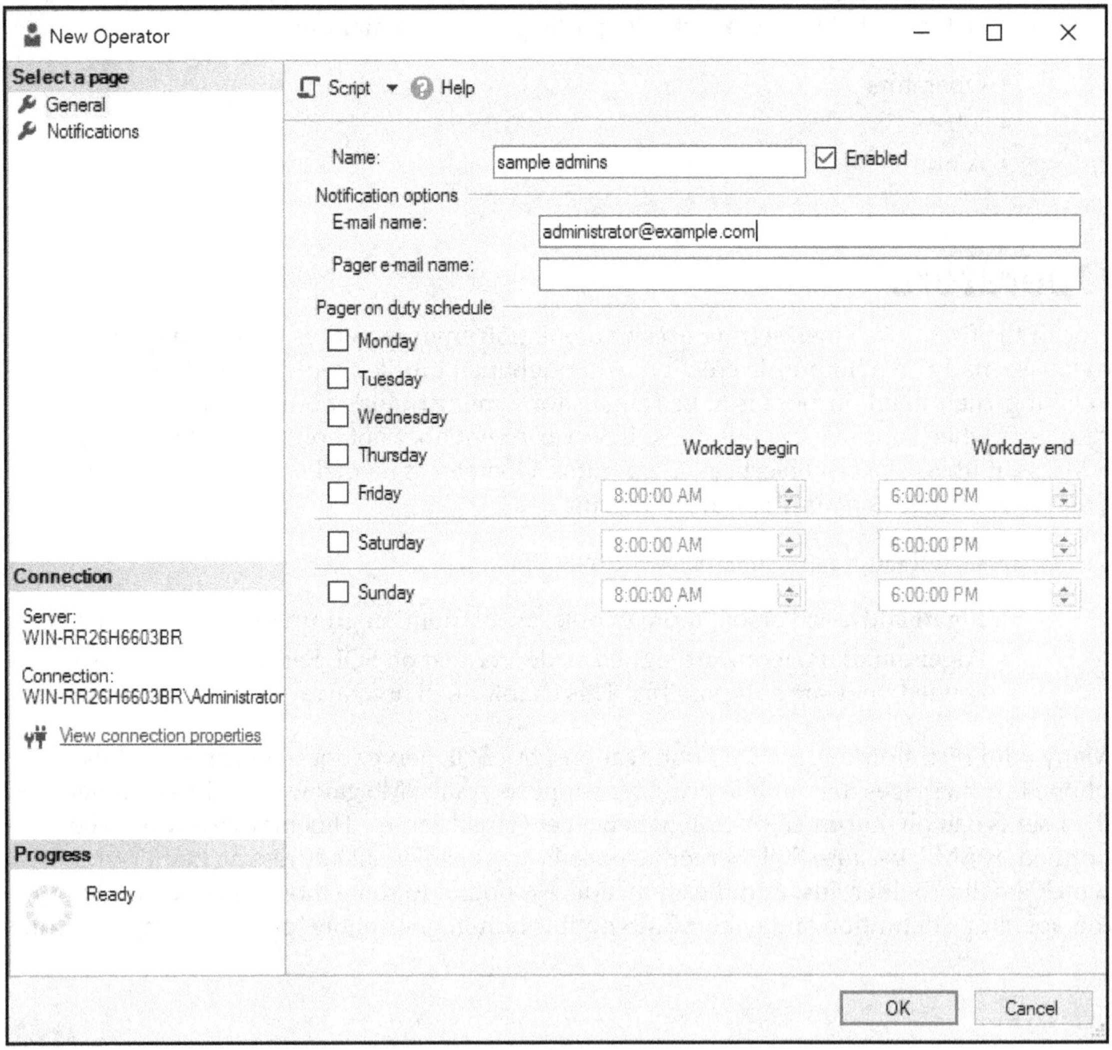

An operator's definition consists of three fields:

- **Name**: Any descriptive name (for example, *sample admins*).
- **Email name**: Any valid email address or address list. When more email addresses are used, they are separated by a semicolon (;) symbol as in a regular email client.
- **Enabled**: This checkbox is turned on by default but if needed, operator could be disabled without the need to erase it completely.

The second tab not seen in the image is called **Notifications**. It's a non-editable list of jobs and alerts about which the operator is notified. The list is maintained automatically when the operator is assigned to some job or alert.

Jobs

A job is an executive object maintained by SQL Server Agent. Job itself is a definition covering one or more **job steps** and usually one or more schedules. The operator can be notified about the whole job result optionally. Let's go through parts of a job's definition in detail.

Job definition

Starting to create a new job is very similar to creating a new operator. In object explorer under the **SQL Server Agent** node is a folder called **Jobs**. A popup menu appears by right-clicking and four interesting options are there:

- **New Job...**: This option will open a window to create a new job.
- **Manage Schedules**: Schedules can be defined within a job definition but they can also be managed separately as shared schedules. If some shared schedules are created from this option, they are just assigned to job definitions.
- **Manage Job Categories**: Jobs can be categorized for better orientation (but job categories are not seen anywhere in Management Studio). If used, the category must be defined before it is used in job definition.
- **View History**: This option opens the **Job History** window to monitor and troubleshoot jobs.

The **Job History** window will be described later in this chapter, schedules and job categories are obvious and straightforward, so let's skip directly to a new job definition. The window used to create a new job is depicted here:

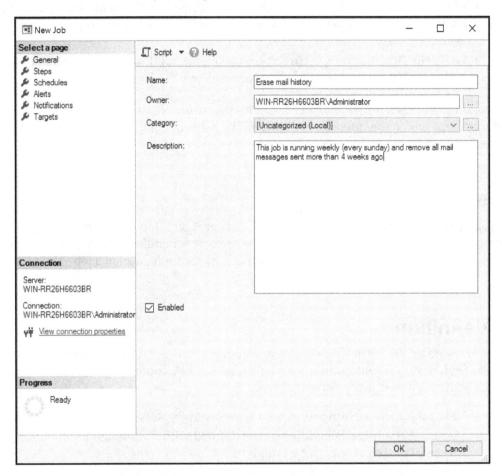

The job definition itself is quite simple. A job has to have a name (for example, `Erase mail history`), may be categorized, has an optional description (description was usually omitted in previous examples but experience says that in this case, description is highly welcome), and can be enabled or disabled. The only tricky field in the dialog is **Owner**. Owner's value determines the user context of the job when it's running. There is an internal rule setting the context:

- When owner is a member of sysadmin server role, job is executed in user context of SQL Server Agent service

- When owner is not a member of sysadmin server role, job is executed within actual user context

However, most jobs are used for administrative purposes, but sometimes some need for application jobs (for example, data load called by end users directly from business applications) will appear and then it's a good practice to think about the actual user context of the job.

A job needs to have at least one step defined because without it, it's something doing nothing. In the next section, we will define some steps.

Job steps definition

The job properties window has several tabs. Let's unhide the next one:

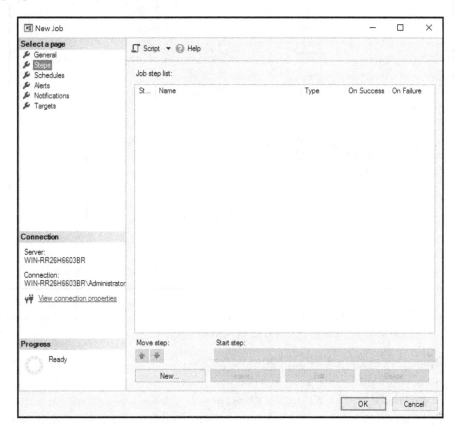

Defining a new job step starts by clicking the **New...** button. A new dialog appears and job step definition is done in the new dialog. This original one then shows a list of steps created within the job. Job steps can be edited, deleted, and sorted by clicking other buttons in this tab.

The job step definition window is seen in the following image:

Every job step must have a unique name within the job definition. The second value to be set is **Type**. It's a dropdown containing these values:

- **Operating system**: Used for command line calls (such as bcp.exe or any third-party command line)
- **PowerShell**: Used for PowerShell scripts, if needed
- **SQL Server Analysis Services command**: Used for data cube maintenance (for example, XMLA calls processing partitions in cube)

- **SQL Server Analysis Services query**: Used for MDX queries
- **SQL Server Integration Services package**: Used to schedule SSIS packages execution
- **Transact-SQL script**: Used in most cases to define tasks such as backing up database or other tasks

In our example, the script in the job step definition picture is used to maintain the `Database Mail` retention period.

> As written in the *Maintenance plan* section, subplans are SSIS packages. When some are created, take a look at the job steps; they are of the SQL Server Integration Services package type.

The **Run as** field may be used for all job step types except the Transact-SQL type. This property sets execution context for certain steps more granularly. To set the context, **SQL Agent Proxy** must be defined before it can be used. SQL Agent Proxy is a pointer to some defined credential objects (credentials are described in the `Chapter 4`, *Securing Your SQL Server*).

Depending on the job step type, the rest of the dialog changes. For our T-SQL type, the database context has to be set in the **Database** dropdown, and the SQL script has to be written to the **Command** field.

> If you are writing a command for the job step, write it in a proper tool such as Management Studio, and then copy-paste it into the **Command** field because the field does not completely test the accuracy of your script.

Alright, the job step has been created and we can continue creating additional steps when needed. When more steps are added, SQL Server Agent executes them one by one in the order they were sorted while being created. By default, when some job fails, the whole job fails as well. We can add some very trivial logic to this behavior by resorting the job steps or setting success and failure action in the **Advanced** tab of the Job step definition window.

When job steps are defined, we can start scheduling job execution. However, it's an optional part of job definition.

Schedule definition

One job definition can contain zero to many schedules. Creating a schedule is a very simple task. Let's take a look at the dialog to create a new schedule definition.

When the **Schedules** tab is selected in the job definition window, a list of schedules is shown and we have two buttons:

- **New...**: This button is used to open the window for the new schedule defined within the job
- **Pick...**: This button is used to open the window with shared schedules already defined

When a new schedule is created, the following dialog window is opened (and it's the same everywhere when a schedule is created, for example, in maintenance plans):

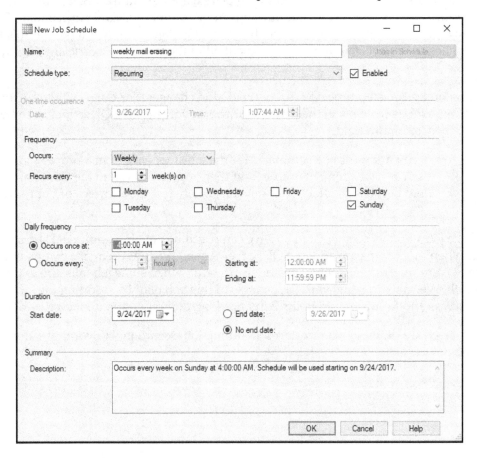

As usual, every schedule has its name, **Schedule type**, and can be enabled or disabled. Schedule type can be the following:

- Recurring
- Start automatically when SQL Server Agent starts
- Start whenever the CPUs become idle
- One time

In our example, the recurring option is selected. Then we can set the frequency. The schedule can start as follows:

- Weekly
- Daily
- Monthly

The rest of the fields are self-descriptive and do not need any extra description.

While troubleshooting why a certain job is not running, always check the **Enabled** field in two places--at the job level and at the schedule level. It's very common to disable not the job, but its schedule.

Notification definition

When a job is finished, some notification(s) may be issued by SQL Server Agent. SQL Server Agent never informs about progress, just about the result of the job.

We can set more notification channels. Let's take a look at the **Notifications** tab:

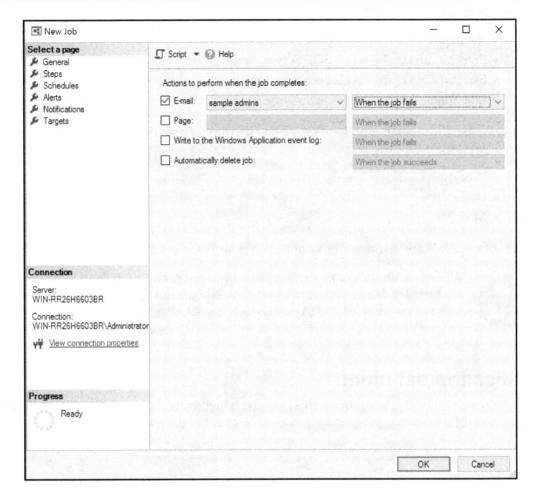

An administrator can choose which channel of notification will be used. **E-mail** or **Page** operators and Windows application log can be set. One extra option is also possible--the **Automatically delete job** option, which is quite dangerous because when a job is deleted, its history is also deleted and diagnostics are not possible in this case.

For every selected notification channel, one more decision has to be taken. It's the condition when the notification has to be issued. It's selected by the rightmost drop-down beside each notification channel. Options are as follows:

- When the job fails
- When the job succeeds
- When the job completes

Now the job is defined completely and it should start doing its job. In a real instance of SQL Server, many jobs are created and executed, so some tool to monitor and troubleshoot is needed. In the next section, we will describe how to diagnose job execution.

Monitoring and troubleshooting jobs

We need to check the correctness of our job's execution and troubleshoot it when things are going wrong. The first approach when jobs are failing is to be informed by email. However, we need to have an overview of all the jobs because it's hard to remember the schedule expiration of every single job.

A good entry point for automation monitoring is the window called **Job Activity Monitor**. This window is accessible from a shortcut placed directly under the SQL Server Agent node in Management Studio's object explorer. When used, a window with a list of all jobs is opened, as follows:

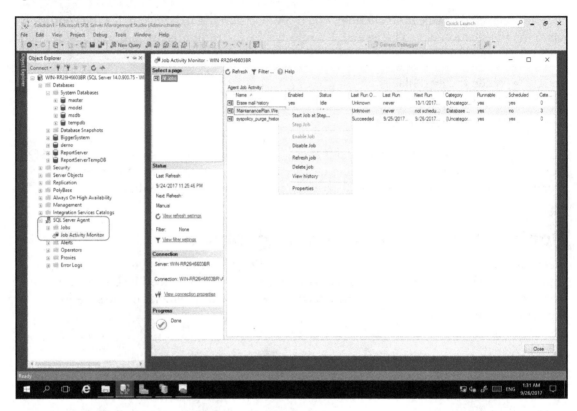

The red rectangle in object explorer shows from where to open the **Job Activity Monitor**. The biggest area is the **Job Activity Monitor** itself. All jobs defined in a certain SQL Server Agent are seen as a list. Every record in the list provides the following information:

- Name of the job
- Current status (running, idle)
- Last run date and time
- Next run date and time
- If the job is enabled and if it's scheduled
- Last run result (success, failed)

The **Job Activity Monitor** is not just a report. We can refresh its content manually or automatically. Manual refresh can be done by clicking the **Refresh** button in the toolbox; automatic refresh must be set from the **View Refresh Settings** link in the left side of the window. Another feature is a possibility to work with a certain job. When DBA right-clicks on the record in **Job Activity Monitor**, a popup appears. It enables one to start the job, enable or disable it, refresh its status, and edit the job through the **Properties** option.

An important diagnostic option is the **View History**. History of job(s) can be shown from more places (from the Jobs folder in object explorer or from a certain job directly) but always opens the same **Log File Viewer** window:

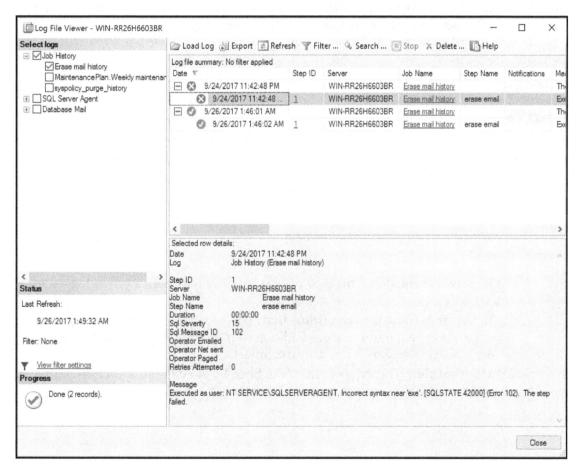

The **Log File viewer** window shows every run of the job with its results. Every run consists of the overall result and, when expanded (runs are collapsed by default), detailed job step results are shown. In the preceding image, two executions are run--the first was successful but the second failed (job executions are sorted by the time of execution in descending order). When recognizing the error, we need to expand the wanted record and click at the detailed record with failure. The actual error message is shown in the bottom part of the window. In our example, a syntactic error was raised when executing the job step, erasing the email history. Now we have to go back to the step definition and correct the problem (it was a typo in this case, keyword .exe was used instead of exec).

Until this moment, we automated regular administrative tasks, usually in a timely fashion. We also need to react to situations that are not raised every night or every week. A helpful type of object maintained by SQL Server is alert. In our last section, we will explore what alerts are for.

Alerts

Alert is an object that is defined to react on certain event. The event can be, for example, some error that is raised on SQL Server. When such a situation occurs, the alert itself just remembers the occurrence in the form of a counter (how many times the error was noticed) and the last time of the occurrence. The benefit of using alerts lies in the possibility to set some **response action**. A response action could be an operator notification, job execution, or both.

We have three alert types:

- **SQL Server event alert**: This type of alert looks for SQL Server errors logged to the error log
- **SQL Server performance condition alert**: These alerts can check the value change of a certain performance condition counter provided by SQL Server (not every operating system performance counter)
- **WMI event alert**: This type of alerts is defined by WMI query and alerts of this type are raised by non-empty result of the query.

When we want to create some alert, we start by right-clicking on the **Alerts** folder under the **SQL Server Agent** node in object explorer. The alert definition window is depicted in the following screenshot:

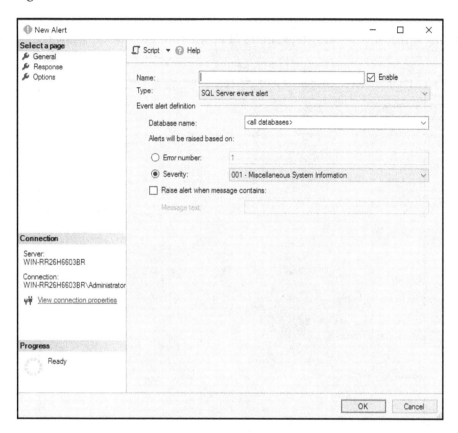

Every alert must have some name and can be enabled or disabled. The critical setting is the **Type** option. It determines the type of the alert. In the preceding screenshot, the **SQL Server event** alert type is selected. It means that the correct error number must be written in the **Error number** field or severity level of errors has to be selected.

SQL Server has more than 13,000 error messages (for a complete set of them, the sys.messages view is present on SQL Server). These messages are divided into categories by their gravity, called severity levels. SQL Server has severity levels from 0 to 25. The bigger the number, the more serious the error. Errors contained in severity level 17 and higher are automatically logged into the SQL Server error log. These errors can be monitored by alerts. Sometimes, it's a better approach to monitor the whole severity level than a single error number because of bigger amount of errors in severity levels.

When defining an alert responding to an error message, we work in the reactive approach of SQL Server monitoring. Sometimes it's quite easy to be reactive, preventing errors before they occur. For such situations, it's very useful to create SQL Server performance condition alerts.

The following screenshot shows an example of how to monitor usage of the transaction log file:

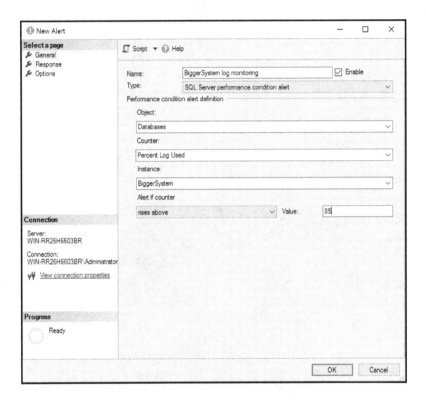

When the **Type** drop-down is switched to the **SQL Server performance condition alert** option, the screen changes its look. Now we need to find the correct object (**Databases**, in our example), counter (**Percent log used**, this counter measures the ratio of log space used/log file space allocated), and also instance of the counter if needed (and it's needed in our example because _**Total** says nothing about actual log usage). Now we must say when the situation becomes dangerous. The last row called **Alert if counter** describes the situation. The counter can rise above, be equal, or fall below some value.

The value is written in the **Value** field. In our example on preceding image, when the transaction log file of the **BiggerSystem** database is used for more than 85%, the alert is executed. It's not proactive yet; we have to set up some response action.

The Response tab of the alert creation window is the place where responses to alerts are set. As seen in the following screenshot, we can switch on the job execution (and also select a job from the list of already existing or create a new one) and switch on the possibility to notify some operator:

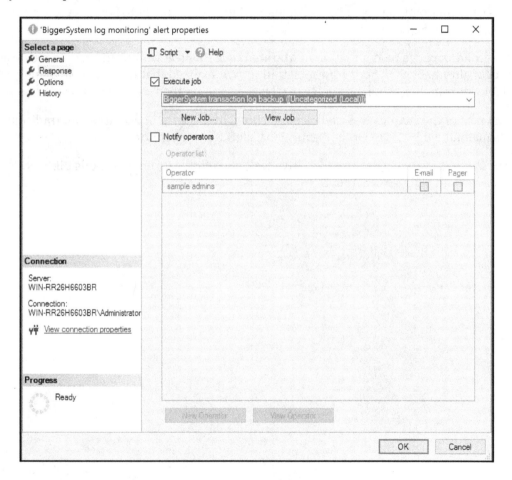

From this moment, every time the transaction log of our `BiggerSystem` database becomes full, transaction log backup is executed along with the regular scheduled execution.

Summary

To imagine an administrator's world without automation is really hard. SQL Server provides a very comprehensive set of tools and techniques to achieve comfortable regular administration and reduce administration to non-regular monitoring or troubleshooting actions.

In the first part of this chapter, we went through `Database Mail` and SQL Server Agent setup. The main point here is to have Database Mail and mainly SQL Server Agent running all the time when SQL Server runs.

In the second part, we paid attention to **Maintenance Plans**, a very useful tool to create a base set of automatic SQL Server administration. We realized that maintenance plans are dividable into smaller subplans, which can be executed on their own schedules.

The last part of the chapter was dedicated to show, in the form of examples, all traditional objects maintained by SQL Server Agent--jobs, alerts, and operators.

We can say that every single administrative task and administrator's responsibility ends as a planned job on SQL Server Agent.

10
Always On High Availability Features

SQL Server high availability includes two main components called **Always On Failover Cluster Instances** and **Always On Availability Groups**. In this chapter, we'll at these two in-depth and explore the possible configurations for the SQL Server environment. Both features use **Windows Server Failover Clustering functionality** (**WSFC**) but have different methods of deployment.

Windows Server Failover Clustering is a server feature available on the Windows Server 2016, which allows for the grouping of computers into a fault-tolerant cluster. In a case where one or more nodes fail, others will keep the service or application available.

Each Windows Server version is bringing new features to the WSFC feature, and many of those can be beneficial for SQL Server deployment. Windows Server 2012 and 2012 R2 have brought many new enhancements and new features to the WSFC, with a strong emphasis on the Hyper-V role used for virtualization. The main new features and improvements for these two versions of Windows Server in regards to WSFC include:

- Shared VHDs
- VM drain on shutdown
- VM network health detection
- Cluster shared volume improvements
- AD-detached clusters
- Dynamic witness
- Cluster dashboard

- Support for SoFS (Scale-out File Server)
- Cluster-aware updates
- Integration of the task scheduler

Windows Server 2016 brings, even more, new functionalities to the Failover Cluster feature, enabling better management, scalability, and performance for the solution. Again, there are many features used by the Hyper-V role which are used for virtualization, including:

- VM load balancing
- VM start order
- Cluster OS system rolling upgrade

Other important features of Windows Server 2016 used in the WSFC include:

- **Cloud witness**: A new type of quorum which uses Microsoft Azure. Like any other quorum, cloud witness has a vote and takes part in quorum calculations. Cloud witness uses Microsoft Azure Blob Storage, which can be configured for multiple clusters as a very cost-effective solution.

Installing Windows Server Failover Cluster

Like any other server role feature, Windows Server Failover Clustering requires careful planning before you begin the installation. There are many things you need to consider, including:

- The number of host nodes
- Networking configuration
- Storage configuration
- Application requirements

Windows Server Failover Clustering is a server feature which can be added via the Server Manager GUI or via the command line. To install WSFC feature via Server Manager, navigate to the **Add Roles and Features** option and select the feature **Failover Clustering**. This feature will allow you to add several sub-features such as a PowerShell module, remote server admin tools for **Failover Clustering**, and so on:

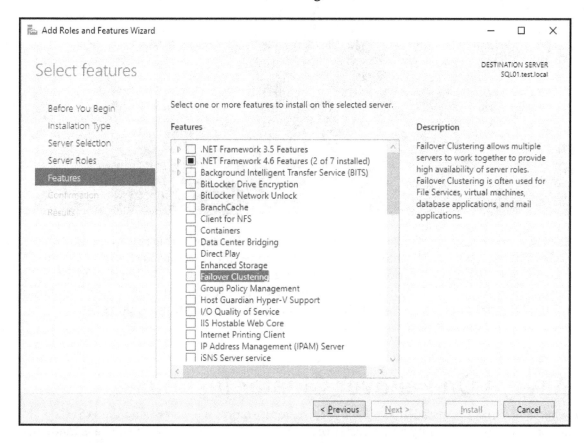

Another option would be a PowerShell command line, where you can run following code to install the **Failover Clustering** feature:

```
Install-WindowsFeature "Failover-Clustering","RSAT-Clustering" -
IncludeAllSubFeature
```

Once you finish the installation with PowerShell, you will see whether or not the installation was successful and if a restart is required. In this installation, we have just added the **Failover Clustering** feature to the server, and there's no cluster configured yet. That's very important to realize. You can deploy the feature with PowerShell using the following scripts:

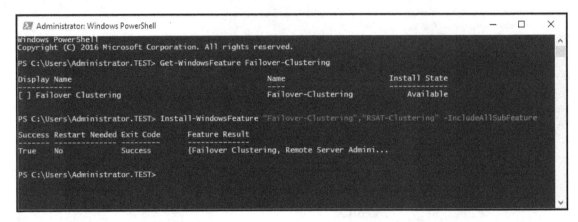

Both the Server Manager GUI and the PowerShell can also deploy this feature to multiple nodes at the same time. The maximum amount of nodes that can form a cluster is 64, but usually, SQL Server clusters don't have that many nodes. There is also a big difference between SQL Server editions in regards to the cluster size supported. SQL Server Standard edition supports only two nodes clusters, whereas Enterprise Edition supports the maximum amount of nodes available in the operating system.

Always On Failover Cluster Instances

When SQL Server is installed as a Failover Cluster Instance, it is leveraging the WSFC feature for high availability and disaster recovery. The Failover Cluster Instance is made up of a set of physical servers which have a similar hardware configuration, operating system, patch level, SQL Server version, and components. They also share the instance name.

Once you have planned your Windows Server configuration, you can start the SQL Server installation process. In Failover Cluster Instance installation, you have several choices, including installation via the setup GUI wizard, available in the installation media, installing with advanced options, or installing as an unattended setup via the command line. To start the Failover Cluster Instance installation, simply click on **New SQL Server failover cluster installation**, which will bring up the wizard to install the SQL Server cluster, as shown in the following screenshot:

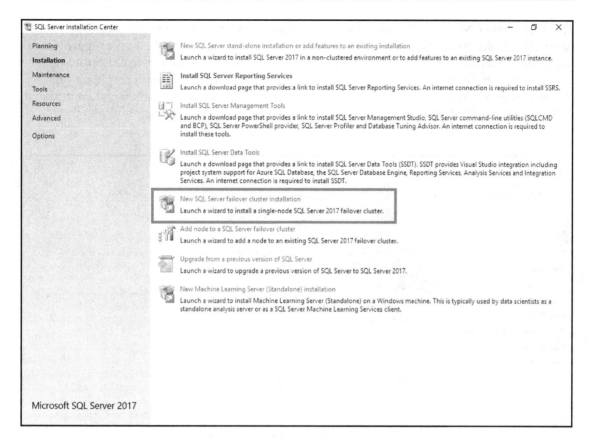

The setup program then goes through an extensive validation process in terms of your environment, and also examines the cluster and the validation of the cluster. You will need to select the features and instance name, and configure the service accounts as with a regular installation. What you will need to configure this differently will be cluster specific information, such as:

- SQL Server network name
- Cluster resource group
- Cluster disks
- Cluster network configuration

The **SQL Server Network Name** is a **virtual network name** (**VNN**) which is used as a connection point to your Failover Cluster Instance. Connection to VNN works regardless of the active node, and the IP address of the VNN always points to the active cluster node hosting the SQL Server services. The configuration can get little bit more complex if the cluster nodes are in different network subnets. If a failover occurs, the VNN is then updated with the virtual IP of the respective subnet for the active cluster node, as shown in the following screenshot:

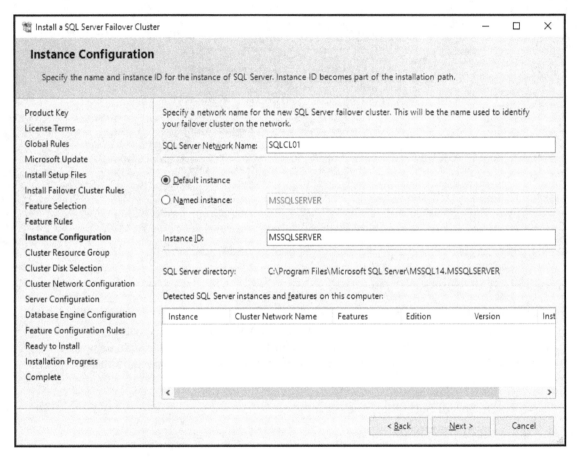

The SQL Server Cluster Recourse group will be used to host SQL Server services, which are installed on the failover cluster. You can either create the group in advance as an empty role in Failover Cluster Management, or the setup program will create a new one for you during the installation, as follows:

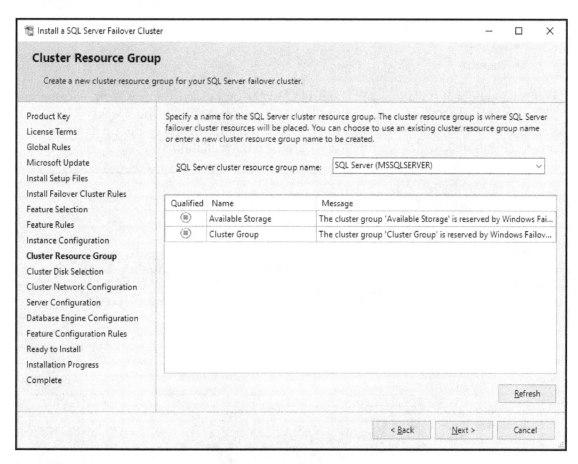

On the next page, you need to assign the disks to your SQL Server cluster, which can have variety of configurations on Windows Server 2016, such as:

- Cluster volume
- Cluster shared volume
- Storage spaces direct

The full disk configuration will usually be prepared by your Windows Server administrator based on your requirements. Based on the disks available, you will need to configure the critical folders for your SQL Server deployment, including:

- Root files
- Data files
- Log files
- Backups

As with standalone installation, you should follow the best practices for SQL Server storage, such as isolating the data and logging and backing up files. Evaluate the storage performance for cluster deployment, as in cluster installation you may end up having more than one cluster disk, which would be more scaled out installation:

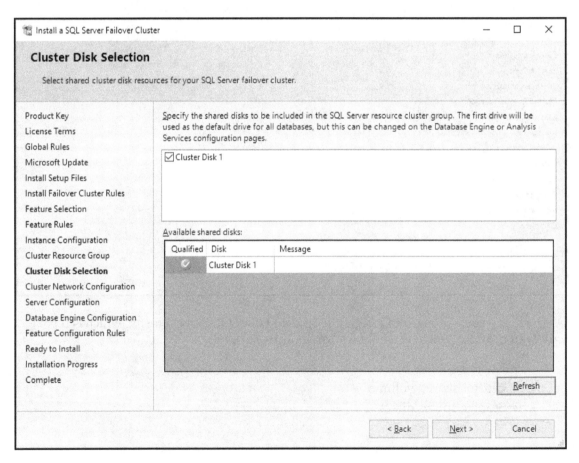

The **network configuration** allows you to select the address for your SQL Server's virtual name, if that will be used with DHCP addressing or if you will assign a fixed IP address, as follows:

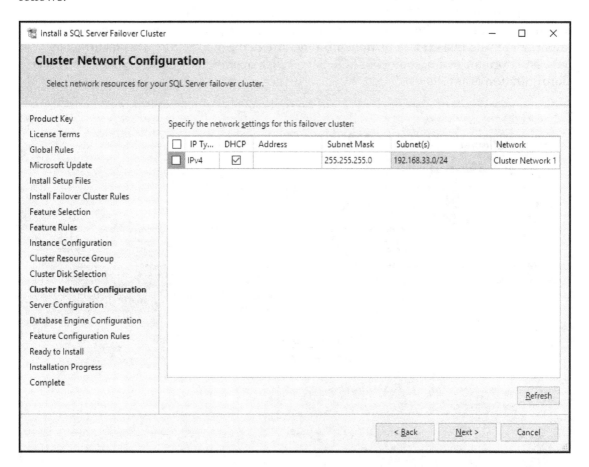

On the **Server Configuration** page, you will need to configure the SQL Server accounts. These accounts were discussed in the `Chapter 4`, *Securing Your SQL Server*. Favorable choices for the cluster would be a domain account or a group managed service account. With SQL Server 2016 and 2017 you can also select the **Grant Perform Volume Maintenance Task privilege to SQL Server Database Engine Service** checkbox, which is important for the **Instant File Initialization** feature of the SQL Server. This feature may have a performance impact on your SQL Server disk operations. The screenshot for **Server Configuration** is as follows:

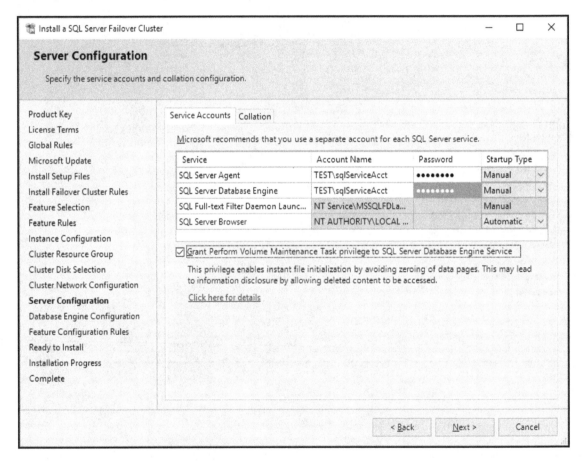

On the **Database Engine Configuration** page, you will configure important server settings including:

- `Authentication`: Mixed or windows
- `Data directories`: Data files, log files, backup folder

- `TempDB` configuration: Amount of files and their size
- `FILESTREAM` configuration

Once you get to the **Ready to Install** page of the setup program, you're set to start the installation. This installation will deploy the Failover Cluster Instance to one of the cluster nodes.

Adding nodes to the SQL Server Failover Cluster

On the other node, you will start the installation with **Add node to a SQL Server failover cluster.** as follows:

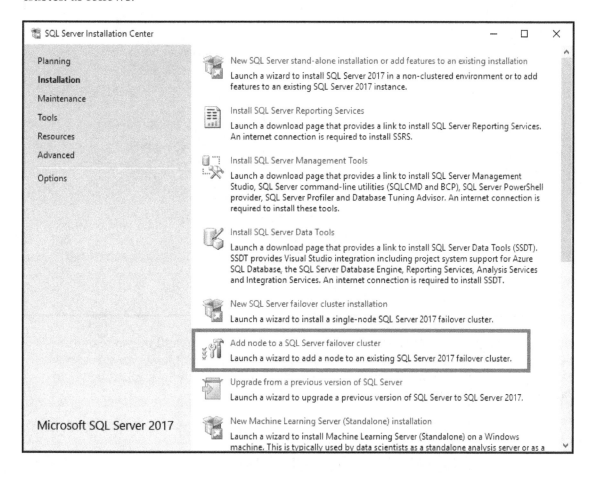

The installation begins as in the regular SQL Server setup, but on the **Cluster Node Configuration** page, you can select the instance name and node to add to the Failover Cluster. On the next page, you will need to configure the networking settings and the **Service Accounts**:

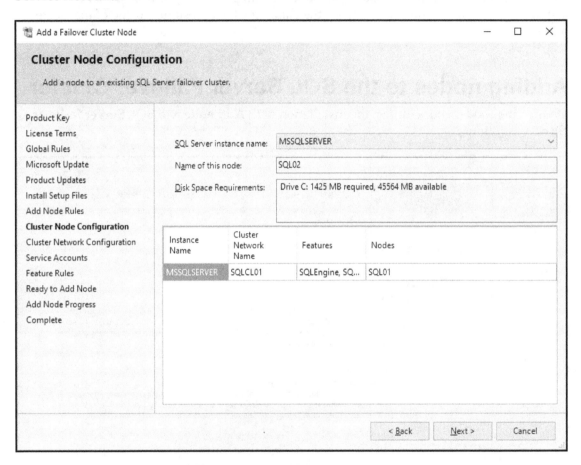

Once you have prepared the installation, you can run the setup to add the node to the cluster that will install the SQL Server instance on this node. The SQL Server services will be configured to start manually on both nodes, and their startup will be controlled by the **Failover Cluster Manager** tool.

Once the installation is finished, you can connect to your virtual SQL Server name which you configured in the first cluster node installation. You can start working with your database server:

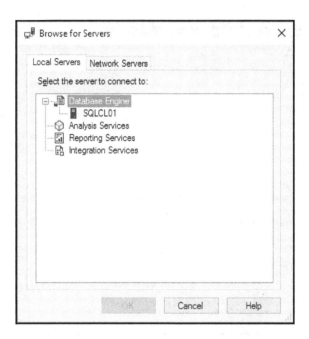

Initiating a failover

Once we have the SQL Server instance up and running with the Failover Cluster, it's protected by the WSFC feature and will be automatically started on another cluster node upon failure. You can perform this failover manually via the **Failover Cluster Manager** tool.

You can use this to move the role of your SQL Server to another node:

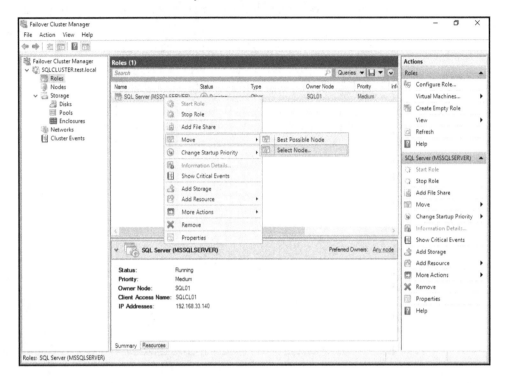

Once you choose a node, and where to move the role, the failover will reassign the resources from the currently active node to the other node. It will move disks, assign names, register IPs and finally start the SQL Server services. In Failover Cluster Instances, the services for a selected instance run only on one node, and the other node or nodes are stopped. Only after a failover to a newly selected active node are the services started on this node, and stopped on all other nodes.

This configuration is frequently referred to as active/passive cluster, where one node is active (hosting the running services) and the other node is up, but all SQL Server services are stopped. Another configuration may be referred to as active/active, where both nodes are hosting SQL Server services which are started, but in this deployment, the two nodes are hosting two different instances. One instance is active on the first node, and the other instance is active on the other node, making both nodes host and run SQL Server services.

Always On Availability Groups

Always On Availability Groups is a high availability and disaster recovery feature that was introduced in SQL Server 2012. This feature, similar to Always On Failover Cluster Instances, requires a **Windows Server Failover Clustering** (**WSFC**) to be configured on the nodes running on the SQL Server. Availability Groups work at a database level, where the Always On **Failover Cluster Instances** (**FCI**) are protecting the whole instance.

We won't focus on the WSFC anymore and just use the common platform to deploy the SQL Server Always On Availability Groups in the following scenarios through the chapter. The WSFC configuration for the Availability Groups is more simple when compared to the FCI infrastructure, since Availability Groups don't require any shared storage and the storage solution depends on the node type. To utilize the Availability Groups, you install the standalone SQL Server on the cluster nodes, but you use the basic SQL Server installation, since the instances in Availability Groups don't share the SQL Server Virtual Network Name and IP, and are independent of each other.

Configuring Always On Availability Groups

Before we start configuring the Availability Groups, we need to make sure all the prerequisites are met on the server, instance, and database levels. Databases for Availability Groups need to do the following:

- Be user databases (no system DBs are allowed)
- Use a full recovery model
- Be read/write databases
- Be multi-user databases
- Have at least one full backup

There are several key terms which we need to define to be able to work with Availability Groups. Availability Group itself is a set of user databases, which is considered a unit for high availability. These databases (or the availability group) fail over to other nodes of the WSFC if there is an issue detected either at the server level or the database level. Availability replica is an instance of the availability group hosted by an SQL Server instance. The replica maintains the copy of the databases which belongs to the Availability Group. The replica can be either a **primary replica** or a **secondary replica**. Different versions of SQL Server support a variety of secondary replicas.

Currently, up to eight secondary replicas can be created. The secondary replica can be a local SQL Server running in the same datacenter, a distant data center, or in Microsoft Azure (Azure replica). The primary replica is the read-write instance of the availability database, and secondary replicas host a copy of the database, which may be configured for read-only access if required by the design.

To start the Always On Availability Group configuration, you first have to verify that your SQL Server instances are properly configured to use the WSFC for Availability Groups. To check the configuration, you can use the **SQL Server Configuration Manager** tool and check the properties of your SQL Server instance:

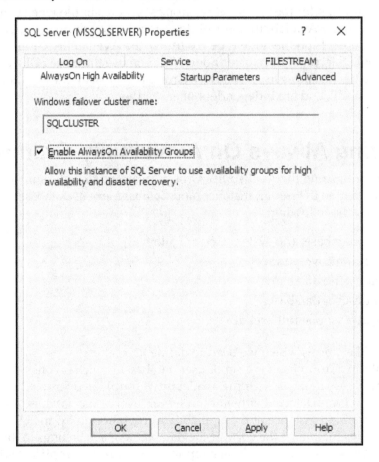

Once you select the **Enable AlwaysOn Availability Groups** checkbox, you will need to restart your SQL Server service to see the effect of such a setting. The main expectation is to have a fully configured WSFC service. All nodes in such a cluster should run the same SQL Server version and edition, and should use the same collation.

Creating an Availability Group

An Availability group is a collection of the databases you would like to host on the availability replicas. You cannot add any of the system databases to the availability group, so this works only for the user databases. The Availability Group can be created from the **SQL Server Management Studio** (**SSMS**), where you can also script out the whole configuration T-SQL script for future reference or larger deployments. In the SSMS, navigate to **Always On High Availability** and start the wizard:

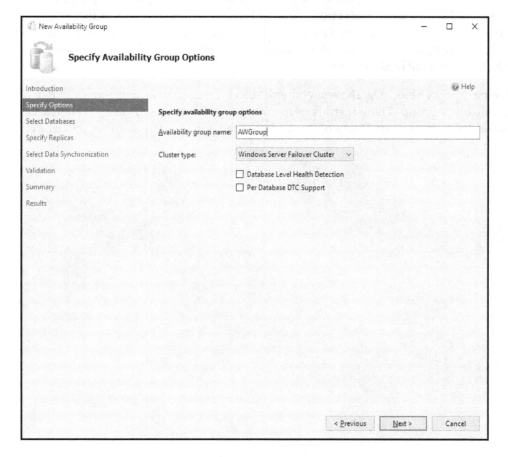

In the **Specify Options** page of the wizard, you have to enter the Availability group name, which can't be longer than 128 characters and will describe the group you are creating. There are then three choices available for you when selecting a cluster type:

- **Windows Server Failover Cluster**: This type is used when SQL Server Availability Groups are hosted on the Windows Server Failover Cluster, a common solution for high availability and disaster recovery.
- **External**: This type is used when the Availability Groups are managed by external cluster technology such as Availability Groups on Linux with Pacemaker.
- **None**: This type is used when there's no cluster technology used for managing Availability Groups.

Two more checkboxes are available for you to configure, and we'll mostly focus on **Database Level Health Detection**. This option enables the failover of the availability group when the database status is no longer *online*. This health detection is applied to the whole availability group, so even if one database has any issues, the whole group will fail over to another node in the cluster.

On the next page, **Select Databases**, you will select the databases you would like to add to the Availability group. The wizard is performing several checks to verify if such a database can be added to the group. If any of those checks fail, you'll see a warning describing what is required:

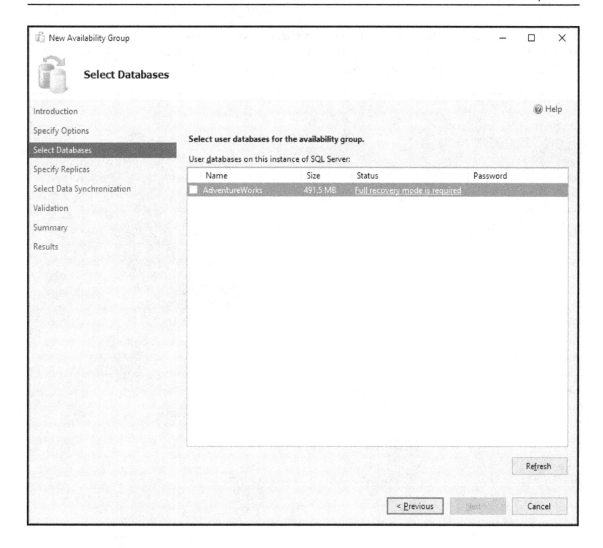

If your database or databases meet all prerequisites, you can move on the next page, called **Specify replicas**. Here you will configure all your nodes that are participating in hosting the availability group, and configure additional features and options:

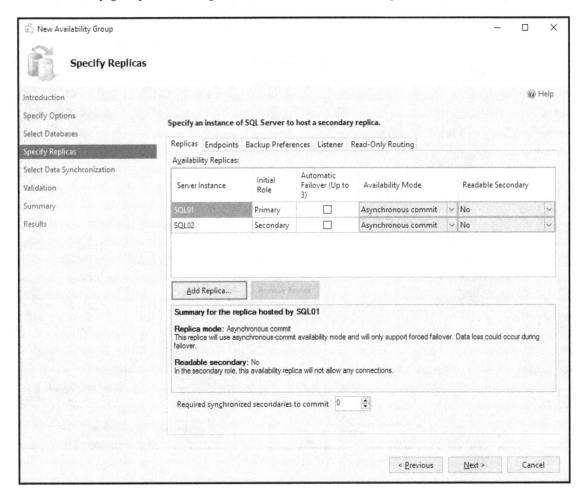

You can see what server instances you have added to the configuration and their initial roles. You can configure one primary and up to eight secondary replicas for the database availability group. Next, to the initial role, you can see an important checkbox, which is used to select which instances take part in Automatic Failover configuration. Out of all the instances, you can select up to three which can be configured for Automatic Failover.

There are two options for synchronization:

- **Synchronous Commit**: Synchronous Commit is a setting where the primary replica will wait to commit the transactions until they have been hardened on the secondary replicas. Synchronous Commit is required for the Automatic Failover option. Usually, Synchronous Commit will be the choice for servers or replicas which reside in the same data center, and it is used as a high-availability option.
- **Asynchronous Commit**: The Asynchronous Commit is generally used for servers in remote data centers for disaster recovery scenarios and for high load systems, where the Synchronous Commit mode would be too slow. Asynchronous Commit does not have to wait, and commits the transaction immediately.

The last column, **Readable Secondary**, is also very important. There there are three options:

- Yes
- No
- Read-intent only

If *Yes* is selected, you can access the secondary replica for read-only, and use the database for reporting purposes or any other read-only access. With the **read-intent only** type of configuration, the replica is available only if the application specifies the Application Intent property with **ReadOnly** in the connection string.

In the next section, called **Endpoints**, you have to configure the TCP endpoints, which will be used for synchronization between replicas. The SQL Server Service accounts will be granted the permission to connect to such endpoints. Notice that the port number is the same as the default mirroring port 5022. Using the **Encrypt Data** checkbox, you can also configure the encryption for the traffic between the nodes:

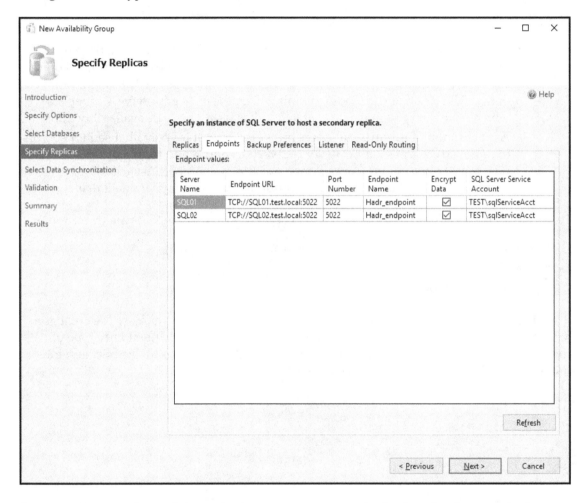

Once you have configured the endpoints, you can set up the **Backup Preferences** in the next section. Here you can configure the preferences for the backup, and you have, again, several options:

- Prefer secondary
- Secondary only

- Primary
- Any replica

The following is a screenshot of specifying the replicas:

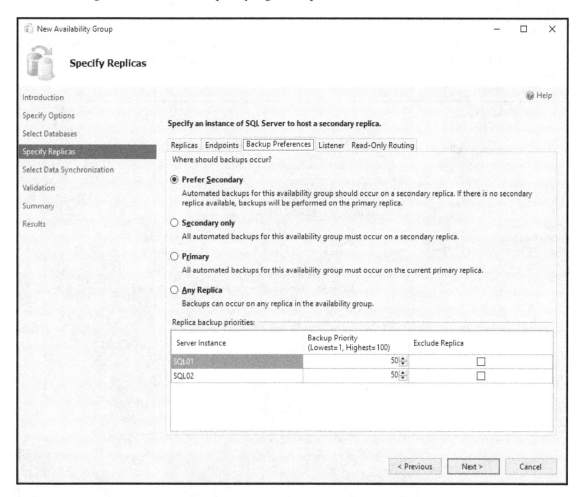

When using **Prefer Secondary**, backups for the availability group will occur on an available secondary replica, based on the priority if there are more secondaries. Only if no secondary replica is available will backup occur on the primary replica. Backups for large databases can consume a lot of system resources, and having a backup on a secondary replica can offload this task from the primary node.

In the next section, you can configure a **Listener**. An Availability group listener is an object that provides set of resources to direct the client connection to the appropriate replica. This replica does not have to be the only primary one, but can also be the secondary replica if the read intent is configured by the application connection string. This listener works like a **Virtual Network Name** (**VNN**) which we have seen already in Failover Cluster Instance configuration. As such, the listener can connect the client to the proper replica, without any need to know the server name. After any failover, you don't have to modify the connection properties in the application, since the listener will point the client requests to the active replica:

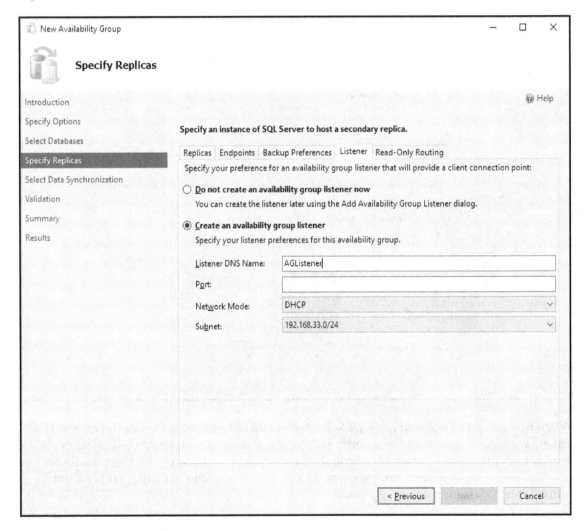

To configure the listener, you need to provide the DNS name, which has to be unique, and the network configuration consisting of the IP address and the port. The IP address can be configured as either static or DHCP configured. The port number can be entered to configure the listener to listen on a specific port, which then has to be configured in the application. If you would like to use the default port 1433, you have to make sure there are no other services using the port, except the default SQL Server instance, which is using the same port and can be shared with the Availability Group listener.

Once the listener is configured, it will become a resource in the WSFC service, together with the VNN and IP address used for the connection to the listener:

The last section can be used to configure **Read-Only Routing**. In this feature, each replica needs to have a URL configured, and the read-only routing list. These are configured on a per replica basis, and each secondary replica will have its own routing URL and routing list. The configuration can be performed either directly via GUI or later on with T-SQL script. The read-only routing works with round robin bases to distribute the read-only load among the secondary replicas.

Once you have configured all the replica options, you have to configure the **Data Synchronization**. This configuration section has many options, and you can choose from the following:

- Automatic seeding
- Full database and log backup
- Join only
- Skip initial data synchronization

The **Automatic seeding** option will create the database on all replicas and synchronize the databases between the primary and secondary replicas. There is, however, one strict requirement for automatic seeding. Database and log file paths have to be the same on all SQL Server instances that are configured as replicas in **New Availability Group**:

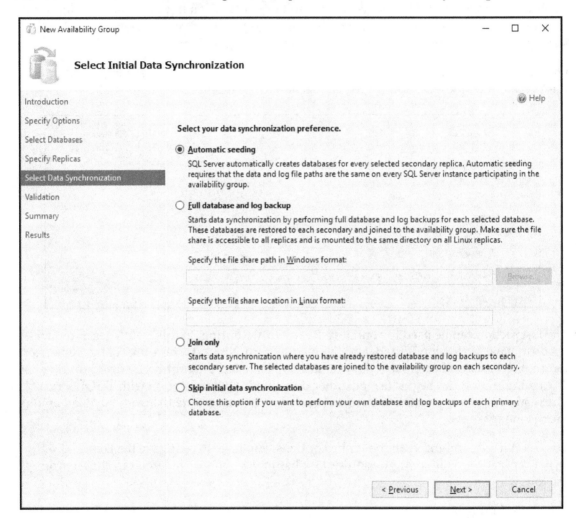

Once you have entered all the options, you are ready to finish the configuration. The wizard will then create all required logins, endpoints, listeners, and databases on the replicas, initiate the automatic seeding, and join the nodes to the availability group. If the configuration is successful, you will have a working Availability Group configured for your databases.

Failover and monitoring

During the configuration of each replica, there will be a new **Extended Session** event created and started to monitor the Availability Groups. Information from these sessions is then used in the **Dashboard**, which you can open to view the basic information about your Availability Groups, databases, and replicas:

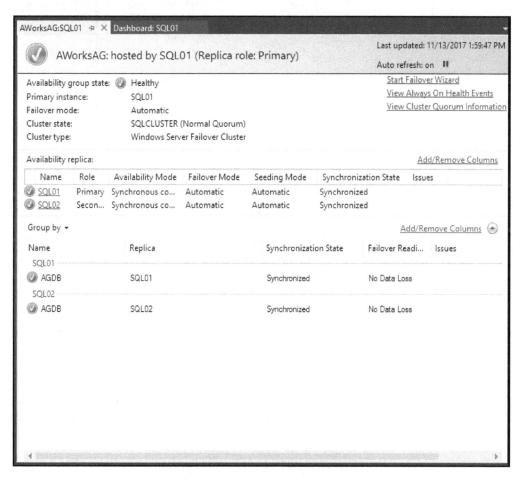

You can whether or not the databases are synchronized and available. When displaying the health events, you can dig deeper into the state of the availability group.

To fail over between replicas you should use the Failover wizard available in the **Dashboard** or the menu item in the SSMS. You can right-click the Availability Group in the **Always On High Availability / Availability Groups** section in the object explorer:

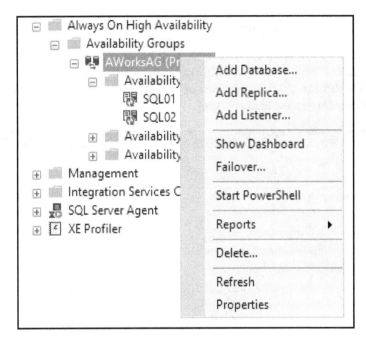

Once you click **Failover**, a new window will open where you can select a new primary replica based on the available replicas in your environment.

You can see which replicas are available and if the databases are synchronized with those replicas:

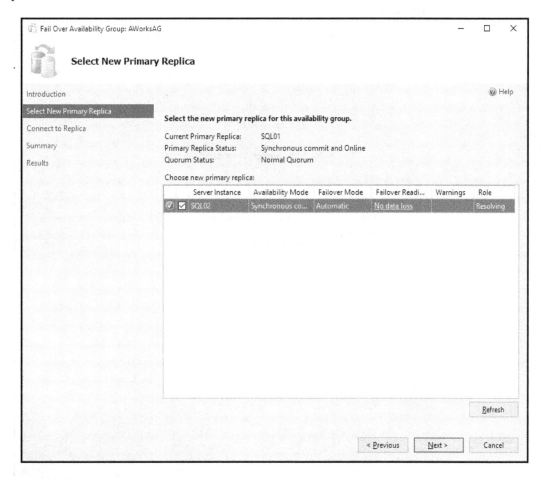

When you select your new replica for failover, the wizard will initiate the failover and follow the required steps to swap the replica roles. In our scenario, we have only two roles, so the primary replica will become secondary and the secondary will become primary:

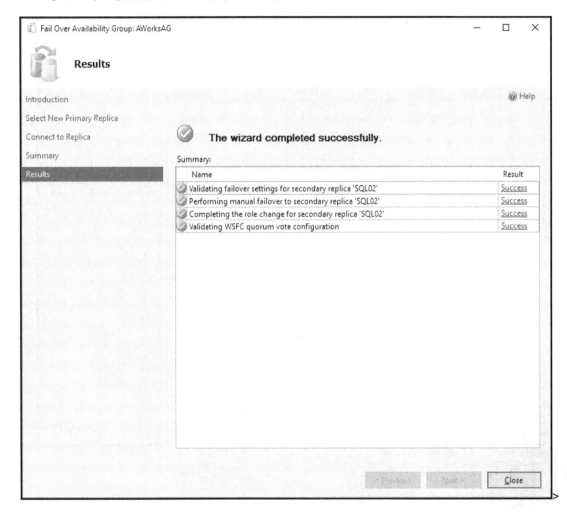

In the **Dashboard**, you can then see that the primary instance has changed to your selected replica, which you chose in the failover dialog window.

Basic Availability Groups

Basic Availability Groups are available in SQL Server 2016 and 2017 as a replacement for database mirroring, which has been deprecated since SQL Server 2012. Although mirroring is deprecated, it's still available and still being deployed in enterprise environments. Basic Availability Groups can offer you similar options to database mirroring.

A database can maintain a singe replica in synchronous or asynchronous commit mode. The secondary replica is inactive and not accessible to users until there is a failover. Failover just swaps the primary and secondary roles between servers, causing the secondary replica to become a primary replica. Basic Availability Groups can even span the environment, and you can configure hybrid scenarios with Azure.

There are several limitations for **Basic Availability Groups**:

- Only one secondary replica

- There is no read access on the secondary replica

- There are no backups on the secondary replica

- There are no integrity checks on secondary replicas

- There is no support for adding or removing a replica to an existing basic availability group

- Supports one availability database

- Basic Availability Groups are only supported for Standard Edition servers

- Basic Availability Groups cannot be part of a distributed availability group

When you are configuring the **Basic Availability Group**, you need to select the **Basic Availability Group** checkbox. This checkbox is not available in the Enterprise or Evaluation Edition of SQL Server, only in Standard Edition:

Distributed Availability Groups

Distributed Availability Groups are similar to **Basic Availability Groups** and are a new feature in SQL Server 2016; they are also available in SQL Server 2017. Distributed Availability Groups are a new type of availability group which can span two separate Availability Groups. Those separate underlying Availability Groups are configured on different server clusters (WSFC). These Distributed Availability Groups are not configured within a cluster and do not configure anything in the underlying WSFC. There is a requirement that the underlying Availability Groups have a listener configured.

This listener will be configured as an endpoint URL for the Distributed Availability Groups. The Distributed Availability Groups have synchronous and asynchronous commit modes, but the data movement is a little bit more complex, since only one database in Distributed Availability Groups can accept the updates to the data. There is a new role named Forwarder, which is a primary replica in a secondary availability group. Forwarder receives transactions from a primary replica in a primary availability group and forwards the transactions to the secondary replicas in the secondary availability group:

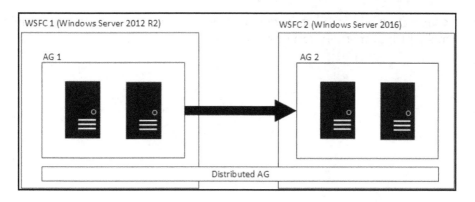

The Distributed Availability Groups are just the SQL Server level configurations, and they need to share the SQL Server version with the underlying Availability groups. However, the version of the operating system for the two WSFC clusters can be different. So, one WSFC can run on Windows Server 2016 and the other can utilize the previous version of Windows Server 2012 R2. This is particularly useful when the two clusters are in different data centers and have different OS level upgrade policies.

Summary

In this chapter, we have looked at two main features for high availability available with SQL Server 2017. As both Always On Availability Groups and Always On Failover Cluster Instances are dependent on the Windows Server feature WSFC, we went through the initial configuration of the failover cluster. As the failover cluster topic itself is quite complex, we have deployed a simple cluster with basic options. Usually, in large-scale environments, there will be a dedicated team to fully deploy and configure the cluster for the database administrator.

The Failover Cluster Instances are an older approach, based on a shared storage; they require more complex cluster configuration. In business continuity planning, you need to consider your options for high availability at the storage and network level, too, since from an SQL Server and cluster perspective, shared storage can become a single point of failure. The deployment of Failover Cluster Instances and Availability Groups is different, so you need to plan carefully regarding which option you would like to manage in your environment. Each has different requirements for licensing. Availability Groups (except the basic option for one database) require the Enterprise edition of SQL Server, in which Failover Cluster Instances can be hosted on SQL Server Standard Edition.

In the next chapter, we will focus on in-memory OLTP technology and the performance improvements which in-memory can bring to your application.

11
In-Memory OLTP - Why and How to Use it

Performance is crucial for every system's success and it's the same for SQL Server. However, as data contention grows all over the world, the traditional method of continuous algorithm tuning and improving from version to version becomes an insufficient approach. Since 2010, Microsoft has been working on a completely new approach of data processing called **Hekaton**. The first version was present on SQL Server 2014 as the In-Memory **OnLine Transactional Processing (OLTP)** feature. It offers new frontiers for developers and administrators to design and maintain very fast applications and also breaks many limits of traditional disk-based data processing.

In this chapter, we will explore:

- **In-Memory OLTP architecture**: A top-level overview of how it works and what's needed for successful implementation
- **Creating In-Memory tables and natively compiled stored procedures**: This section will provide an overview of how to create In-Memory tables and how to enhance their performance with natively compiled stored procedures
- **In-Memory OLTP usage scenarios**: In this section we will look at some useful usage scenarios

In-Memory OLTP architecture

The architecture of In-Memory OLTP on SQL Server is completely different from everything seen before on SQL Server. Authors of the solution proceeded from the assumption that everything that could be done on the disk-based part of the data engine was just an evolution of the data processing optimization, so some kind of revolution was needed. In this chapter, we will explain what In-Memory OLTP is, we will describe the top-level architecture, and then we'll jump deeper into the details of In-Memory OLTP.

To see the benefits gained when using In-Memory OLTP, we need to consider the differences between two areas of work: data storage architecture and user request processing phases.

Data storage differences in OLTP

Disk-based data is stored in classic files (.mdf or .ndf) and divided into small 8 KB parts called data pages. Those data pages are registered within other data pages called **Index Allocation Maps** (**IAMs**), and other types of data pages are used for identification, for example which data pages have free space and so on and so forth.

SQL Server uses all data page types to find out proper parts of data needed for request fulfillment, moves the data pages to the buffer cache, and does what's needed according to the user request. The movement of data pages back and forth between the physical disk and the buffer cache incurs significant overhead.

The second big issue occurs when data pages have to be protected against accidental reading or changing by concurrent sessions. Session isolation and protection invokes locking as an protective mechanism, used by SQL Server to avoid situations such as non-repeatable reads, dirty reads, or phantom reads.

 In-Memory tables, on the other hand, neither use data nor locking architecture. Structures of In-Memory tables are actually C-structures like other application objects and they are held in memory all the time when SQL Server is running. This omits the need for reading data from the disk when the data is required by a user request.

Even if it seems that In-Memory tables are somehow similar to structured buffers, In-Memory tables can be persisted on physical disks but in the form of sequential data saved into a dedicated filestream filegroup, also called a **memory optimized filegroup**. The persisting is done by SQL Server outside of regular user request processing, so the performance from the user's perspective is not affected by it. SQL Server has two ways of handling the data durability of In-Memory tables:

- **Full durable In-Memory tables**: These tables are ACID compliant, and when SQL Server is restarted, table content is reconstructed from the memory optimized filegroup.
- **Nondurable In-Memory tables**: The content of such tables is lost when SQL Server is restarted. That's why this type of In-Memory table is not ACID compliant.

Both types of In-Memory table have their purpose—some scenarios are mentioned in the last section of this chapter.

ACID is a shortcut for four basic transaction properties: **Atomicity**, **Consistency**, **Isolation**, and **Durability**. The last property is broken when we use non-durable In-Memory tables.

Another big difference is the mode of concurrency control. Records, or group of records of In-Memory tables, are not locked. SQL Server uses row versioning for concurrency control. This means that every record in a certain In-Memory table has two hidden columns called **Begin timestamp** (**BTS**) and **End timestamp** (**ETS**). When a record is inserted, the first version of the record is held with BTS containing the record time and ETS containing the special **infinity** symbol.

When the record is updated, SQL Server creates new version of the same record. The old version has the infinity symbol in ETS replaced by the so-called transaction timestamp value, and the same transaction timestamp value is used in the BTS of the new record version. When the transaction is committed, the transaction timestamp is replaced by the actual timestamp value in both the old and new version of the record. So the old version has ETS filled with the actual timestamp of the end validity, and at the same time the new version remains valid, with ETS set to infinity.

Old versions of records are scrapped by garbage collector asynchronously, so row versioning does not invoke memory consumption growth.

We can summarize the comparison as shown in the following table:

	Disk-based tables	In-Memory tables
Data storage	Data pages saved to disk	C-structs held in memory
Data movement	Huge movement between disk and memory	No data movement
Concurrency control	Locks and latches, pessimistic concurrency	Row versioning, optimistic concurrency

When approaches from the table are compared, In-Memory OLTP improves the performance of data storage and concurrency control up to ten times more than disk-based processing. But data storage and concurrency are not the only areas of improvement. Another area of improvement is **request processing** itself, and we will explore that in the next section.

Request processing differences in OLTP

User requests processed in traditional disk-based processing are received by the data engine and then several steps are carried out before a result of the request is sent back to the session's output buffer:

1. **Parsing**: Parsing is a syntactical check of the request validity. The result of the parse phase is a syntactical tree.
2. **Binding**: Binding checks for existence, user permissions, and valid usage of objects used in the query. During this phase the data engine reads the metadata of used objects.
3. **Algebraizing**: This process finds out and substitutes logical operators which represent certain actions declared in the request (for example, WHERE predicates or JOIN operators). The result of this phase is a so-called algebraizer tree containing the first form of the latter execution tree.
4. **Optimizing**: The optimization phase is probably the most complicated phase of request processing. SQL Server uses known metadata such as data types, indexes, statistics, and relative costs of operators used in algebraizer trees, and builds the execution tree. The optimization is highly affected by the state of the database, especially the timeliness of statistics.

5. **Compilation and execution**: When the query tree is optimized enough, SQL Server compiles the tree to the form known as an execution tree. The execution tree contains physical operators which are interpreted during execution by functions developed inside SQL Server's core. The execution tree is often cached into a memory section called the **procedure cache** so it can be reused.

The summary of user request processing is mentioned because we can now think of places where some performance enhancements can be done. From the preceding listed points, two areas are possible—optimizing and execution:

- When SQL Server optimizes a query, it uses more than 90 different factors or measures to recognize and create a good enough execution tree. The weights of those measures are changing slightly as versions of SQL Server are released and optimizing algorithms adjusted. Nowadays, it can increase performance by a tenth of a percent.
- The second area of enhancement is the execution part of query processing. The optimization of functions interpreting physical operations over data has probably the same minor benefit as the optimization adjustments themselves.

In SQL Server 2014, natively compiled stored procedures were introduced. This first attempt covered stored procedures but in later versions the set of objects programmable in a natively compiled manner was enhanced to scalar functions and triggers. Yet we still speak about natively compiled stored procedures.

A natively compiled stored procedure has some particularities and limitations because it is not interpreted such as traditional SQL statements, even though it is still writen using T-SQL language. When a natively compiled stored procedure is created, it's actually compiled into a set of C instructions and then, when called by a user, it's executed directly by the CPU without any additional overhead resulting from the necessity of optimization and compilation.

Comparing these two approaches of request processing—natively compiled versus traditional objects—we can see an improvement up to twenty times more than when using natively compiled stored procedures.

As written in this and previous sections, SQL Server is not one but two data processing engines now. The following section describes how those two parts of the data engine are working together.

Cooperation of disk-based and memory-based parts of SQL Server

In-Memory OLTP was incorporated into SQL Server as a second hidden engine, but from a client's perspective nothing has to be changed. Let's explore the architecture depicted in the following diagram:

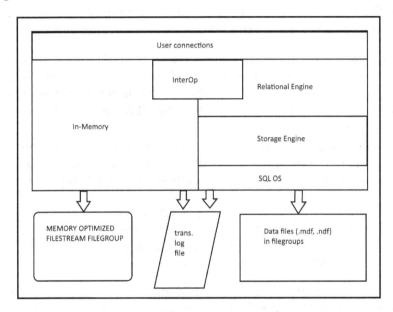

As seen in the the preceding diagram, the top layer is called **User connections** and covers the rest of engine so users are connected in the same way. When a user sends a request, the **InterOp** component serves as a sign post for In-Memory or disk-based processing. When the request is disk based, it's taken by **Relational Engine** for parsing, binding, and optimizing. Then it's sent to the **Storage Engine** which resolves execution in cooperation with **SQL OS**. Data is persisted in traditional data files, and transactions are logged in the transaction log file.

The **InterOp** component resolves parts of interpreted SQL requests using In-Memory tables. When a user calls the natively compiled stored procedure, **InterOp** sends the request completely to the In-Memory part and the request is processed in the way it was described in the previous section. Data is read by the natively compiled stored procedure. When the transaction is executed, SQL Server uses the same transaction log file for transaction logging. This feature covers transactional consistency across both In-Memory and disk-based parts of the database.

Both engines must share the same memory given the limits of the edition of SQL Server installed. For Enterprise Edition, the memory limit for In-Memory OLTP is up to 2 TB. For other editions, the limit is computed as 1/4 of the memory limited by the edition.

For example, let's look at the standard edition. Its memory limit is set to 128 GB, so the In-Memory OLTP could occupy an additional 32 GB of memory. Beware of sufficient memory present on the OS, because the In-Memory OLTP is quite aggressive. The following diagram shows what will happen when the memory of the OS becomes low:

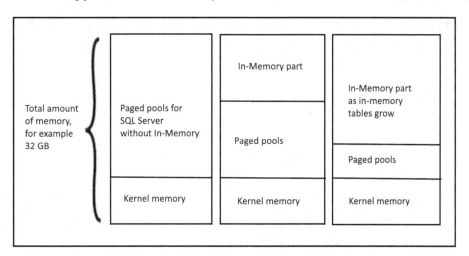

As seen in the preceding diagram, the In-Memory part of memory steals memory from paged memory pools, so In-Memory could occupy almost all the memory dedicated to SQL Server.

In-Memory OLTP limitations

As explained in the previous section, In-Memory tables have limits for memory usage set by the edition of SQL Server. But it's not the only limit we have to keep in mind. There are many more limitations, and they are as follows:

- In-Memory tables cannot have data types such as XML, geography, or geometry.
- In-Memory tables cannot be indexed by full-text indexes
- In-Memory tables cannot be used in replications
- In-Memory tables cannot refer to disk-based tables by foreign key constraints
- In-Memory tables cannot use computed columns

- In-Memory tables are always bound to the memory optimized filegroup, hence they cannot be placed into partition schemas
- In-Memory tables cannot be filetables

Natively compiled stored procedures also have limitations. The biggest limitation of natively compiled stored procedures is that they can handle In-Memory data only, yet traditional SQL queries, stored procedures, or other objects can use both disk-based as well as In-Memory data. Other limitations are, for example:

- Transactions cannot be controlled, everything is closed to the atomic block
- A lots of syntactical limitations are present, for example common table expressions, cursors, temporary tables, the SELECT..INTO construct, and so on.

All these limitations have to be considered when we want to migrate some functionality of our databases to In-Memory OLTP.

At this moment we know that In-Memory OLTP consists of tables intended for fast data contention, held in memory and using optimistic concurrency approach. Also we knew natively compiled stored procedures, triggers and scalar functions, which can handle data in in-memory tables. Both together, in-memory tables and natively compiled objects, maintain very fast data access in situations when classic disk-based tables and T-SQL procedural objects reach their performance limits. In the next section we will go through the procedure for setting In-Memory OLTP on the server and the database.

Creating In-Memory tables and natively compiled stored procedures

The previous section was about the top-level architecture of In-Memory OLTP. Knowing the architecture will help us to be familiar with all the steps needed to set up environment for In-Memory OLTP applications, and to create objects within it.

In the following section we will go through creating memory optimized filegroups and then we will create some tables, indexes, and natively compiled stored procedures. All these tasks will be described in the form of walk through examples.

Preparing for In-Memory OLTP

The first step is to create a memory optimized filegroup. The following screenshot shows you how to use the **Properties** dialog for the database, opened by a right-click on the database in **Object Explorer**:

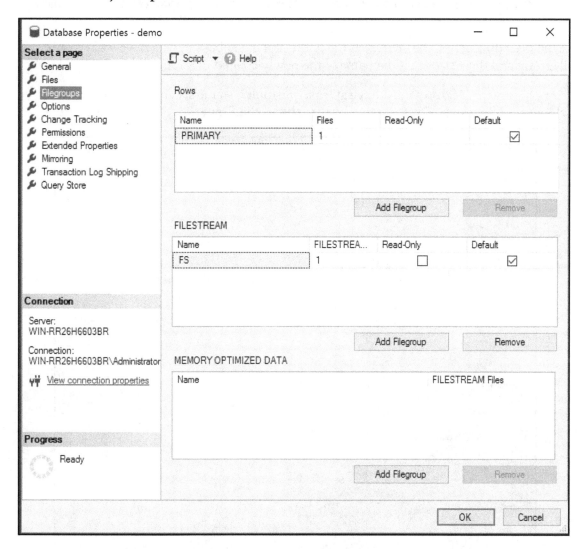

As seen in the preceding screenshot, the well known **Filegroups** tab is divided into three lists. The last list, labeled **MEMORY OPTIMIZED DATA**, is dedicated to creating the memory optimized filegroup.

Every database can contain one memory optimized filegroup only, so when the filegroup is created by the **Add Filegroup** button, the button is disabled and no additional memory optimized filegroups can be created. The second option we can use to create memory optimized filegroups is to use a simple script, as follows:

```
ALTER DATABASE [demo] ADD FILEGROUP [INMEM] CONTAINS MEMORY_OPTIMIZED_DATA
GO
```

In the preceding script, the [demo] is the name of the database to which we want to add the filegroup and the [INMEM] is the name of the newly created filegroup.

Every filestream filegroup must have at least one folder, so the second step is to add a folder to the filegroup. The following picture shows the **Properties** dialog one more time:

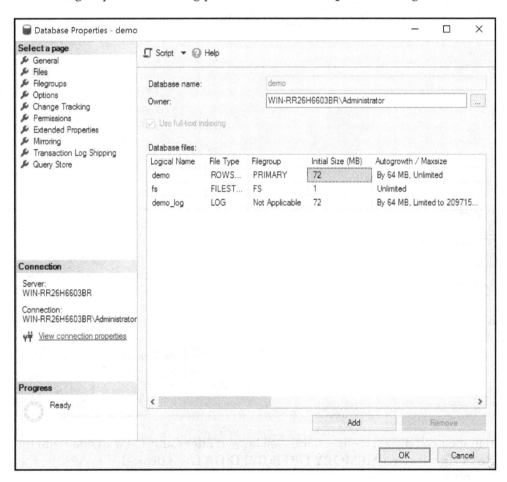

In the preceding screenshot, the **Files** section is selected. By clicking the **Add button** a new row is added to the **Database files** list and we have to fill in these columns:

- **Logical name**: The name used for administrative purposes such as backup.
- **File Type**: It could be rows, a log, or a filestream. The last choice is the most suitable one.
- **Filegroup**: The name of the memory optimized filegroup from the dropdown.
- **Path** (not visible on the screenshot): The path to an existing folder which will contain data persisted the from In-Memory tables.

The second option is script, as follows:

```
ALTER DATABASE [demo]
ADD FILE
(
  NAME = N'inmem_file',
  FILENAME = N'F:\DATA\inmem'
)
TO FILEGROUP [INMEM]
GO
```

Here are some short explanations about the preceding script:

- [demo] is the name of the sample database
- inmem_file is the logical name of the folder which is added to the filegroup
- F:\DATA\inmem is the path to the folder containing data
- [INMEM] is the name of the memory optimized filegroup

After doing the steps described in this section, the environment is prepared and we can start to create objects.

Creating In-Memory OLTP objects

Two types of objects are created within In-Memory OLTP—tables with indexes and natively compiled stored procedures. Now we'll go through their creation.

Creating tables with indexes

The basic syntax for creating tables is almost the same, but we have to consider some extras:

- Index is a part of table creation
- Clustered indexes are not allowed

In other words, we are creating indexes together with CREATE TABLE or ALTER TABLE statements.

 In earlier versions of SQL Server, the ALTER TABLE statement was not allowed in an In-Memory environment. It was introduced in SQL Server 2016.

The syntax for creating a table is as follows:

```
create table Ratings_InMem
(
Id int not null identity primary key nonclustered
, UserId int not null
, MovieId int not null
, Rating tinyint not null
, index ix_Users (UserId)
)
with
(
memory_optimized = on, durability = schema_and_data
)
```

As seen in the script example, the base syntax is very similar to disk-based table creation. The exceptions are:

- In-Memory tables don't support clustered indexes. That's why the primary key is marked as nonclustered.
- Indexes are a part of an In-Memory table; they are not created separately by the CREATE INDEX statement. The last row in the table structure shows us how to create the index. When indexes have to be changed, the ALTER TABLE statement is used.
- The ON keyword is used for placing a new disk-based table or disk-based index into the right filegroup, and is prohibited when creating In-Memory tables.

- The WITH keyword says that the table will be in memory. Its definition consists of:
  - A memory_optimized option set to on.
  - A durability option. This option sets whether the table will be fully durable (it's the value schema_and_data as seen in the script; it's also a default value) or if it will be a non-durable table (the value is schema_only in that case).

Tables can be accessed by traditional interpreted T-SQL statements. This is necessary because otherwise In-Memory tables would stay separated from the rest of the database. For some operations, using In-Memory tables is very good to enhance performance when using natively compiled stored procedures. The next section shows you how to write such a procedure.

Natively compiled stored procedures

Natively compiled stored procedures are written in T-SQL. When such a procedure is created, it's saved into metadata and compiled into C. It makes natively compiled stored procedures very efficient, but the C compilation also causes a lot of limitations. Let's take a look at the following example:

```
create proc procNativeModification
  (@Id int
  , @UserId int
  , @MoveiId int
  , @Rating int)
with native_compilation, schemabinding
as
begin atomic with (transaction isolation level = snapshot, language =
N'English')
  if @id is null
    insert dbo.Ratings_InMem (UserId, MovieId, Rating)
    values (@UserId, @MoveiId, @Rating)
  else
    update dbo.Ratings_InMem
    set UserId = @UserId, MovieId = @MoveiId, Rating = @Rating
    where Id = @Id
end
go
```

This procedure does a very simple thing; when a record does not exist yet in the table called `Ratings_InMem`, it's inserted, otherwise it's updated according to the key value provided in the `@Id` parameter.

Let's explore this, which differs from regular stored procedures. The first syntax mandatory for every natively compiled procedure are in the header. This declare that the procedure is natively compiled (the `native_compilation` keyword), and the procedure also must be schema bound (the `schemabinding` keyword). The schema binding forces the writer of the procedure to use two phase names inside the procedure (not just `Ratings_InMem` as a table name but `dbo.Ratings_InMem`).

The body must be enclosed in an atomic block. As seen in the preceding code, it's traditionally the `begin .. end` block but it's marked by the keyword `atomic`. The atomic block has additional properties: `language` and `transaction isolation level`. The `language` property can be set to almost any language and the `transaction isolation level` is always set to `snapshot` because it means that updates will be row versioned.

Natively compiled stored procedures cannot access disk-based tables, so when creating them we must keep in mind this limitation. If we still want to profit from the efficiency of these procedures, we have to migrate all tables used in transactions to the In-Memory area.

Natively compiled stored procedures offer big performance gains and they are suitable for cases when new transactions are coming frequently (for example, thousands of transactions every second).

At this moment, we know how In-Memory tables and natively compiled stored procedures are working together. In the next section we will briefly describe how to monitor In-Memory contention.

Migrating disk-based objects to In-Memory OLTP

Lots of systems were built a long time before In-Memory OLTP was born. Such systems would enhance performance but maybe the traditional method of optimization would fail. For these cases, Microsoft offers reports and wizards helping with migration of tables and stored procedures to the In-Memory environment.

The first question is which tables are suitable to be migrated to the In-Memory OLTP to improve performance. The second question is how expensive the migration could be. The migration of tables and stored procedures to the In-Memory OLTP has to be transparent to the applications using it, otherwise significant effort will be needed to remake some part of the client applications due to the need for physical design changes on the database side. As was mentioned in the *In-Memory OLTP limitations* section, not all data types or constraint types are supported, and sometimes it's hard to consider all of the limitations.

Both questions are answered by a report called the **Transaction Analysis Performance Overview**. This report is reachable via SSMS by right-clicking the database in **Object Explorer** and selecting this report from the list of reports. When opened, the report provides a signpost as seen in the following screenshot:

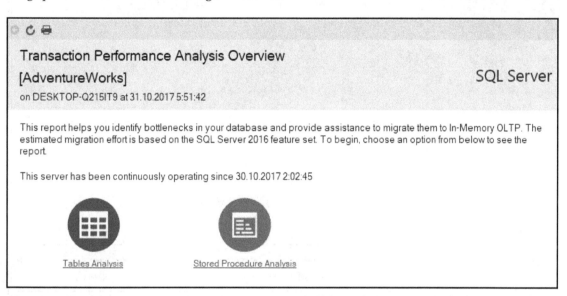

When we want to inspect tables which are candidates to migration, we will click through the left option labeled **Table Analysis**, and for migration candidates from stored procedures we will use the right link labeled **Stored Procedure Analysis**.

When using the **Table Analysis** link, a report called **Recommended Tables by Usage** will be opened, as follows:

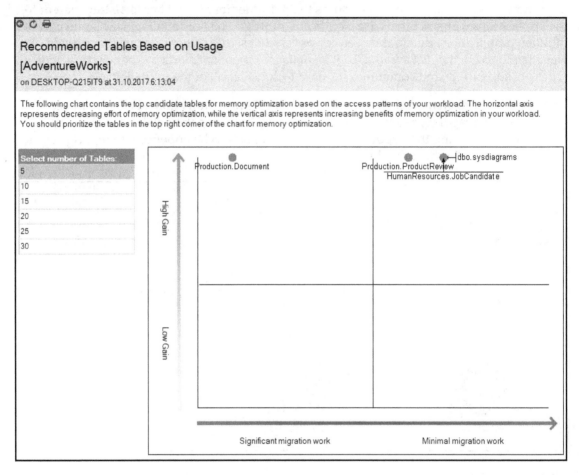

The preceding report shows a selected number of tables which are probably good for migration to In-Memory. The left table with numbers allows us to select how tables will be seen in the diagram on the right side. The diagram itself shows tables as blue points. As the point when a certain table moves to the right top corner, the migration of the table is considered useful from a performance perspective and the effort needed for migration is relatively small. If tables are shown in the top left corner, they are still heavy loaded but the migration effort will be big. Tables in the bottom half of the diagram are not good candidates for migration at all.

When we need more detailed information about migration blockers, we can click certain tables in the diagram and a new report appears:

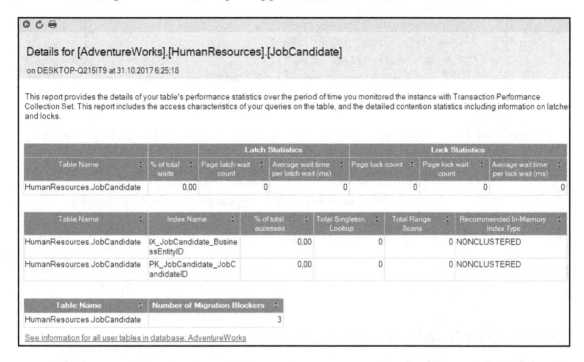

The preceding picture shows the **Details for table_name** report. It summarizes actual wait statistics, which is good criteria for decisions about migration (more waits are issued, so it's a better idea to migrate the table) and it also summarizes existing indexes and the total number of potential migration issues. Unfortunately, this report does not show which issues have to be resolved prior to migration. We can try to find out all the blockers. In this example, the three problems are:

- **A clustered index created by the primary key constraint**: We have to create a non-clustered primary key
- **A foreign key referring to another table**: Here we have to decide if we will migrate the parent table as well or if we'll drop the foreign key constraint
- **A column of the** xml **data type**: This is the most serious issue because we must drop the column and save the data to another disk-based table; this action means effort for all client applications using this table

The following screenshot shows the structure of the table spread in the **Object Explorer**:

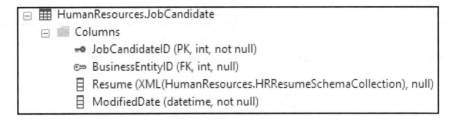

If all roadblocks are removed, we can start the migration itself. It can be done by using a simple wizard. The wizard is accessible this way:

1. In the **Object Explorer**, spread the **Tables** node under your database.
2. Right-click on the desired table and from the popup menu select **Memory Optimization Advisor**.
3. The wizard is open, so follow its steps.

The reports described in this section help us to recognize tables which could be moved into the In-Memory OLTP. In next section we will take care of memory consumption.

Monitoring In-Memory OLTP

As was mentioned in the *Cooperation of disk-based and memory-based parts of SQL Server* section, memory consumption of the In-Memory part of the database can be huge and aggressive. That's why it's necessary to monitor memory amounts occupied by In-Memory objects regularly. The simplest way to obtain an overview of In-Memory size is to use reports in the Management Studio:

1. Right-click on a database in Management Studio and select **Reports** in the appearing popup menu
2. Under the **Standard Reports** option, select **Memory Usage by Memory Optimized Objects** in the list of reports

The report shown by this option is depicted in the following screenshot:

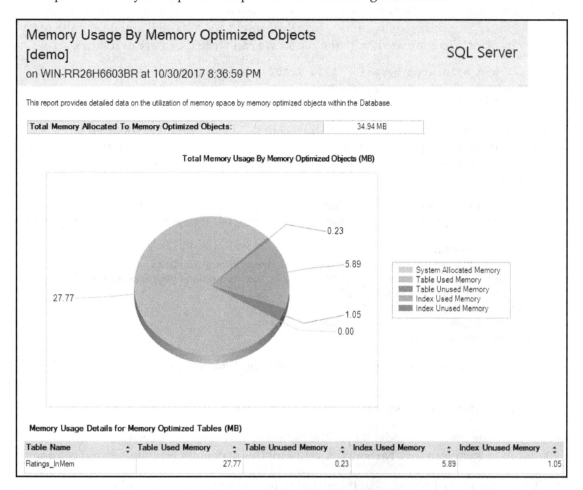

The first row shows the total amount of memory consumed by objects created by the user. The diagram shows several sections of In-Memory allocation such as tables and indexes. The table at the bottom of the report shows the size of each In-Memory table within the indexes.

But there are also internal objects used by SQL Server for internal purposes. For a better overview of complete In-Memory content, we can use a dynamic management view called `sys.dm_db_xtp_memory_consumers`. This DMV shows the allocated and used parts of memory by object. To compare it with the report we can write the query as follows:

```
select sum(allocated_bytes) / 1024 / 1024. as TotalObjectsMemoryInMB
from sys.dm_db_xtp_memory_consumers
where object_id > 0
```

This query returns a number exactly the same as in the **Total Memory Allocated to Memory Optimized Objects** field in the first part of the previous report. In the same way, we can try to compute numbers in the rest of the report. The following code is provided as an example:

```
select object_name(xtp.object_id) as ObjectName
    , iif(grouping_id(object_name(xtp.object_id), xtp.memory_consumer_desc)
> 0
        , 'TOTAL'
        , xtp.memory_consumer_desc) as MemoryConsumerDesc
    , sum(xtp.used_bytes) / 1024 / 1024. as UsedMemoryByObjectInMB
    , sum(xtp.allocated_bytes) / 1024 / 1024. as
AllocatedMemoryByObjectInMB
from sys.dm_db_xtp_memory_consumers as xtp
group by grouping sets
(
    (object_name(xtp.object_id), xtp.memory_consumer_desc)
    , ()
)
having sum(xtp.used_bytes) / 1024 / 1024. > 0
```

Let's explain the preceding code. It uses the same `sys.dm_db_xtp_memory_consumers` dynamic management view. The `select` clause of this statement contains several columns.

The first column is just `object_id` translated to the object name by the built-in `object_name` function.

The second column is three nested functions. The first function used is `iif`. This built-in function is used here for the creation of a summary row description of the result set. The first parameter of the `iif` function tests the level of grouping. It uses the `grouping_id` function. This function is very useful when an aggregate query is written with more combinations of grouping criteria, as seen in the `group by` clause. When the lowest level of grouping is computed on a certain record, the function returns zero.

When a grouping column is omitted by SQL Server, in other words, when a higher level of aggregation is computed on a certain row, the function returns an integer value bigger than zero. In our case, the `grouping_id` function returns three when the total row is computed, otherwise it returns zero. The second parameter, the so-called true block, returns the word `TOTAL` when the grouping level is the higher one. The third parameter returns the `memory_consumer_desc` column when the `grouping_id` returns zero. Simply said, the second column shows the concrete memory consumer description or the word `TOTAL`.

The third and fourth columns are the results of the aggregation. The third column shows the MB actually used by all memory consumers one by one, and the fourth column shows the memory allocated by the consumers.

The results of the query look like this:

	ObjectName	MemConsumerDesc	ObjectUsedMemoryInMB	ObjectAllocatedMemoryInMB
1	NULL	256K page pool	2.500000	2.500000
2	NULL	4K page pool	0.007812	0.015625
3	NULL	64K page pool	0.125000	0.125000
4	NULL	Database internal heap	0.058593	0.375000
5	NULL	Hash index	0.210937	0.210937
6	NULL	Logical Root table	0.003906	0.187500
7	NULL	Physical Root table	0.000976	0.062500
8	NULL	Range index heap	0.000976	0.625000
9	NULL	Storage internal heap	0.008789	0.562500
10	NULL	Storage user heap	0.005859	0.062500
11	NULL	Tail cache 256K page pool	38.500000	38.500000
12	Ratings_InMem	Range index heap	5.891601	6.937500
13	Ratings_InMem	Table heap	27.767578	28.000000
14	NULL	TOTAL	75.086914	78.664062

As seen in the preceding screenshot, SQL Server allocates and uses more memory objects than just tables and indexes. The actual memory consumed by the In-Memory functionality of SQL Server is in surrogate record with the `TOTAL` in the memory consumer description (`MemConsumerDesc`) column, and in the fourth column labeled `ObjectAllocatedMemoryInMB`. Its value is approximately double the **Total Memory Allocated to Memory Optimized** column of the **Memory Usage by Memory Optimized Objects** report.

If you want to compare the values shown on the report with values received by querying the DMV, add all values from the `ObjectAllovatedMemoryInMB` for the `ObjectName` to the `Ratings_InMem` value. You will obtain a 34.9375 value; when rounded up it is 34.94 MB. Now add on all the values from the bottom table of the report. You will get 34.94 MB. This means that the DMV computes exactly the same data as the report shows, but in the report, memory consumers are limited to user objects.

At this point, all information about In-Memory OLTP has been explained. In the next section we will explore some useful use cases.

In-Memory OLTP usage scenarios

The upcoming sections are going to show you some useful scenarios for In-Memory OLTP usage. The sections are designated as walk through examples. We will work with a large amount of data into In-Memory, then we will change the scope to heavily updated data, and in the next exercise we will add a system versioning feature. In the last example we will divide OLTP and OLAP workloads to cooperate in separate areas on top of quickly incoming data.

Assignment of the user story sample

To provide a consistent use case, we will use an imaginary water management company. Such companies have geographically spread tube networks delivering water across a whole region. The network has to be monitored constantly because the company has to be informed about every abnormality or disorder as soon as possible.

That's why there's approximately 100,000 sensors measuring the amount of water flowing through the network. Every sensor sends records with it's own identification and measures flow rate every 5 seconds. It means 20,000 simple transactions per second. This scenario is typical for In-Memory OLTP applications as the amount of transactions processed in regular disk-based OLTP causes the enhanced risk of locking conflicts.

The company also requested reports showing trends, history, and statistics about water flow rates over time:

1. Our first example will resolve the amount of transactions by capturing all new information sent by the sensors using INSERT statements only, so it will work as a log.

2. The second example will do the same task using INSERT or UPDATE statements.

3. The third example will add the functionality to be able to show real-time information about current state of the network.

Example 1 – inserting incoming data into In-Memory tables

This first sample shows probably the most traditional method of data capture for production tracking or monitoring systems. It originates from traditional disk-based data processing. What we need is a table living in In-Memory and also very simple natively compiled stored procedures to achieve the best possible performance.

Our first code sample shows the table creation. We can still have to keep in mind that the database prepared for such table must have memory optimized filegroup:

```
create table SensorData
(
Id bigint not null identity primary key nonclustered
, SensorId uniqueidentifier not null
, RecordTime datetime2 not null default(sysdatetime())
, WaterFlowRate decimal(7, 2) not null
)
with
(
memory_optimized = on
)
go
```

The previous code sample shows the creation of very simple table without indexes, except the primary key. For data handling, we need to develop a natively compiled stored procedure. The creation script is shown in following code block:

```
create procedure procAddSensorData
(
  @sensorId uniqueidentifier
```

```
    , @waterFlowRate dec(7, 2)
)
with native_compilation, schemabinding
as
begin atomic with (transaction isolation level = snapshot, language =
'English')
insert dbo.SensorData (SensorId, WaterFlowRate) values (@sensorId,
@waterFlowRate)
end
go
```

As seen in the preceding code block, the procedure does only one action—inserts new record.

The first example seems to be ready to go live, but that's not true. We must consider In-Memory limitations with regards to the edition of SQL Server, and we have to decide how much memory will be dedicated to In-Memory tasks. That's why one more requirement needs to be fulfilled. We have to develop a retention policy.

The retention policy is simply an action, moving data from an In-Memory table to a disk-based table. It could be done as in following script:

```
create table SensorDataHistory
(
  Id bigint not null primary key
, SensorId uniqueidentifier not null
, RecordTime datetime2 not null
, WaterFlowRate decimal(7, 2) not null
) on [primary]
go

create proc procMoveSensorData
  @recordsBefore datetime2
as
begin try
  begin tran
    insert SensorDataHistory (Id, SensorId, RecordTime, WaterFlowRate)
    select Id, SensorId, RecordTime, WaterFlowRate
    from SensorData
    where RecordTime <= @recordsBefore

    delete SensorData where RecordTime <= @recordsBefore
  commit
end try
begin catch
  rollback;
  throw;
```

```
end catch
go
```

The previous script consists of two steps. In the first step, a table called `SensorDataHistory` is created. This table will contain all historical data. The second step is the creation of a stored procedure called `procMoveSensorData`. The procedure invokes regular explicit transactions controlled by the `try..catch` block. The transaction itself inserts data intended for deletion from an In-Memory table to a classic disk-based table, and then deletes copied records from the In-Memory table. If some errors occur, all the action is rolled back correctly.

 This procedure is working with both In-Memory and disk based-data; that's why it cannot be written as natively compiled. For better performance, the procedure could be rewritten into two procedures. The first one would copy data into a disk-based table, with the second stored procedure nested into the first one—it could be natively compiled and could just delete data from In-Memory table. Transaction consistency will be kept by the first procedure.

The last step is to schedule the calling of the procedure, for example for everyday. It's just two rows of code to be written into a job step. Let's look at the script:

```
declare @timeBefore date = getdate() - 1
exec procMoveSensorData @timeBefore
```

As seen in the preceding script, deletion time is computed as a current date and time minus one day. Then the procedure is executed. This example will move all the data inserted before yesterday.

Let's summarize how the assignment was satisfied:

- Data was stored in a fast, lock-free structure so no conflicts nor waits were expected
- Data was moved from the In-Memory to disk to keep the environment healthy, but we needed to make some extra effort to manage the retention policy
- Statistical reports were selected against the disk-based table with no regards to constantly incoming data (data delays would then occur)
- Real-time analytics were selected against an In-Memory table

Given the third point, we have to find a better solution, and the solution will be provided in next section.

Example 2 – updating data in an In-Memory table

The previous sample involved big data contention with the need for a regular retention policy. This sample is going to start at almost the same point. Let's create an In-Memory table which is similar to the previous one, as follows:

```
create table SensorData2
(
SensorId uniqueidentifier not null primary key nonclustered
, RecordTime datetime2 not null default(sysdatetime())
, WaterFlowRate decimal(7, 2) not null
)
with
(
memory_optimized = on
)
go
```

As seen in the preceding script, the table does not need an extra surrogate key (compared to the table from the first example), as every sensor is registered once. The rest of table definition remains the same. Bigger changes have to be done in the stored procedure's definition, as follows:

```
create procedure procUpdateSensorData
(
  @sensorId uniqueidentifier
  , @waterFlowRate dec(7, 2)
)
with native_compilation, schemabinding
as
begin atomic with (transaction isolation level = snapshot, language =
'English')
  update dbo.SensorData2 set
    WaterFlowRate = @waterFlowRate
    , RecordTime = default
  where SensorId = @sensorId
  if @@rowcount = 0
    insert dbo.SensorData2 (SensorId, WaterFlowRate) values (@sensorId,
@waterFlowRate)
end
go
```

The preceding script creates new stored procedure called `procUpdateSensorData`. This stored procedure tries to update a record according to the parameters provided. If the record does not exist (a new sensor was installed), then a new record is inserted. This conditional `insert` ensures that the new sensor's data will be saved correctly.

This design does not cover the requirement for statistical reports as it overwrites data time after time. Fortunately, SQL Server provides a feature called **temporal tables**. The idea of temporal tables is to catch every data change done in a table and save the changes to a separate table with the same structure. Aside from this functionality, the T-SQL language provides a syntax for querying the original table with the possibility of time shifts as needed.

The following script shows you how to modify the table structure to start the change capture:

```
alter table SensorData2
add
StartDate datetime2 generated always as row start,
EndDate datetime2 generated always as row end,
period for system_time (StartDate, EndDate)

alter table SensorData2
set
(system_versioning = on (HISTORY_TABLE = dbo.SensorData2History))
```

The preceding script has two steps. The first step adds two new columns which will set a range for record version validity. Those columns must be of the `datetime2` data type and both columns also must have the adjective `generated always`.... Also, the `period for` ... is mandatory. Even though the first step modifies the structure of the table, this kind of change is transparent to other database objects and client applications. But the table is not the temporal table yet. The second step is the moment when the data change capture is turned on.

> The history table could be created as a standalone table with the same structure as the original table and bound to the temporal table feature later. It's good when a lots of changes are done because we can create the history table more precisely, for example to partition schema.

From now on, we can write simple queries against the In-Memory table itself to retrieve current values, for example to select `select SensorId, RecordTime, WaterFlowRate from SensorData2,` or we can write queries still against the In-Memory table but returning a state from history. An example of such a query is shown in following script:

```
select SensorId, RecordTime, WaterFlowRate
from SensorData2 for system_time as of '2017-02-11 00:00'
```

The preceding script will move us back to the time provided in the `system_time as of` clause. If we want to have a set of record versions for some time range, we can use a similar query with a slightly different `system_time` clause. An example of the query looks like this:

```
select SensorId, RecordTime, WaterFlowRate
from
SensorData2 for system_time between '2017-02-11 00:00' and '2017-02-11
01:00am'
```

Temporal tables offer very comfortable ways of exploring changes in data over time.

Let's summarize this example:

- Data was stored in fast, lock-free structures so no conflicts nor waits were expected
- Data was relatively small because the insertion of new records was dramatically reduced
- We didn't need to manage the data retention policy
- Statistical reports were selected using the `system_time` clause in the select statements so no data delay would occur
- Real-time analytics were selected against In-Memory tables

This sample took us one step higher because of less memory consumption and natively created historization, so all points of assignment are fulfilled now. But real-time analytics still are subject to improvement. The last sample will show you how to ultimately improve performance.

Example 3 – improving real-time analytics

The previous examples relied on the performance ensured by memory storage. But if data contention is actually huge, it's a good idea to improve the read load and at the same time not affect write load. In this example, we will just enhance the solution described in the previous section.

When we think of real-time analytics, we can imagine some kind of aggregation queries which are issued by a client frequently. As an example, we can use a regularly (and often) refreshed dashboard. Such dashboards or any other aggregate queries requested can often profit from `columnstore` indexes. SQL Server enables us to create `columnstore` indexes over an In-Memory structure. The sample script looks like this:

```
alter table SensorData2 add index cs_SensorData2 clustered columnstore
```

Its only action we need to improve is the querying of In-Memory tables. The `columnstore` index is described briefly in the `Chapter 6`, *Indexing and performance*, as an object, which is very useful for analytical queries with long full and range scans.

As in the previous examples, we have to summarize what was done:

- Data was stored in fast, lock-free structures so no conflicts nor waits were expected
- Data was relatively small because the insertion of new records was dramatically reduced
- We didn't need to manage data retention policy
- Statistical reports were selected using `system_time` clause in select statements so no data delay would occur
- Real-time analytics were selected against In-Memory `columnstore` indexes

This third sample showed us the complete functionality which could be used to create efficient and extremely powerful solutions.

Summary

This chapter provided a detailed overview of a very valuable part of SQL Server called In-Memory OLTP. The biggest advantage is the In-Memory nature of the solution; the biggest risk we have to consider is the memory consumption.

In the first section, we went through an architectural overview and also a comparison between disk-based data processing and In-Memory data processing. This comparison showed how different approaches to both parts of SQL Server are used when handling requests.

The second section was a guide to tasks which have to be done before In-Memory OLTP implementation, and then we started to create objects hosted by the In-Memory OLTP part of SQL Server.

The last section was a real-world use case of In-Memory implementation. This section described some samples of In-Memory usage step by step.

The next chapter will explain another set of advanced scenarios, and the cooperation of an on-premises SQL Server with cloud technologies.

12
Combining SQL Server 2017 with Azure

Cloud technologies have been growing over the last couple of years and nowadays they are able to cover every global, technical, or business need without compromise. SQL Server can be completely hosted in cloud environments; we would also have Microsoft SQL Server provisioned on-premise but we still use the advantages of cloud environment. In this chapter, we will provide an overview of what's possible in Azure when manipulating data, and then we will go through hybrid scenarios combining on-premise instances of SQL Server with Azure.

The main outcomes of this chapter are:

- **Overview of data related technologies in Microsoft Azure**: In this chapter, a set of server and serverless technologies will be described
- **Microsoft SQL Server 2017 and hybrid scenarios**: This chapter offers end-to-end and step-by-step samples of several features such as StretchDB, data files in Azure, backup to URL, and also managed backup to Azure

Overview of data related technologies in Microsoft Azure

Cloud technologies profit basically from the so called all independent concept. It means a cooperation of many computers, disk arrays, server network switches, and many other elements collectively called nodes.

When some node is not available, the rest of the nodes fully cover its absence. In such moments the whole system must not be unstable or it could go down.

To build such an environment in-house leads to an overkill of expenses. Years ago big players came with an offer to provide fully supported services using the cloud concept. It reduces the expense IT solutions because hardware and software are maintained by the provider, and the customer always pays just for the feature and performance level they need. One of the most basic properties of every tenancy is pay-as-you-go charging mode, which enables to pause, stop, or completely remove features or technologies not needed at the moment. When new web applications, storage, whole Windows servers, or any other service is needed, it's usually just a few clicks away from the tenant. This pay-as-you-go concept supports very good predictability of expenses of IT.

Microsoft also started to offer huge cloud-based technology and named it Microsoft Azure. Nowadays Azure is covering all IT needs and also offering a step-ahead with very new technology such as AI, IoT, data science tools, and so on. It's very hard to describe all of the technology offered by Microsoft in a couple of words, we can imagine SharePoint servers, Active Directory in cloud, and also virtual servers with many operating systems and services on it. In addition, the scale of products and technology is still growing and every existing technology found in Azure is continuously improved.

In the following sections, we will just focus on data related technology such as Azure SQL database, Azure SQL Server, Azure SQL DWH, Cosmos DB, and Data Factories. In every section, a short sample will be provided. If you want to try it yourself, remember that you need an Azure account. If you don't have one, it's simple to create a trial account at `https:/ /azure.microsoft.com/en-us/free/` (this link was working during writing of this book at fall of 2017, maybe it will slightly change in the future).

Understanding Azure SQL database

In simple terms, Azure SQL database is a typical relational database which behaves to an users as a database without an SQL Server instance. It's not true, however, because actually the database is hosted in SQL Server cloud environment in the form of a **partially contained** database.

The database containment can be used on-premise as well. The partially contained database is a SQL Server database that has some server level properties inherited to itself. That's why such databases are also called self-contained databases. Using self-contained databases on on-premise SQL Server instances enables DBAs to create users with passwords. It bypasses traditional authentication and authorization models described in Chapter 4, *Securing Your SQL Server*.

The user with the password is a kind of user that is not authenticated by an SQL Server instance, but it's authenticated directly by a certain database. It could be very useful for scenarios such as hosting web databases or having some database often migrated between more server instances.

Starting with Azure portal

Everything in Azure is basically done through a web application called Azure portal. It's placed on the following URL `https://portal.azure.com`. We will visit it very often throughout the next sections and chapters. For those of you who have never used Microsoft's web technologies before, you need to create a new LiveID account. Then the user is signed in with the LiveID or with an organizational account. Azure portal shows a dashboard and on the dashboard the work starts. The following screenshot shows how to get oriented in the portal:

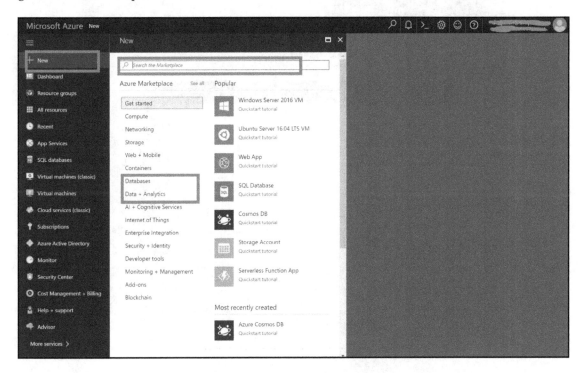

When Azure portal is accessed, it shows a dashboard in the main area and a set of the most favorite features that could be requested. When you click on the **New** link in the top left corner, a screen with a more complex set of features and technology appears.

It can be filtered by categories (**Databases** and **Data + Analytics** are highlighted in the red rectangle in the middle), but sometimes it's easier just to start typing the feature name into the search box at the top of the screen (highlighted in the red rectangle at the top).

For example, let's write a word `database`. Several options will be shown such as **Azure Database for PostgreSQL** or **Azure Database for MySQL**, but also the **SQL Database** label will appear. When selected, the screen offering technology creation disappears and it's replaced by a screen for Azure SQL database creation. The following screenshot shows this screen:

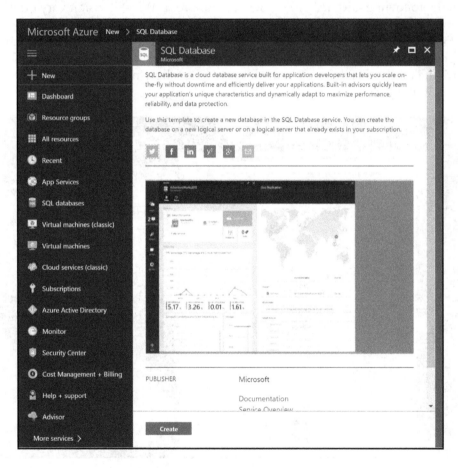

The only control available on the screen is the **Create** button. The rest of the screen mainly offers an overview of how the database looks and also links to documentation, and so on. It's the same for all features being created from the portal. The next section will describe how to create a complete and ready-to-live Azure SQL database.

Creating the Azure SQL database

The previous section was focused on basic orientation in the Azure portal. Now we are going to continue with the Azure SQL database creation. When we click the **Create** button, a new screen will be shown as seen in the following screenshot:

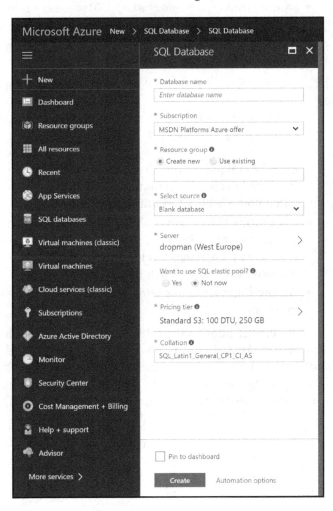

Let's describe fields on the screen depicted previously one by one:

- **Database name**: Just the name of the new database.
- **Subscription**: Subscription is account for payments and invoicing. One login can have more subscriptions.
- **Resource group**: It is an organizational unit, not an SQL Server! One resource group can hold all resources belonging to the same solution or application.
- **Select source**: This drop-down list offers three values:
    - **Blank database**: New blank database prepared for content provision
    - Sample (`AdventureWorksLT`): Database containing sample data about a non-existing company called Adventure Works
    - Backup: Database recreated from existing backup of the same or other Azure SQL database.
- **Server**: The server property is not about creation of a new instance of SQL Server. It provides:
    - The first part of the name used as a server name when connecting to Azure SQL database. The link is always in a form `selectedservername.database.windows.net` form. This name must be unique within all of Azure. Besides the name, if it already exists red exclamation mark is shown, else a green tick is shown when name is choosen uniquely.
    - Geographical location of the newly created database (for example Western Europe, West Central US, and so on). Select this property with care, a database created in location high distance slows response times down dramatically.
    - Admin login and password: it's not `sa` login, the login behaves more such as a dbo user.
- **Want to use SQL elastic pool?**: When the answer is **Yes**, we can set fix pricing for a group of databases created within the same elastic pool. It helps when each of the databases in the same elastic pool has its peak hours in a different time. If we want to control pricing for just one database (or the database has more or less constant load), the answer for the question is **No**.

- **Pricing tier**: How much performing database we need, so how much we have to pay. The pricing tier is set in **Database Transaction Units** (**DTUs**); unit composed from memory consumption, CPU consumption, reads and writes, and the maximum storage amount. For example, the cheapest database has 5 DTUs and maximum storage 2 GB and is about $5 per month. The most expensive database is 1000 DTUs and maximum storage 1 TB. But it's more than $800 per month. This property can be changed anytime, so if you are not sure how expensive the database should be, start with cheaper settings and when needed, add more resources, DTUs, storage, or both.
- **Collation**: Default database collation. This property is the same as in on-premises databases.

When all properties are filled, we can check the **Pin to dashboard** checkbox. It pins the database on the dashboard and it's useful for overview or when the database settings are often visited. The last action could be **Create** for immediate creation of the database, or the **Automation option** link. The **Automation option** link generates a full JSON description of the newly created database. It helps when resources are created or configured in Azure by using **Azure Resource Manager** for provisioning automation of different resources. Clicking the **Create** button starts the database creation. It lasts a couple of minutes and then a new screen appears with an overview of the database. The overview is shown in the following screenshot:

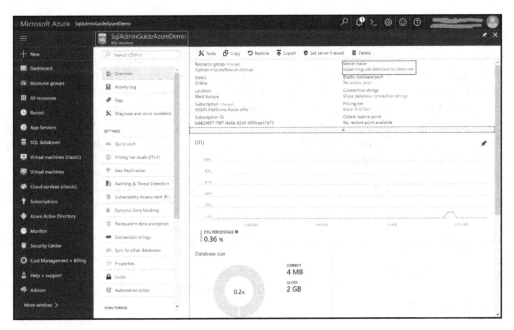

There's a lot of options that could be configured, but it's beyond the scope of this book. But the two main properties are highlighted by red rectangles; the database name as a label of the screen, and the server name as a link on the top part of the overview. This information is important for accessing the database from client tools such as Management Studio.

When connecting, a user must provide server name and also database name, because they are not going to connect a real SQL Server, but an alias created for him. And the database name is needed to provide which database will authenticate the user.

Nowadays Azure SQL databases provide almost the same feature set as on-premise databases, but with one important exception. Even if they are hosted on the same server (and let's keep in mind that the term *server* means alias of a whole group of SQL Servers maintained by Microsoft) they are the accessible points for connections. That's why it's not possible to combine more databases in one connection. In other words, the USE database_name command is not allowed against Azure SQL databases and also statements can be executed only against the database to which the user is already connected. But on the other hand, Azure SQL database is fully maintained in a cloud environment without any care about SQL Server instances from the DBAs side.

This section went into a bit more detail of using Azure portal itself. In the next section, we will not focus that much on Azure portal, rather we will focus more on Azure SQL Server.

Understanding Azure SQL Server

Azure SQL Server uses a completely different way of database hosting in cloud. It is a regular virtual machine that has SQL Server installed. A good point is that administrators are completely aware of licencing and high availability of the machine itself, but on the other side, we still have one more SQL Server instance and it's completely up to DBA to maintain it correctly in a form of database checks, rebuilding indexes, and so on, as it is described in Chapter 6, *Indexing and Performance*, and also Chapter 9, *Automation - Using Tools to Manage and Monitor SQL Server 2017*.

Azure SQL Server breaks limitations of Azure SQL database because it's a regular instance of SQL Server. Let's consider other properties of Azure SQL Server:

- Azure SQL Server could be incorporated into an Active Directory when the Active Directory has to be hosted in Azure as well
- Azure SQL Server is a better decision than Azure SQL database when we need a highly available machine with more databases for Line-of-Business (LOB) applications

- The performance of the machine is settable through its price level
- Azure SQL Server could serve as a secondary replica for AlwaysOn and it's really good because we can spread our availability groups outside organization for a case of physical disaster

In the next section, we will create a sample Azure SQL Server.

Creating Azure SQL Server

The creation of Azure SQL Server starts in the Azure portal in the same way as was described in the previous section. When finding a correct option, we need to use search term SQL Server 2017, because SQL Server 2016 is already offered. Azure portal will show a list of many options, but basically, we need to decide between three editions of SQL Server:

- Enterprise
- Standard
- Web

When the choice is done, we are asked for **Deployment model**. The deployment model decides if we will create a resource (virtual machine in our case) existing independently of other resources, or we can group more resources together logically. Deployment model can be:

- **Classic**: Newly created resource is independent.
- **Resource Manager**: Resources could be grouped together. It's useful when provisioning some solution using more resources such as SQL Server, web applications, and other resources together. This is a newer option and one of the enhancements is the possibility of using an SSD disk for storage.

The procedure of Azure SQL Server creation consists of five steps. The first step for virtual machine creation is shown in the following screenshot:

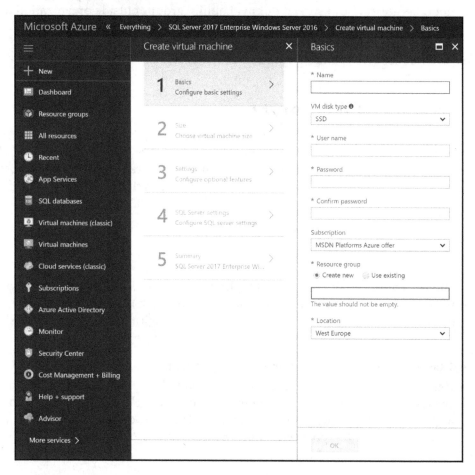

Let's describe all the properties:

- **Name**: Just a name of the newly created virtual machine.
- **VM disk type**: This option is SSD or HDD. This option is not seen when **Classic** deployment model is selected.

- **User name**: Name of the administrator of the server who will be able to connect the server through a remote desktop.
- **Password and Confirm password**: Password for the administrator user. Password must be at least 12 characters long.
- **Resource group**: The server can be added to an existing resource group or it can occupy its own.
- **Location**: Geographic location of the new server.

When all properties are filled correctly, the **OK** button is enabled and the virtual machine creation continues to the second step. This step is used to configure size, performance, and the price level, however. It is depicted in the following screenshot:

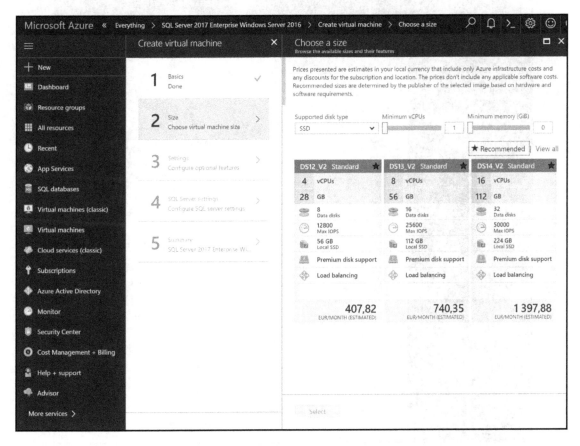

When the second step is shown, Azure portal offers three recommended pricing tiers, but we can click the **View all** link and see more (and also cheaper) pricing tiers. How it's seen in the previous screenshot, every tile shows the performance, resource consumption, and its price very clearly. The size is selected by clicking on some of the tiles. The controls above the tiles are just filters. When we have our own size requirements, we can set it by the filters and corresponding tiles will be shown.

The third step is about additional optional configurations. This is shown in the following screenshot:

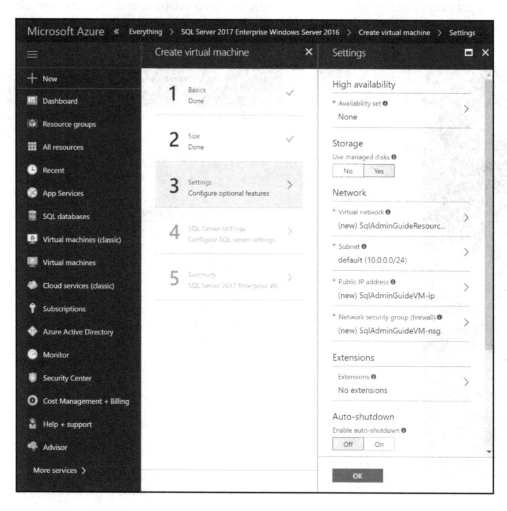

The **High availability** section enables server redundancy for a case of sudden or planned downtime. The **Storage section** enables usage of managed disks—it's built-in storage redundancy. Then network configuration could be adjusted, extensions such as antivirus protection can be added and diagnostic features can be switched on.

The fourth step is about SQL Server instance configuration. It's shown in the following screenshot:

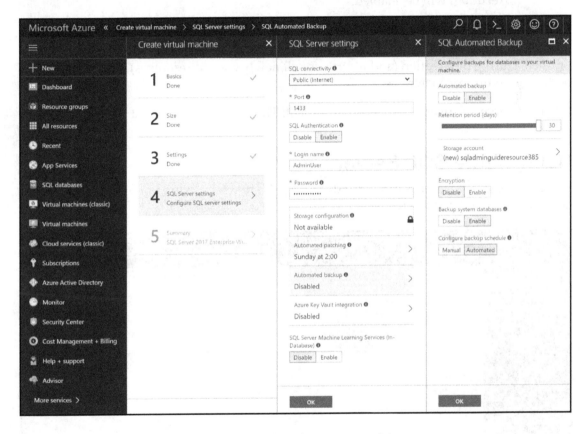

These are the options that are used in the fourth step to configure:

- **SQL connectivity**: From inside the virtual machine, over VPN or publicly.
- **SQL Authentication**: Ability to use standard authentication. The user and password is prefilled from the first step.
- **Automated patching**: When Microsoft will patch the virtual machine.

- **Automated backup**: This option continues in the far right side when several options are configured, such as to enable backup encryption, whether to enable system database backup, and whether to create our own backup schedule or not.
- **Azure Key Vault integration**: This option could be used in conjunction with Azure Key Vault storage, for example, for TDE or the Always Encrypted feature.
- The last option says that machine learning services (support for R or Python code execution) will be enabled.

The last step is just a summary and confirmation of all properties set during previous steps. Then creation starts and we just have to wait a couple of minutes until the creation is finished. During the creation (and it's true for all newly created resources) we can leave the portal and return back later.

When the server is created, we can start to use it. The next section is about the usage.

Using Azure SQL Server

When the virtual machine is created, a dashboard is shown in Azure portal. The dashboard is shown in the following screenshot:

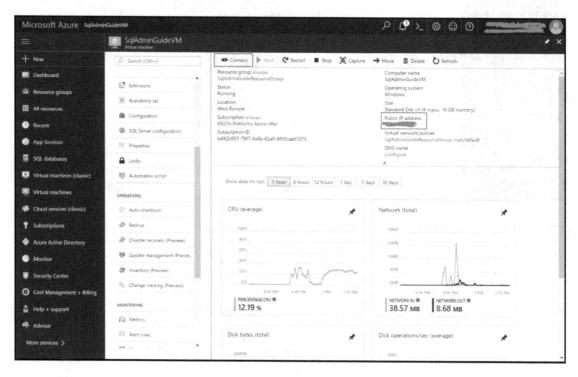

The dashboard contains a set of configuration properties on the left side and also diagrams showing CPU or network utilization as well as disk utilization. The main two controls on the dashboard are highlighted in red rectangles. The first is the **Connect** button on the top toolbar. When it's clicked, an RDP configuration file is downloaded and we can access our virtual server over our remote desktop using the username and password set in the first step of creation. When we are connected to the server, we can configure the operating system and SQL Server services. The remote desktop does not contain Management Studio, but we can install it.

The second highlighted place is in the right column of configuration properties and it is the IP address of the server. It's useful for accessing the SQL Server via Management Studio from outside the virtual machine.

> The Azure SQL Server is installed with a full feature set and with default settings at the instance level. After provisioning in Azure portal is finished, review Service Manager services and instance properties in Management Studio first, as it was mentioned in `Chapter 1`, Setting up SQL Server 2017.

Azure SQL Server is a good option for larger LOB applications, as a secondary replica in AlwaysOn groups, and it could also serve for reporting or traditional analysis via Analysis Services. But for data warehouses with really big contention, Microsoft prepared a special resource called Azure SQL Data Warehouse. Keep on reading to the following section.

Azure SQL Data Warehouse

Data warehouse workload means a very big database with a lot of range or full scans. Against it, everything must be subject to the response time. Azure SQL Data Warehouse fulfills these requirements through its very complex design.

The following screenshot shows the SQL Data Warehouse architecture:

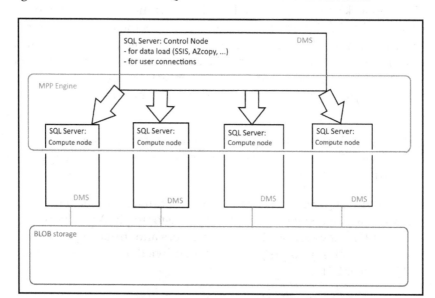

The only point of contact with Azure SQL Data Warehouse is an SQL Server instance called **control node**. Control node responds to user requests and also receives data incoming during ETL executions. The control node itself plays the main role in the distribution of load between **compute nodes**. Every compute node is an SQL Server instance holding part of data loaded into Azure SQL Data Warehouse. The amount of compute nodes could be up to 60 SQL Servers, that's why everything is done by **massively parallel processing** (**MPP**). The MPP engine is internally **Polybase**.

Polybase is a technology with two usage purposes:

- Controls MPP processing
- Enables connection between relational databases and Hadoop applications such as HDInsight (also present in Azure)

Polybase topology can be installed on-premise as a part of SQL Server Enterprise Edition, but it's beyond the scope of this book.

The last part of every node in Azure SQL Data Warehouse is **data movement service** (**DMS**). This feature starts to work when data used in the same query is not stored together in one node.

Creating Azure SQL Data Warehouse

The creation of Azure SQL Data Warehouse is also done on Azure portal. The best search term when creating a new resource is just **SQL Data Warehouse**. Once found, the resource type by an administrator and creation is started, and a screen with several properties appears, as shown in the following screenshot:

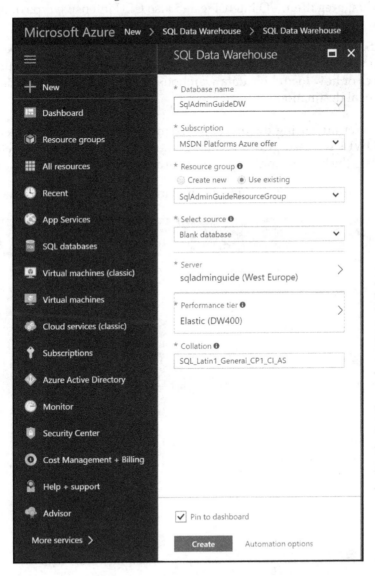

All properties such as **Database name** and **Resource group** seen in the preceding screenshot are self-descriptive. The **Select source** property enables the creation of a blank database prepared for new schema and ETL data load, sample database, or database from (Azure) backup. The most tricky property is the **Performance tier**. The performance is rated in **data warehouse units** (**DWU**). It's quite complicated and consists of three parts:

- **Search/aggregation**: I/O intensive and also CPU intensive type of operations.
- **Read**: I/O intensive type of operations.
- **CTAS**: This shortcut means create table as select. I/O intensive operations and also a way how to load data to the data warehouse from non-relational data sources or how to archive data warehouse data off the relational database to non-relational destination.

The computation formula using the preceding factors is not publicly documented. But as the number of DWUs we need grows, so more expensive the SQL Data Warehouse service will be. And this is the biggest and maybe only disadvantage, this service is expensive!

Let's take a look at the following screenshot showing how to set up a performance tier:

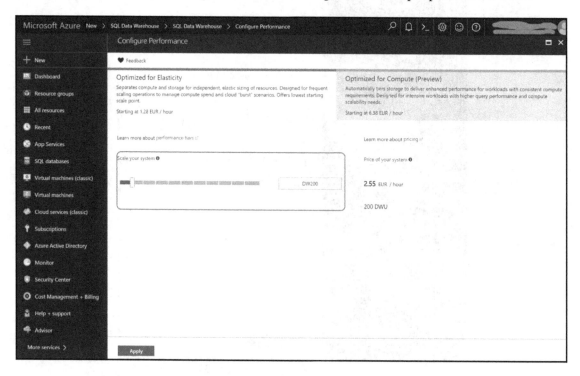

The most important place when sizing the performance tier property is highlighted in the red rectangle. Moving the bar to the left or to the right changes the maximum capacity of DWUs. And as seen in the preceding screenshot, even if we have a very small amount of DWUs set, the price is computed not per month as it is in Azure SQL database, but per hour. Once the performance tier is set and the administrator clicks the **Apply** button, all properties are set and provisioning can start.

When the Azure SQL Data Warehouse is created, overview is shown with a summary of basic properties and with tiles for quick start. The overview is shown in the following screenshot:

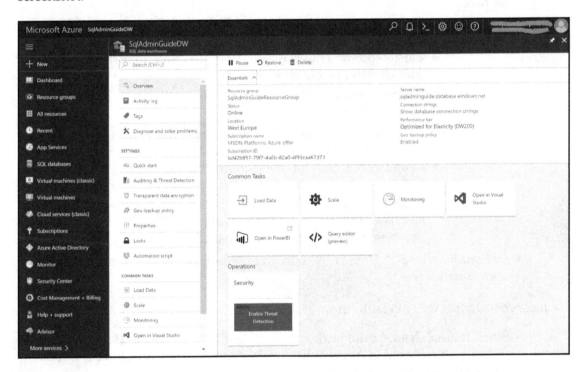

As seen in the preceding screenshot, there's a lot of possibilities with the Azure SQL Data Warehouse like starting to load data, monitor its state or connect to SQL DWH via PowerBI. If we want to access Azure SQL Data Warehouse with Management Studio, we need the server name property as a path to a server, but we also need to fill the database name, which is written in the header of the page. In other words, when connecting to Azure SQL Data Warehouse, the connection is done the same way as when connecting to an Azure SQL database.

Using the Azure SQL Data Warehouse needs a a few more things to be considered. This information is summarized in the next section.

Using Azure SQL Data Warehouse

Azure SQL Data Warehouse was designed to support a huge amount of big read operations and full scans. That's why the physical design of tables has three extra differences against common SQL Server databases:

- **Storage**:
    - By default, every table stored in Azure SQL Data Warehouse is clustered `columnstore` index
    - Clustered B-tree index is also supported, and it must be explicitly defined within table creation
    - Heap is also supported, and it must be explicitly defined within table creation
- **Distribution**: As massively parallel technology, every table is distributed across all compute nodes. The distribution could be solved in two modes:
    - **Round-robin**: Default mode of distribution. Control node distributes data randomly and evenly across all compute nodes.
    - **Hash**: Non-default mode of distribution based on user-defined hash key. This mode of distribution can lead to so called data skewness (data is not spread across all nodes evenly).
- **Statistics**: Azure SQL Data Warehouse does not support auto create and auto update statistics.

We must consider not using defaults in several cases:

- **Small tables**: Those should be heaps or clustered B-tree indexes (Microsoft think of small tables stored in Azure SQL Data Warehouse when they have less than 100.000.000 records).
- **Dimension tables with selective random searches**: Those tables should be clustered B-tree indexes.
- **Tables joined often together**: When those tables are distributed randomly in round-robin mode or are not distributed by the same hash key, data movement service is forced to move data from one instance of compute node to another to get data of joined tables together. We should minimize the work of data movement service, that's why the hash distribution is the best practice in these circumstances.

In addition to the issues listed previously, an ETL developer has to know that Azure SQL Data Warehouse does not create and update column statistics automatically. When a table is loaded, column statistics must be created or updated manually using the CREATE STATISTICS or UPDATE STATISTICS command.

This chapter could continue on and on describing other data-related Azure technology such as Data Factories, Hadoop services, or serverless Cosmos DB storage. But an overview of main technology was provided and so now let's move to the next section about hybrid SQL Server scenarios.

Microsoft SQL Server 2017 and hybrid scenarios

While the previous section showed several clear Azure deployments of SQL Server, SQL Server is traditionally hosted on-premise. As the data contention grows over time, administrators face a challenge of handling the increased storage space needed for data or for backups as well as with RTO and RPO objectives.

Migration to Azure environment is not always easy or possible at all. That's why Microsoft incorporated many enhancements to SQL Server to help DBAs to succeed when challenging mentioned situations. In the following sections, we will go through these enhancements and show how to use them. Every section contains appropriate situations for using them, and also a detailed description of the implementation.

The first described feature was introduced in SQL Server 2016, continues in SQL Server 2017, and it is called StretchDB.

StretchDB

StretchDB is a feature that enables us to store data from tables placed in on-premise databases to cloud. A typical scenario is when users keep data forever, but rarely access it. Such historical tables with huge amounts of records tend to run out of space and also maintenance requirements such as backup size becomes an issue. In other words, StretchDB is intended for cold OLTP data. It's not a good idea to stretch data warehouse tables even if they are big.

StretchDB offers a transparent way of data movement to a dedicated Azure SQL database. All data could be moved, but also the filter function can be written to decide how many records will stay on-premise. Everything is set up on the SQL Server site, the only requirement is to have an active Azure subscription.

When setting up StretchDB, a selected table is going to be stretched. At the start of the process, the linked server is created by SQL Server to Azure on an on-premise instance. This linked server is not accessible for regularly distributed queries, it's dedicated only for StretchDB features.

To use StretchDB, it must be enabled on instance level first. The following script shows the action:

```
use master
go
exec sp_configure 'remote data archive', 1
go
reconfigure
go
```

The second prerequisite is to have an existing Azure SQL database. The database will not be used finally, but an on-premise SQL Server needs to have an existing **logical SQL Server** in Azure. The logical SQL server serves as a virtual instance of SQL Server, which is actually just host for Azure SQL databases, it is never used for other purposes.

Logical SQL Server can be created without databases in Azure portal, but on-premise SQL Server is not able to connect to it. That's why it is a good practice to create an empty Azure SQL database, use the logical SQL Server as a host for StretchDB, and then delete the empty database, because StretchDB will not use it and will create its own.

Once an instance is enabled and Azure is prepared, we can start to enable certain databases. The first step is to create **database scoped credential**. Its identity is used by the StretchDB feature to access and secure communication between the database and the cloud. Database scoped credentials are secured by the database master key in the database, which has to be stretched. The script for the database master key and the database scoped credential creation is as follows:

```
use <database name>
go
create master key encryption by password = '<$0me $tr0ng pa$$w0rd>'
go
create database scoped credential <credential name>
with identity = '<identity>' , secret = '<secret>'
go
```

The preceding script does not seem so complicated, but we must take care about the `identity` and `secret` properties. The `identity` property is a username of the Azure SQL database, it's not a username used for logging in to Azure portal. Secret is a password associated with the username. In other words, database scoped credentials will be used by SQL Server as a user of Azure SQL database created for StretchDB.

When security prerequisites are fulfilled, the database itself must be configured to allow StretchDB. The script is shown as follows:

```
use master
go
alter database <database name> set remote_data_archive = on
(
    server = 'tcp:<your logical SQL Server
name>.database.windows.net,1433',
    credential = <credential name>
)
go
```

The statement depicted previously has a `server` property, which is a connection string to the logical SQL Server. Even if a common logical SQL Server address used when connecting by, for example, Management Studio is in a form `nameoftheserver.database.windows.net`, this doesn't work when enabling StretchDB. That's why the `tcp:` prefix and port number at the end are provided.

When executing the statement, on-premise SQL Server creates a hidden linked server and also creates a dedicated Azure SQL database. Hence the statement is executed several minutes. When it's successfully finished, we can go to Azure portal to see the newly created Azure SQL database with a name looking like `RDA<on premise database name>80762919-0C12-4CE5-A99A-CC5B2C4F66D0`.

At the moment:

- The original Azure SQL database could be deleted via Azure portal to save money
- The new Azure SQL database created by the `alter database` statement starts to consume money

When something goes wrong, it's tricky to unhide the root cause. The simplest way is to drop credentials and the database master key in an on-premise database, reset the password for logical SQL Server in Azure portal, and repeat the procedure one more time.

When a database is enabled for StretchDB, the last step is to choose and start StretchDB on the table level. The StrechDB feature is enabled table by table. Every table can be stretched entirely or filtered. When a table is entirely stretched, all data is transparently moved to a cloud and only metadata of the table will stay on-premise.

In some scenarios, we can have tables with hot and cold parts of data. Hot data we would have on-premise, older and rarely used data we would move to a cloud. For this case, a filter function can be written. An example of a filtered stretch of a table is shown as follows:

```
use demo
go

create function dbo.fn_StretchMovieRatings (@Rating int)
returns table
with schemabindings
as
return select 1 as is_eligible whene @Rating <= 5
go

alter table MovieRatings set
(remote_data_archive = on
(filter_predicate = dbo.fn_StretchMovieRatings (Rating),
migration_state = outbound))
go
```

The function as seen in the preceding script, is a regular table value function. When used as a `filter_predicate` in an `alter table` statement, the appropriate column from the table is used as a parameter to this function. Microsoft recommends writing simple conditions into the filter function because StretchDB internally uses the CROSS APPLY operator to evaluate the function.

In some cases, we would have to pause the StretchDB on a certain table. The `migration_state` property in the `alter table` statement is used to set the state of StretchDB. It could be outbound (the data movement works) or paused (StretchDB is set, but data movement is not working). The script for pausing StretchDB is shown as follows:

```
alter table MovieRatings set (remote_data_archive = on (migration_state =
paused))
go
```

If we don't need to use the StretchDB anymore, we will switch the feature off for every stretched table. When disabling StretchDB on the table level, we must decide what to do with data already moved to Azure. We have two options; bring the data back or leave the data in Azure. Both possibilities are shown in the following script:

```
-- bringing data back
alter table MovieRatings set (remote_data_archive (migration_state =
inbound))
go

-- leaving data in Azure
alter table MovieRatings set
(remote_data_archive = off_without_data_recovery
(migration_state = paused))
go
```

When StretchDB is disabled on the table level for all tables, we can disable StretchDB for a whole database. The command is as follows:

```
alter database <database name> set remote_data_archive = off
```

When StretchDB is not needed anymore and it's turned off, Azure SQL database still exists on Azure and also still consumes money. We don't have to remember to delete unwanted databases or all the virtual SQL Server from Azure via Azure portal.

For actions described in this section, Microsoft provides nice and readable wizards in Management Studio. At the time of writing, using the wizard for creating complete StretchDB infrastructure leads to failure.

Using StretchDB is useful in scenarios when some tables grow beyond limits and storage becomes insufficient, or backup operations grow too much. Data moved to cloud is not a part of regular `backup database` statements, SQL Server relies on Azure reliability. From a users perspective, a stretched table is transparent, user still queries the same structure, even if records are actually stored in Azure. When the query is resolved as a combination of on-premise data and data stored in Azure, it can be slower depending on network capabilities.

In next section, we will explore another hybrid scenario called data files in Azure.

Data files in Azure

Data files in Azure is a topology in which SQL Server is running on-premise or as an Azure VM, metadata of user databases is stored in its master database, but files of these user databases are hosted in Azure blob storage. This feature is useful in scenarios when some database is often migrated between instances or we want to divide the instance and the data. This topology also benefits from the ability of snapshot backups, which will be mentioned at the end of this section.

First of all, the **Storage account** has to be created. It's done in Azure portal, as shown in the following screenshot:

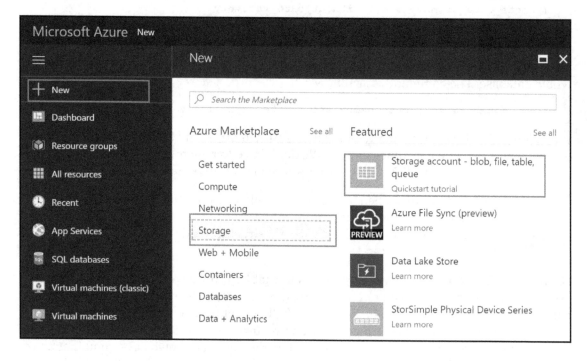

The procedure goes from the left to the right, following places highlighted by red rectangles in the preceding screenshot. We have to fill several properties such as name and placement for the **Storage account**, and in a couple of moments, the **Storage account** is prepared and empty. We have to go into the **Storage account** and create a container. A container is a physical place for placing files, we could think of it as a folder. The following screenshot shows how to do it:

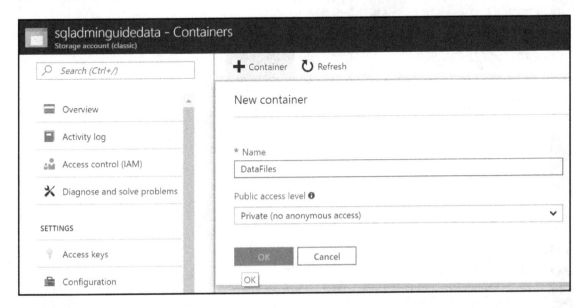

The container has a name (that has to be lower case) and also a **Public access level** property. It should be set to private as it's seen in the screenshot. When the container is created, access policy should be created for it with at least Read, Write, and List permissions. Delete permissions are preferred for a case of dropping a database later. The access policy is created in Azure portal on the container's level.

During previous steps, the cloud storage was prepared itself, in the next steps we will prepare other security prerequisites for using data files in Azure. SQL Server needs to be authenticated against certain containers. It's done by a server credential. The credential needs to have a secret created for the container in Azure.

Azure portal does not help to correctly create the secret. Fortunately, a free and often used tool exist. It's called **Microsoft Azure Storage Explorer** and it solves this issue in Azure portal. The **Microsoft Azure Storage Explorer** is a desktop application and it is shown in the following screenshot:

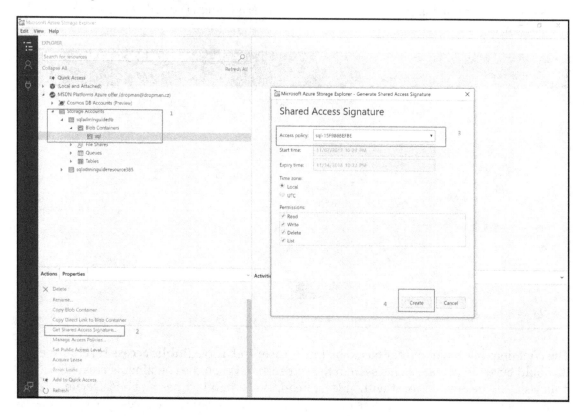

As seen in the preceding screenshot, once connected, **Microsoft Azure Storage Explorer** shows all storage types created within Azure subscription. But we have to stay focused on the highlighted places. They are numbered for better orientation:

1. After connection, we have to expand **Storage accounts** - certain storage account (**sqladminguidedb** in our example) - **Blob Containers**, and then we'll see a container created in the Azure portal (its name is **sql** in our example), or we can create one by right-clicking on the **Blob Containers** node.

2. When the **sql** container is selected, the bottom part appears with two tabs; **Properties** and **Actions**. The **Properties** tab is shown by default. The **Actions** tab contains a set of links for certain actions. We have to click **Get Shared Access Signature**.

3. When the **Get Shared Access Signature** (SAS) link is clicked, a dialog is opened for the SAS creation. In this dialog we have to select our access policy created for the container in Azure portal.

4. When the access policy is selected and the **Create** button is clicked, the dialog window is changed and shows the newly generated SAS.

The new look of the dialog is shown in the following screenshot:

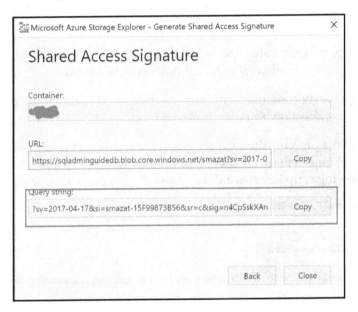

The field in the red rectangle contains the complete SAS used in the next step. We have to copy it before closing the dialog:

 Azure portal also contains a Shared Access Signature link, but on the **Storage account** level. It's too high and when used for credential, it does not work! SAS on container level must be created.

When SAS is created, we can switch to Management Studio and create the credential. It's not a database scoped credential, it's created in the database `master` database. The script is as follows:

```
use master
go

create credential [https://sqladminguidedb.blob.core.windows.net/sql]
```

```
with
identity='SHARED ACCESS SIGNATURE',
secret =
'sv=2017-04-17&si=sql-15F986BEFBE&sr=c&sig=4d*******************3D'
go
```

Let's dive deeper into the preceding script. The credential's name has to be a complete link to the container. In our example, the base link to the **Storage account** is `https://sqladminguidedb.blob.core.windows.net`, and the container's name is just `sql`.

The `identity` property with value `SHARED ACCESS SIGNATURE` is constant informing SQL Server that this is the credential used for Azure container access.

And the `secret` property contains a query string generated in the previous step. Keep in mind that the leading question mark must not be there.

At this moment all the prerequisites are done and the last action is just to create the database. The script for database creation is definitely identical to any other database creation. The following script creates a database with files placed to Azure:

```
create database FilesInAzure
on
(
name = 'FilesInAzureData',
filename =
'https://sqladminguidedb.blob.core.windows.net/sql/masterfile.mdf'
)
log on
(
name = 'FilesInAzureLog',
filename = 'https://sqladminguidedb.blob.core.windows.net/sql/logfile.ldf'
)
go
```

When the database is created, we can go back to the **Microsoft Azure Storage Explorer** or to the Azure portal and we will see that files are created into the container.

Creating databases with files placed in the Azure blob storage is the same for on-premise and also for Azure virtual machines. From on-premise instances, worse response time could be issued when Internet connection is not capable enough, but when combining Azure SQL Server VM with data files in Azure, the response is very good. The only limitation is that such a database cannot be bigger than 1 TB.

Using data files in Azure offers a very good feature called snapshot backup. The next section will describe all hybrid backup types and also this snapshot backup. Keep reading.

Backups to Azure

This section is going to show how backup operations could be executed placing backup files directly to Azure. Using this approach of backups provides several advantages:

- Backup files are stored reliably due to native Azure data redundancy.
- Backup files are highly accessible from around the whole world. It helps with database migrations.
- Cost of on-premise storage is always higher than Azure blob storage.
- Depending on the backup scenario, restore can be done extremely quickly.

Managed backup to Azure

Managed backup to Azure is probably the first feature of SQL Server, which profits from cloud technologies. However, we can back up databases locally and plan backup strategies by jobs created on SQL Server Agent, managed backup to Azure offers automated way of regular backups to Azure blob storage. It is a very good option for backups because we don't need to maintain local storage. We pay only for the amount of space consumed in Azure. Managed backup to Azure was introduced in SQL Server 2012 as a fully automated way of doing backups. From the time the managed backup to Azure was enhanced. Nowadays we can set our own time schedule for backups, or we can back up on demand whenever we need.

For using managed backups to Azure, these prerequisites must be fulfilled:

- Azure blob container must be created
- SAS must be generated for the container
- Credentials must be created on SQL Server

All three prerequisites were described in the previous section, so read on to start with managed backup to Azure. The following screenshot shows **Object Explorer** in Management Studio:

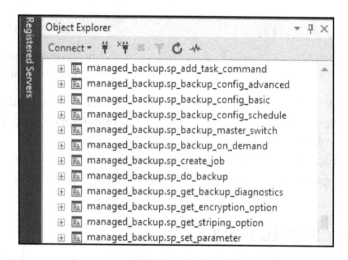

The preceding screenshot shows a part of the stored procedures created in the msdb database in the **managed_backup schema**. A full description of all stored procedures is at https://msdn.microsoft.com/en-us/library/dn449493(v=sql.120).aspx, but a simple example will follow. Let's use the demo database and Azure blob storage container https://sqladminguidedb.blob.core.windows.net/bck. We want to back up database demo with a default schedule and we want to keep backup retention for seven days. The following script shows the solution:

```
-- credential has to be created
create credential [https://sqladminguidedb.blob.core.windows.net/bck]
with
identity='SHARED ACCESS SIGNATURE',
secret = 'sv=2017-04-17&si=bck-15F9EE*****************Fdw%3D'
go


-- procedure managed_backup.sp_backup_config_basic is executed to setup and
start backups
exec msdb.managed_backup.sp_backup_config_basic
  @database_name = 'demo'
  , @enable_backup = 1
  , @container_url = 'https://sqladminguidedb.blob.core.windows.net/bck'
  , @retention_days = 7
go
```

The preceding script shows the credential creation, and then the procedure `managed_backup.sp_backup_config_basic` is executed. Let's explore parameters of the procedure:

- `@database_name`: Basically the name of a certain database. It can be set to `NULL`, and it means that all databases including system databases (except the `tempdb` database) will be backed up.
- `@enable_backup`: This parameter is just switched; when set to 1, backup starts, when set back to 0, managed backups are stopped.
- `@container_url`: URL to the Azure blob storage container.
- `@retention_days`: Number of days for which backups will be kept in the Azure blob container. Default (and the longest retention) is 30 days.

When we want to stop all managed backups to Azure, one more procedure exists for it. The following code shows how to stop all managed backups to Azure at once:

```
exec msdb.managed_backup.sp_backup_master_switch @new_state = 0
go
```

Restoration of a database from a managed backup to Azure is the same as described in Chapter 3, *Backup and Recovery*. When the database is in a simple recovery model, just one full backup is used to restore and recover the database. When the database is in at least a bulk-logged recovery model, the database could be restored and recovered to the most recent state.

Managed backup is mostly an automated mode of database backup. Another option is to use backup to a URL, which will be described in the next section.

Backup to a URL

Against the managed backup to Azure, backup to a URL is just regular backup. It's exactly the same as every other regular backup as described in Chapter 3, *Backup and Recovery*. The only exception is that we don't use `DISK`, but `URL` as a backup device. Also we need the credentials for the access to the Azure blob storage. Let's use a database called `SimpleDemo`, which we want to backup using Azure blobs as backup storage.

First, we need to create credentials with shared access policy for the container. The same procedure is described in the previous section. Then we are going to write the following statement:

```
backup database SimpleDemo to url =
'https://sqladminguidedb.blob.core.windows.net/bck/simpledemo.bak'
with init
```

With backup to URL we can establish any backup strategy using any backup types just according to our backup needs.

When restoring the database, the restore procedure and statements are exactly the same, again the only exception used is the device type. The following script shows how to restore the database `SimpleDemo` from a URL:

```
restore database SimpleDemo from url =
'https://sqladminguidedb.blob.core.windows.net/bck/simpledemo.bak'
with recovery
```

As seen in the preceding script, as it was already mentioned, the only difference against restores described in Chapter 3, *Backup and Recovery*, are that the restore statement is `restore... from url = 'https://...'` instead of `restore ... from disk = 'L:\...'`.

The next section will discuss using backups and restores of database files already stored in Azure blob storage.

Snapshot backups

In Chapter 3, *Backup and Recovery*, a process of point-in-time recovery of the database is described. It contains restore in sequence from full backup, then from differential backup (if it exists), and from all transaction log backup in sequence. This process is most probably time-consuming and it affects the **recovery time objective** (**RTO**) negatively.

When we want to ensure the best possible RTO, we can use so called **backups with file snapshots**. This type of backup is possible for databases having its files placed in Azure blob storage. Backups, when executed, then create pointers to snapshots of files only. It's very fast and efficient. Backups must also be placed in the Azure blob storage. In other words, from a DBAs perspective backups are the backups to URLs described in the previous section.

Using backups with file snapshots provides a possibility to recover a database to a certain point in time by using just two backups. That's why there's no need to go through all the regular processes described in Chapter 3, *Backup and Recovery*.

From DBA's perspective, a snapshot backup is a regular backup to a URL. The only prerequisites are:

- To have credentials for access to Azure blob storage
- To have files of the database placed in Azure blob storage
- To have a database in full recovery model

Let's have a database called FilesInAzure, the database has its files placed into Azure blob storage, and the database has also set a full recovery model. We want to use file snapshots for backup. The first backup has to be a full database backup. Sample script is as follows:

```
backup database FilesInAzure to url =
'https://sqladminguidedb.blob.core.windows.net/bck/FilesInAzureFull.bak'
with file_snapshot
```

The file_snapshot backup option seen in the preceding script makes the difference between regular backups and snapshot backups in Azure.

The same option is used in a transaction log backup statement. Let's see the following script:

```
declare @url nvarchar(255) =
'https://sqladminguidedb.blob.core.windows.net/bck/FilesInAzureLog_'
set @url = @url + convert(sysdatetime, 'yyyyMMddhhmm') + '.bak'
backup log FilesInAzure to url = @url
with file_snapshot
```

The preceding script has one extra feature; it computes a filename for consequential log backup files to keep each log backup in its own file. The declare statement in the script is just variable declaration and initiation with a constant part of the device path, the set statement adds a date and time as a formatted string, and also a file extension is added to the @url variable.

When the need for the database restore appears, we need to have three backups:

- The full backup
- The last transaction log backup when we want to restore the database to the most recent moment

- The first transaction log backup after the time of failure

Let's consider the `FilesInAzure` database. This database has files placed in Azure blob storage and it is also regularly backed up to URL. When we need to restore the database because we encountered some error in data, the following script shows the process of recovery:

```
restore database FilesInAzure from url =
'https://sqladminguidedb.blob.core.windows.net/sql/FilesInAzureFull.bak'
with norecovery, replace

restore log FilesInAzure from url =
'https://sqladminguidedb.blob.core.windows.net/sql/FilesInAzureLog_20171108
2300.bak'
with recovery, stopat = '2017-11-07 03:00pm'
```

From the preceding script, SQL Server recognizes which backups must be restored. The restore and recovery are then very fast and the database has minimal possible downtime.

Summary

Microsoft offers a complete and still growing cloud ecosystem for data processing in Azure. In this chapter, we mentioned all of the SQL Server and SQL database scenarios, but there are also other technologies such as Data Factory for ETL processes, machine learning for building of predictive models and analytics, and so on and so forth, but those technologies and features are out of the scope of this book.

In the first section, we summarized scenarios of a data platform fully placed into the cloud. The first of them, Azure SQL database, is provided as a service hosting isolated databases. The second option is Azure SQL Server as a virtual machine hosted in strong and extremely reliable cloud virtual environment. The last of them is a very powerful Azure SQL Data Warehouse service used to maintain a load balanced and massively parallel data warehouse fulfilling the most demanding performance requirements.

In the second section, we came across hybrid scenarios combining on-premise instances of SQL Server with Azure technologies. At the start of the section, we created an on-premise database with its files placed in Azure blob storage. The sub-sections following this described several backup and recovery scenarios profiting from an almost bottomless amount of storage capacity provided in Azure.

Index